MW00463505

AMERICAN
FLYGIRL

AMERICAN FLYGIRL

Susan Tate Ankeny

CITADEL PRESS
Kensington Publishing Corp.
www.kensingtonbooks.com

CITADEL PRESS BOOKS are published by

Kensington Publishing Corp.
900 Third Avenue
New York, NY 10022

Copyright © 2024 by Susan Tate Ankeny

All Kensington titles, imprints, and distributed lines are available at special quantity discounts for bulk purchases for sales promotions, premiums, fund-raising, educational, or institutional use. Special book excerpts or customized printings can also be created to fit specific needs. For details, write or phone the office of the Kensington sales manager: Kensington Publishing Corp., 900 Third Avenue, New York, NY 10022, attn Sales Department; phone 1-800-221-2647.

CITADEL PRESS and the Citadel logo are Reg. U.S. Pat. & TM Off.

10 9 8 7 6 5 4 3 2 1

First Citadel hardcover printing: May 2024

Printed in the United States of America

ISBN: 978-0-8065-4282-9
ISBN: 978-0-8065-4284-3 (e-book)

Library of Congress Control Number: 2023951533

For my mother

CONTENTS

PROLOGUE

1943

What good are wings without the courage to fly?

—ATTICUS

THE TEXAS SUN REFLECTED OFF THE AIRCRAFT lined up on the flight line, and Hazel raised her hand to block the blinding glare. Her khaki coveralls—men's size 42, the only size available—enveloped her small frame. Even with the sleeves and pant legs rolled up and a belt cinched tight around her waist, the one-piece suit engulfed her. She had worn the coveralls in the shower before hanging them to dry outside during breakfast, but they were already covered in a layer of dust like everything else around the airfield.

Two Army Air Corps lieutenants walked onto the tarmac, and she held her breath watching them approach. No one had said anything yet about her mishap yesterday. Maybe her instructor hadn't had time to file a report, but that seemed unlikely. These men were coming to tell her she'd washed out and order her to leave. Disappointment formed its fist in her stomach.

A month into training and already too many students to remember had washed out, been dismissed and sent home. There had been three last week. The commanding officer wasn't kidding on the first day when he'd said, "Look left and right. Only one of you will be here for graduation."[1] Some were due to illness; one had an ear issue during descents; another received two demerits for being late to classes; and one hadn't passed a flight check after refusing to go on

1

a date with her instructor. Dating between students and instructors was strictly forbidden. It didn't matter. He failed her, and she was sent home.

Hazel's eyes followed the two officers as they continued walking past, wishing her a good morning. She gave them a wide smile and exhaled. Feeling reckless, she pulled a red lipstick tube from a pocket and walked to her plane. Pressing gently, she formed the Chinese characters of her name on the nose beneath the window. She was going home today, that much she knew, and without an opportunity to say goodbye to her friends. When she returned from this morning's practice flight, if she would even be allowed one more practice flight, her belongings would be packed and waiting, her bed rolled up and empty. Marking the plane with her name might bring luck. She had nothing to lose.

Falling out of a plane was not good.

Yesterday afternoon had been clear and bright, with the usual wind blowing steady from the north. Charlotte Mitchell had stepped outside to watch the student trainees being tested on aerial maneuvers. A tiny dark speck in the sky caught her attention. As it continued floating downward, a training airplane came skidding up to the flight line, and the pilot sprang from the open cockpit yelling, "Lost my girl! She fell out!" The back seat of the biplane was empty, and the gosports hung over the side. "She took us into a spin and suddenly she wasn't there anymore!"[2]

Two test pilots jumped into a jeep and tore off in the direction of the descending parachute. For half an hour, a crowd paced the flight line waiting, until finally the jeep returned, with Hazel and her crumpled parachute in the back seat. The twenty-five-knot wind had carried her four miles, and after she landed, the billowing chute dragged her fifty feet. Her feet were bare, her face scratched, and she wore a grin. With one hand over her head, she waved her D-ring parachute handle. As concerned trainees circled around, Hazel explained, "I popped the stick and before I knew it was soaring out over the windscreen. My seatbelt latch came unfastened."[3]

Hazel wasn't shaken; she'd been preparing to walk back to the base when the jeep arrived. Not fastening a seatbelt securely was a rookie mistake, and she wasn't a rookie; she had more flying experience than the others in her class. She berated herself for what might cost her the training program. Most of all, she dreaded the disappointment her failure would bring to the Chinese community back home who had sponsored her and paid for her training. She remembered the old men, members of the Chinese Benevolent Society, posing for photographs beside her after graduation from training for aerial combat in China. They were so proud. "A girl!" they said to one another as if they had to repeat it aloud to believe it; a Chinese girl flying a plane and going to China to fight against the invading Japanese would bring honor to them all.

So far nothing had turned out as she'd hoped. There would be no honor to share with her benefactors, and worst of all, worse than not being able to fly because there were no flying jobs for women, if she failed, her little sister, and other girls like her would question whether they could accomplish their dreams. They might give up before they even tried, believing the cards were stacked against them in a world determined to keep them down. Hazel intended to show them that girls were just as capable as boys, if not more so.

1

LITTLE HERO

1920

Among all the marvels of modern invention, that with which I am most concerned is, of course, air transportation. Flying is perhaps the most dramatic of recent scientific attainment. In the brief span of thirty-odd years, the world has seen an inventor's dream first materialized by the Wright brothers at Kitty Hawk become an everyday actuality.[1]

—AMELIA EARHART

ON A STREET IN CHINATOWN, Portland, Oregon, a cluster of children stood together, reluctant to go home. School had ended for the summer, and the long twilights, too sweet to squander, allowed them to stay outside until bedtime. One, an eight-year-old girl with short black hair and a large toothy smile, was called Hazel. "Beat you to the end of the corner!" she yelled and bent forward with a hand on her knee. The girls stepped back to watch as the boys took their places in a line, each certain they would win this time. Hazel was only a girl, after all. Her older brother Harry bent down beside their younger brother Victor. Little sister Florence stood on the sidelines and called out, "Ready? Set? Go!"

Hazel shot forward, pumping her legs and arms ferociously. Her hair flew across her face, her shoes slapped the pavement, and she smiled, reveling in her own speed. Reaching the corner, she hugged the lamppost and turned back toward the others as one by one they joined her huffing and bending over to catch their breath.

The soft drone of an engine caused Hazel to look up. A yellow biplane, luminous against the darkening sapphire sky, seemed to float, pulled along by an invisible thread. As the other children walked away, Hazel watched the plane descending over the rooftops until it disappeared. What would it be like to be high up in the sky and alone, looking down on everyone? She imagined sailing over the city with the wind blowing her hair. Someday, she promised herself, she would fly.

In 1920 the world had become obsessed with the new phenomenon of aviation. Seventeen years had passed since the Wright brothers took their first flight, and now families spent their Sunday afternoons at airfields watching airplanes spiraling nose-first toward the earth. Crowds of thousands gathered at air shows to watch spellbound as pilots performed seemingly impossible twirls and loops, even leaving their cockpits to climb out onto the wings. The ending of the First World War had made a surplus of aircraft available, and pilots returning from Europe supported themselves by flying into small towns and showing off their skills, often taking paying passengers for rides.

The airplane, while a novelty and an exciting machine good for sport and leisure activities, was still years away from being seen as a reliable means of transportation. In May 1919, the first transatlantic flight had been successfully completed in stages, and the first nonstop flight happened the following month in June. Daring aviators, both men and women, broke and set aviation records in speed and distance while capturing the public's imagination. Flying was one of the most dangerous pursuits in the world, and pilots were the swashbuckling heroes of the day.

The Roaring Twenties had just begun. And with the Nineteenth Amendment's ratification, white women gained the right to vote. Empowered, women began to tentatively emerge from the shadows. It would become a decade of prosperity, jazz bands, bootleggers, bathtub gin, flappers, marathon dancers, and aviation. And one eight-year-old girl named Hazel Ying Lee stood at the corner of Davis and Fourth Streets ready to embrace it all.

Hazel and her siblings made their way home along the sidewalks, passing old Chinese men dressed in long, black mandarin-collared coats and speaking soft Cantonese. One held a Chinese newspaper and pointed with a gnarled finger, causing the others to nod and make sympathetic noises. Just a few blocks north of the downtown district, where white men in business suits hurried importantly and well-dressed women carried string-tied boxes, was like stepping into a foreign world. The air carried the rich scent of char siu bao—barbecued pork buns—and fresh-cut lumber. Delivery vehicles honked as the trolley clanged up Fourth Street past newspaper boys shouting today's headlines as they hawked *The Oregonian* newspaper.

The streets of the second largest Chinatown on the West Coast, after San Francisco, were lined with businesses like the traditional Chinese theater, a laundry, a grocer, the herbal shop, secret-but-not-so-secret gambling dens, saloons, pawn shops, the popular Chinese lottery office, apartment buildings and boardinghouses, and the residences of prominent Chinese merchants. Iron balconies, wooden awnings, brightly colored curved canopies, and restaurants with rounded windows transformed the small corner of Portland into a bustling, self-contained Chinese community.

Discriminatory housing practices kept the Chinese in this small section of town. Most Euro-Americans viewed the Chinese as a completely alien people who refused to assimilate into American society or embrace American culture, while ignoring the fact that

Americans actively sought to keep Chinese immigrants apart from mainstream society. Americans valued the entrepreneurial spirit and hard work of the Chinese but considered them a class apart from European immigrants, due in large part to their religious traditions, language, dress, and appearance.

◊ ◊ ◊

The small, crowded apartment where Hazel lived with her parents and six siblings was a second-floor walk-up at 67½ Fourth Street. With three children under the age of eight, the home offered scant privacy. Hazel and her siblings preferred to be outside. Their sister Rose looked up from the stove as they came in and slipped off their shoes. Despite being the oldest, her siblings called her "Little Sister" because she was the shortest among them and resembled a doll with her sweet face and short, curly hair.

Her siblings seated themselves around the table. Harry, who was thirteen, fell into a chair beside two-year-old Frances, busy working a chunk of cabbage into her mouth, while eight-year-old Florence began a card game with six-year-old Victor. Hazel snatched baby Howard from the floor and began to bounce him to a rhyming song she made up about a hairy baboon. He laughed and she touched her nose to his.

Her mother stopped folding clothes and said, "Ah Ying, you watch him for me tomorrow morning." The family spoke Cantonese at home. In the afternoons, after regular school, Hazel attended Chinese School, where she received instruction in language and Chinese traditions and customs.

"I can't, Ma, I'm going swimming." Hazel made a noise like an airplane engine and held baby Howard aloft over her head and told him, "Someday I'm going to soar through the sky in an airplane."

"Maybe I gave you too strong a name, Little Hero. You are not afraid of the wind. You are not afraid of the water."[2] This was a common refrain from her mother. "What becomes of a daughter with no fear? Some fear is a good thing." Hazel did not agree. Fear was limiting. She did not want her younger siblings to fear ghosts haunting their apartment or the Shanghai tunnels that ran beneath Chinatown, where it was rumored people disappeared, smuggled onto ships to work as slaves and never to be seen again. Someone had to be brave, and Hazel appointed herself.

Moving on to another topic, her mother asked, "Why are you always racing with the boys? Let them run. You are a girl. Girls stay put." Hazel turned her head so her mother couldn't see and made a face at Howard.

◊ ◊ ◊

Hazel Ying Lee had been born on August 25, 1912, a month after thousands had crowded the streets of Portland just blocks from her home to watch their first airplane flight. Twenty-four-year-old Silas Christofferson took off in a brand-new Curtiss Pusher, a bright yellow biplane, from the roof of the twelve-story Multnomah Hotel and flew north for twelve minutes before landing at Fort Vancouver on the Washington side of the Columbia River. It's likely Hazel's father was among the crowd, as few Portlanders missed the exhibition.

A female physician, Dr. Jessie M. McGavin, delivered Hazel at home. Maybe Hazel's mother gave her daughter the Chinese name Ying, meaning hero, because she believed the woman doctor's auspicious presence at her daughter's birth was a good omen, a sign of future opportunities for little Ah Ying that had not been available to her. Regardless, Hazel's birth just blocks from where a young man had risked death to fly an airplane off a tall building and her delivery by a woman at a time when few women were doctors, as well as the name her mother chose, all suggested a foreshadowing of her destiny.

Hazel's father, Yuet Lee, had immigrated to Portland in 1880 while he was in his early twenties, fleeing China soon after fighting broke out between the Nationalists and the Communists. Yuet became a merchant, importing mah-jongg cards and other Chinese goods, like baskets. In 1902 he returned to China and married his second wife, Shee, who at nineteen was more than twenty years his junior. It is unknown what became of Yuet's first wife, but their two children stayed in China and may have been grown when Yuet remarried. The first children born to Shee and Yuet were Rose and Harry, who were born in China before their parents came to live in Portland.

Like most immigrants, Yuet had believed in a better life in America. But in the United States at the turn of the century, Asians were subjected to unjust discrimination and denied the rights granted to Euro-Americans. The years between 1882 and 1943 are known as the Exclusion Era in Oregon. During this time, the law banned entry into the United States of essentially all Chinese. Although merchants, diplomats, professionals, and students were exempt, all Chinese seeking entry to the country were assumed to be laborers and subject to a complicated process to prove otherwise. They could not vote, own land, live outside designated Chinese communities, serve on a jury, apply for citizenship, or attend public schools. Consequently, the Chinese population in Oregon declined from over ten thousand in 1900 to two thousand in 1941. Most occupations outside Chinatown were not open to them, and many places of business were completely off-limits. Every Chinese American, even children who were born in the United States, was required to carry identification. Yuet learned that all men being created equal only applied to white men.

By 1924 the Lee family, with the birth of Daniel, had expanded to include eight children, four girls and four boys. Yuet was nearly seventy years old and shared ownership of the Golden Pheasant, a Chinatown restaurant popular with dockworkers. Like other Chinese fathers who worked long hours, he was not often at home.

In a family photograph taken in 1927, Yuet and Shee, seated and surrounded by their eight offspring, appear bent forward as if weighted down by lives of hard work. The three oldest girls, teenagers

Hazel and Florence and twenty-four-year-old Rose, who was married, stand behind their parents wearing white capes with mandarin collars. Mother sits wrapped in a traditional brocade mandarin jacket. All the boys, even little Daniel, who was only three, and Father wore dark Western suits.

Yuet stares out from the photo with troubled eyes as though he has seen the future. A man who would never stop working or know his children well, his haunted expression suggests resignation. To provide for his family, he became a stranger in his own home.

2

CHINESE NOT PERMITTED

1930

The air is the only place free from prejudice.[1]

—BESSIE COLEMAN

IT WAS A RARE WARM DAY ON THE OREGON COAST. Waves roared under a turquoise sky, and the air smelled of sand, seaweed, and salt water. Children, having touched the cold water, ran away from the frothy tide screaming, while others, carrying buckets and shovels, dug holes in the sand near their families. Hazel, wearing her new skirted swimsuit, stood ready to dive into the ocean. The rough surf and numbing temperature didn't concern her; she was a strong swimmer. In fact, by the time she had graduated high school, she'd earned a reputation as an outstanding competitive athlete. She excelled at tennis and was unbeatable at handball. Although Chinese were not permitted to compete in the local tennis tournaments at the Irvington Tennis Club or the Multnomah Athletic Club, she honed her skills at Benson High School's public courts, skills that would have made her equal to the top players in the state had she been allowed to play them.

Hazel dove beneath the waves to deeper water. After the initial shock, she loved her weightlessness in the water, like being held

12

by something powerful. She and her sisters, Rose and Florence, had arrived yesterday after a long journey on the steam train affectionately called the "Daddy Train" because it brought white fathers to the coast on weekends to join their families who spent the summers escaping the inland heat. The trip took six hours from Portland to Astoria and then south to Seaside. Neighbors from down the hall had invited them on the trip. At seventeen, Hazel had not been many places outside Portland. There were no vacations for the Lee family, only occasional visits to the Hing's Farm, where she and her brothers and sisters caught crawdads in the Tualatin River.

Since graduating from Portland's High School of Commerce, an independent high school with a focus on business education, Hazel had worked in her family's restaurant, becoming an experienced cook. She wanted more. In high school she had learned stenography, accounting, and bookkeeping along with a regular high school curriculum. The problem was that the only positions available to Chinese outside of Chinatown were those where they would not be seen by the public—invisible jobs, like working in the back with stock. The office work Hazel wanted and had been trained to do existed only in her dreams.

And to further complicate matters, the Roaring Twenties had abruptly ended after the stock market crash in 1929. Only a year into the Great Depression, and Americans were out of work in alarming numbers that continued to rise steadily. Nearly a million people were homeless, and there was no telling when the hard times would end. Whether you were rich or poor, the fear and uncertainty about tomorrow hung like a cloud over everyone.

Aviation continued to enthrall the public. The thrill of watching pilots perform stunts provided an escape from humdrum lives and uncertain futures. Airplanes provided the perfect distraction, and it cost nothing to take the family to an airfield and watch death-defying acts in the sky right overhead. Hazel had read an article in *Cosmopolitan* magazine written by Amelia Earhart called, "Try

Flying Yourself." Earhart, and other female pilots like her, gained inspiration from aviators such as Charles Lindbergh, who in 1927 had made the first nonstop solo flight across the Atlantic. The following year, Earhart became the first woman to cross the Atlantic, and even though she called herself nothing more than "baggage" on the flight, because she had not been allowed to fly the aircraft, her trip drew attention to women pilots. And in 1932 she would accomplish the flight solo.

Flying in her closed-cockpit Vega, Earhart had recently set three world speed records for women. Using aviation as an example, she hoped to prove that women could succeed in traditionally male-dominated occupations. Her message rang loud and clear; if a man could do something, why couldn't a woman? She challenged the common belief that women shouldn't fly under any circumstances due to their fragile constitutions and unstable mental capacity. The argument against women flying had gained momentum in 1911 when Harriet Quimby became the first woman to earn a pilot's license in the United States, and the second in the world. Less than a year later, during a race, she fell out of her plane and to her death in Boston's Dorchester Bay. The accident was witnessed by more than a thousand spectators, and a cause was never found. Sabotage, something like sugar in the gas tank, was suggested but dismissed without proof. Clearly, it seemed to everyone, Harriet Quimby's mishap proved women just didn't have the temperament or capabilities required for flying.

Amelia Earhart, Louise Thaden, and Blanche Scott consistently attempted to break records in speed, altitude, and endurance and challenged other interested women to do the same. Women pilots had to prove they possessed the unlimited energy, courage, quick eye, clear judgment, and physical dexterity of their male counterparts. In trying to be accepted, early women pilots changed their behavior, acting more assertively and speaking in a lower register to demonstrate to skeptics they were as capable as men, while being careful to not go too far and be called "mannish." They walked a thin line to dispel misconceptions about women and to avoid gender bias.

Amelia Earhart's soft-spoken, humble manner and petite frame, and her uncanny resemblance to Charles Lindbergh, endeared her to the public, especially women. The fledgling aviation industry sent her across the country as a glorified salesperson, hoping Amelia would demonstrate that flying was so easy even a woman could do it.

A new age was dawning, and for the first time the idea that more than child-rearing and homemaking might be available to women began to take root. Some women, brave enough to go against convention, found themselves willing and eager to exchange traditional roles to become pilots and explore new opportunities in aviation.

Hazel and her sisters had been looking forward to seeing the elegant Hotel Seaside they'd heard so much about. After a walk along the promenade skirting the wide sandy beach, they crossed the hotel's manicured lawn and climbed the steps onto its veranda to gaze out on a sweeping view of the Pacific Ocean and forested Tillamook Head jutting into the sea to the south. Their clothes had been carefully chosen. Hazel wore a new cream-colored calf-length skirt and loose-fitting yellow blouse ruffled around the neck and sleeves. Her low-heeled pumps, also new, had been an extravagant purchase. Now that she was out of high school, she was growing out her side-parted pixie to something more modern, like Carole Lombard's short, sculpted waves in the movie *High Voltage*. She imitated Carole Lombard's tough, no-nonsense attitude and deep-voiced, lazy drawl that suggested she knew her own mind and played nobody's fool.

At the hotel's main entrance, they were greeted by a doorman who held up his hand. He cleared his throat, focused his gaze beyond them, and said, "Chinese are not permitted inside." The girls stood motionless while disappointment turned to embarrassment, although this was not their first experience being refused admittance based on their race. Hazel and her friends had been asked to leave restaurants in Portland, and she knew better than to try to go to certain places, like the tennis clubs where she couldn't play and wasn't allowed to watch either. But no matter how many times it happened, she never got used to it. Hazel took her sisters' arms and turned to go back down the steps. Two women, wrapped in fur coats and wearing expressions of distaste, stopped and watched them leave.

Because of widespread anti-Chinese sentiment, some of Hazel's friends tried to disassociate themselves from their heritage, hoping to better fit in. But Hazel loved the Chinese culture and customs, while at the same time embracing everything new and exciting and American. In every way she was a modern American teenager. But wherever she went, and no matter what clothes she wore, there was no escaping her skin color, her eyes, her hair, her Asian appearance. Like most second-generation Chinese Americans, Hazel lived with a foot in each culture. She was both American and Chinese—and yet neither.

In that summer of 1930, when she wasn't at the restaurant or helping at home, Hazel spent her free time with her friend Elsie Chang. They were the same age and had gone to school together and known each other all their lives. With four brothers and no sisters, Elsie could easily have been a "tomboy" like Hazel, but instead she exuded the femininity fostered and prized by Chinese mothers. Even her round face and delicate V-shaped smile suggested a sweet and gentle disposition. Leaving the movie theater where they'd spent two hours lost in *The Divorcee* with Norma Shearer and Robert Montgomery, Hazel and Elsie meandered along the sidewalk wearing the new white, high-waisted pleated shorts that were snug at the waist and billowed out around their legs. Shorts had been banned on public streets in a few small towns in the United States, but in Portland the new "short pants" were now popular among young women after having been acceptable previously only for sports. That they were generally considered a disgrace and too risqué only made them more exciting to wear.

Hazel and Elsie had walked the two-mile distance because Elsie wasn't allowed to be driven in Hazel's car. A friend had recently taught Hazel how to drive and she had obtained a driver's license. Few women drove, and most of Hazel's friends had never ridden in a car. Elsie wanted to ride in Hazel's car more than anything but couldn't get permission from her father. "He's afraid you'll have an accident and kill us both."[2]

Hazel, undaunted, offered to teach her to drive, but Elsie was too obedient to go behind his back, and her father never changed his mind.

Freedom beckoned to the younger generation, excited by all the modern innovations like the automobile that offered a new independence. Cars offered dating couples privacy away from family and chaperones, and the radio brought people from all over the country together to hear the same news, soap operas, and music. News was no longer days old, but immediate. And everyone heard it together at the same time, which provided a shared connection to the world that hadn't existed before.

Passing the grocer, a newspaper headline caught Hazel's eye. She grabbed Elsie's arm to pull her closer. Paul Mantz, the stunt pilot, had broken an international record flying his Fleet biplane through forty-six consecutive outside loops in Palo Alto, California. Outside loops were even more difficult than inside loops because the plane went into the loop nose toward the ground instead of nose toward the sky. In an outside loop the pilot was on the outside and centrifugal force tried to throw the pilot out of the airplane. The feat earned front-page coverage, and in fact, Mantz's record stood for fifty years.

The girls crossed Burnside Street and passed under the watchful-eyed lions on their pedestals guarding the arched entrance gate to Chinatown. A fire had destroyed the old part of the neighborhood, and hammers provided a background beat from dawn to dusk. As Hazel and Elsie passed a construction site, the workers began to whistle at them and yell suggestive remarks about Chinese girls being wild and uninhibited, and how they'd like to see if those rumors were true. Hazel immediately stopped, turned toward them, and with her hands on her hips and feet planted wide proceeded to yell at them to shut up and show some respect. Their mouths fell open at this unexpected behavior from a woman, and an Asian woman at that, and her perfect, unaccented English. One by one, they looked down at their boots and returned to work.

"There! They'll think twice the next time!" Hazel said, linking arms with Elsie.

"Hazel always had something to say," Elsie would remember with a smile and a twinkle in her eye many years later.

In early September of 1931, the Lee family stood side by side holding dripping umbrellas at the graveside of their father. Rain poured in a heavy torrent, unusual for Portland in late summer. The coffin, carefully chosen by his wife, was lowered into the ground. Breathing in deeply the scent of freshly dug soil and rainwater, Hazel remembered a devoted, hardworking father, with never a harsh word, leaving those to his wife. And yet she couldn't remember a time he'd ever shown any affection. He'd been largely a stranger to her. His age made him more like a grandfather, and she knew little about him other than what he did to support his family and the few stories he had told about his life in China.

Twenty family members circled the open grave in Block 14, the Chinese section of Lone Fir Cemetery, one of the few places someone of Chinese descent could be buried in the city, located miles from their home on the other side of the Willamette River. Next to Mother stood six-year-old Daniel and ten-year-old Howard wearing stoic expressions and looking like miniature businessmen in their small suits. Hazel was sad to think that they had lost their father while still so young.

Standing in the rain, her shoes and feet as wet and cold as if she stood in the river, Hazel wondered how her large family would survive. Maybe her older brother would take over the restaurant partnership, although the restaurant business had suffered during those uncertain times, with people eating out less.

Hazel caught the eye of her cousin, Emily Kee, wearing under her coat the beautiful cream-colored silk mandarin-collared dress, the style they both wore when volunteering as interpreters. The rain would damage, if not ruin, the delicate fabric. Her father would have been pleased at Emily's show of respect. Beside Emily, Hazel's oldest sister, Rose, was trying to quiet her son, a chubby-faced two-year-old named Irving. Although Rose had married, she and Irving were living with the family while her husband looked for work in New York. With all the Lee children living at home, the small apartment now housed ten people. It occurred to Hazel that her quiet father's absence would make little difference to their claustrophobic conditions. He had rarely been home anyway. But his presence had been felt in all the many things he would not allow.

That was about to change.

The rain stopped and a patch of blue sky appeared overhead, and then a few rays of sunshine reached down toward the family gathered under the skyscraping Douglas firs.

And suddenly Hazel knew what she wanted to do someday. Someday . . . she would travel to China and visit her father's family and the half brother and half sister she'd never met, and bring her father's blessing to them. She had no idea how this would happen, but she would make sure that it did.

3

THE INVISIBLE GIRL

Flying is an indescribable feeling. There's no way I could tell you how free and how wonderful it is to get up there all by yourself. The world is so big! The bug bit me.[1]

—Violet "Vi" Thurn,
WASP, class 43-W-4

Hazel reached out and put her hand on the yellow nose of the biplane. Being so close to an airplane for the first time, her heartbeat quickened. The nose felt cold, and although it only sat two in its tandem cockpit, it was larger than she had expected. A voice broke her communion with the plane. "Want a ride?" It was the pilot who had just landed in the beautiful machine after performing breathtaking acrobatic maneuvers that had stunned the crowd.

"Right now?" She couldn't believe her luck.

"Right now. No charge." He produced a crooked smile at her enthusiasm.

His name was Charles Hanst. Hazel had come to the air show with a friend who was taking flying lessons from Hanst, a former World War I pilot. The air show took place at Christofferson Airport, one of many small airports scattered around the area to facilitate mail delivery. Located east of Portland, it had been named for Silas Christofferson, the man who had flown an airplane off the Multnomah Hotel in downtown Portland the month before Hazel was born. In his short lifetime he went on to become an Oregon aviation pioneer. In 1916, at the age of twenty-eight, Christofferson, while test flying a new biplane prototype in Northern California, experienced engine failure at two hundred feet and died from his injuries a few hours later.

Hazel donned the leather cap and goggles Hanst provided and climbed into the biplane's front seat. With the propeller activated, Hanst hopped into the seat behind her, and they were off. The engine picked up speed and the plane lifted, almost imperceptibly at first. Then her stomach fluttered as the ground sank away, and the Columbia River appeared flowing on both sides of tree-covered islands. The plane rocked from side to side climbing through the choppy air. Hazel turned her attention to the horizon. She had never looked out from anything higher than a third-story window, and now she saw the snowy dome of Mount St. Helens and, behind it, Mount Rainier. On the eastern horizon Mount Hood's familiar craggy blue rocks and white glacial expanses stood sentinel, and to the northeast was Mount Adams.

It was 1932, and since graduating from high school, Hazel, unable to find work in an office, had been working at the restaurant. She was bored and restless. She played on a girls' basketball team and continued to play tennis, but she wanted so much more.

The Depression had changed life for everyone and showed no signs of abating. People were saying it could be twenty-five years before the economy recovered. Adolf Hitler, refusing to comply with the Treaty of Versailles, was rearming his country, and although Americans tried to look away from the troubles in Europe, they couldn't help wondering if another world war loomed darkly on the horizon.

Hazel's family struggled like everyone else's, but having never been well off, perhaps they had a bit of an advantage. A sadness hung over everyone, though; even children seemed to sense it. After the latest report about yet another business failure, yet another bankruptcy, yet another ruined person taking his own life, questions hung in the air unanswered. "Where will we go? What will we do?"

The biplane rose and dipped like a boat riding swells, reminding Hazel of the weightless sensation of swimming. No race or tennis match she'd ever won could compare to soaring like a bird through the sky. This was where she belonged, but not in the passenger seat. She wanted to pilot the biplane.

They followed the Columbia westward as it weaved its way between Oregon and Washington until it met the Willamette River. Banking into a left turn, they sailed south over fields of grazing cows on Sauvie Island, one of the largest river islands in the United States, carpeted in bright green fields of spring vegetables and berries and peach orchards lush and leafy in late May. Suddenly, the plane dipped, and Hazel smelled sweet, fresh-cut grass on the wind. In the dense vegetation along the island banks the Willamette disappeared into narrow channels before widening again. They flew over downtown Portland, with its Douglas fir–covered hills on the western horizon. Cars creeping along the streets looked like toys, and Hazel wished her little brothers could see the sight. South of the city the plane turned sharply at the Ross Island Bridge to follow the two rivers back along the path they'd come. Hazel wondered how she would describe flying to her family who had never experienced anything like it. More importantly, how could she earn the money to take lessons?

Hazel thanked the pilot. "Things are heating up in China," he told her unnecessarily, as the Chinese community talked of little else these days.

Hanst proceeded to tell Hazel all about a newly formed flying school for Chinese American pilots taking place in Portland. The students would be required to have a pilot's license, which they would have to fund themselves, but the training program would be free. Hazel had heard rumors and believed they were just fanciful dreaming on the part of the boys in Chinatown who bragged that they were going to be trained to fly for China's Air Force and defeat the Japanese. Now she wanted to hear more, and Hanst assured her the program was very real, but of course girls were not permitted to apply.

As it happened, Hanst worked as an assistant instructor to Al Greenwood, who had been granted enough money by the Chinese Benevolent Society and businessmen in Portland to train thirty-six Chinese American pilots to go to China and help defend against the invading Japanese. These young men would become a vital part of Generalissimo Chiang Kai-shek's gallant stand against the invasion. Kai-shek was the head of the Nationalist government in China. He and his party were trying to establish control in a nation divided among revolutionists, nationalists, indigenous warlords, a developing Communist army and government, and now Japan's determination to take China's resources. Chinese Americans supported Kai-shek and believed he would help China emerge from years of strife and discord.

The invasion and occupation of Manchuria in northeastern China, and the subsequent destruction of Shanghai that caused the deaths of thousands, mostly civilians, had deeply humiliated the Chinese, both abroad and in the United States. It was clear to them that Japan was not going to be satisfied with Shanghai but would continue a larger invasion of China.

China's fledgling air force, with barracks and hangars still being constructed in the north, was easily defeated by the Imperial Japanese Army Air Force. The Chinese Air Force needed pilots. Delegates were sent to the United States to scout flying schools that could teach young Chinese American pilots to fly for China. Branches of the Chinese Consolidated Benevolent Association in cities around the United States agreed to help raise funds to train the young men.

The association, made up of local merchants and businessmen, had been established in 1882 with the purpose of aiding and protecting Chinese citizens in the community by providing assistance with housing and jobs and other issues that arose. Portland residents Dr. Chan Lam and Dr. Ting Lee made impassioned speeches to raise money for an aviation school to train young Chinese American pilots and send them to help China. Chinese flight schools opened not only in Portland, but in Chicago, New York, San Francisco, and Los Angeles. In total, two hundred Chinese American pilots would be trained at these schools before joining China's defense against Japan.

In Portland, the Chinese delegates and Benevolent Society members visited flying schools and discovered Allan D. Greenwood, a flight instructor at the Adcox Aviation School with a reputation of being one of the best. In 1918, at the tender age of nine, Al Greenwood had left Wisconsin and gone west. Like other boys his age, he became enamored with the World War I flying aces he read about in the newspapers. When the war ended and the government released its unwanted airplanes, the barnstormer came into being. Named for the farm fields or barn roofs where they landed, the first barnstormers were ex–World War I pilots looking to make money. The rock stars of the 1920s and '30s, these showmen, and women like Amelia Earhart and Bessie Coleman, traveled around the country performing stunts such as exchanging cockpits with another flier at one thousand feet or walking on the wing of their plane to retrieve a handkerchief dangling from the landing gear. They performed mock dogfights almost as dangerous as the real ones had been in combat. In a popular stunt called the "death dive," the pilot dove, spiraling straight toward the ground, before pulling up at the last minute.

One day young Greenwood had watched a plane land in a cow pasture. That moment changed his life. From then on, he knew he wanted to become an aviator. He became a member of the first class of Tex Rankin's, the well-known aerobatic pilot, barnstormer, and air racer. A natural, Greenwood soloed after only four hours of instruction. By 1927 he was performing as a barnstormer all over the Northwest. He was well known for his luck—more like lucky misses. The planes were primitive, and he flew out of cattle pastures, stubble fields, and ball parks. Broken wheels, blown-out tires, and blind landings were just a few hazards he walked away from without serious injury.

In 1930 Greenwood founded a business called the Sunset Flyers and originated the penny-a-pound racket in the Northwest, which charged passengers wanting rides one cent for each pound of their weight. In 1931 he was flying on fire patrol, which required the most skill and courage of any piloting. As he described it, "With eyes and lungs burning from smoke, the pilot must use all his strength and skill to retain control of his ship in the billowing heat waves that roll up from the big fires. Rarely is there a place to land in case of trouble."[2] Around Oregon he was the man responsible for marking roofs with town names and arrows to help pilots navigate.

If he would agree, the delegates wanted him to find Chinese students to train. Greenwood enthusiastically agreed. He placed advertisements in newspapers across the country seeking student applicants. Greenwood's attitude about the war in China and the Japanese invasion is unknown, but it's likely he was not unsympathetic, while possibly more interested in the money and potential notoriety the work provided. Furthermore, he had taught Chinese Americans to fly at Adcox Aviation School and been vocal about his positive impression of their abilities as pilots. In short, he admired his Chinese American students, disapproved of the common racial biases of the day, and looked forward to training them for combat.

Applications poured in not only from the Northwest but from all over the country, including Hawai'i, Chicago, Los Angeles, San Francisco, San Diego, Tucson, and New York. Requirements to be accepted to the school were a pilot's license and Chinese ancestry.

Here was an opportunity for applicants to be adventurous, and help the country of their parents' birth. A sense of duty toward and willingness to sacrifice for China was typical in Chinese American communities.

The heroic exploits of the Washington State flier Robert McCawley Short further inspired the prospective fliers. Bob Short had graduated as a lieutenant pilot in the United States Army Air Corps Reserve in 1928. While he was flying airmail between Spokane and Seattle and performing stunts on the side, a private company asked him to fly fighter aircraft to China, where he would train pilots for the newly emerging Chinese Air Force. Having once told a newspaper reporter that he hoped to die in the cockpit of a fighter aircraft, Short immediately accepted. In China, despite being under contract only to train pilots and demonstrate aircraft, he could not stand by as the Imperial Japanese Army Air Force attacked China. He became the first American to engage in combat against the Japanese.

Short had only recently been shot down and killed after downing three Japanese planes. It was believed by many who witnessed the crash that he sacrificed himself to break up the raid and save civilian lives. After his plane crashed and burst into flames, Japanese pilots, so impressed by Short's courage, flew over the crash site and dipped their wings in salute. His death went mostly unreported in American newspapers outside of Washington State. Reportedly, a half million people lined the streets of Suzhou on the day of his funeral. The first American casualty in the war with Japan, he is still revered as a hero in China today.

What had previously been the Adcox School of Aviation became the Chinese Flying Club of Portland, although everyone called it Al Greenwood's Chinese Flying School. It was a revolutionary enterprise at a time when the average pilot was more like millionaire Howard Hughes than a Chinese American kid with immigrant parents. The first group of students began with nineteen in training, out of which four would not finish.

The school was originally at Christofferson Airfield, where Hanst fought to keep it, but the Chinese benefactors decided to move the location to Swan Island, a joint civil-military airport closer to Portland and to Chinatown, where the students lived. Problems plagued the school in the beginning, with Hanst and Greenwood butting heads over leadership despite Greenwood having been chosen to head the program. Upset over the move of the Chinese Flying School activities to Swan Island, Hanst attacked Greenwood one day in what *The Oregonian* newspaper called "Portland's first hit and fly case." Hanst struck Greenwood over the head with a blackjack, a flexible steel rod used by police, at Swan Island airport and then escaped in a plane. The front-page headline read, "Charles Hanst Accused of Felling Fellow Flier: Alleged Aggressor Then Takes Off in Aircraft, Allan Greenwood, Victim Tells Police."[3] Greenwood suffered a head contusion and was taken to the hospital but was not seriously injured. *The Oregonian* reported that Greenwood planned to get a warrant for Hanst's arrest. Somehow they settled their differences in a more civil fashion, since the record shows that Greenwood continued to use Hanst as an assistant instructor at the Chinese Flying School.

From that first flight, Hazel was captivated. She later told a reporter, "Like Amelia Earhart, when I had my first ride in an airplane, I decided that I just had to learn to fly."[4] Less than a week before Hazel's first flight, Amelia Earhart became the first woman, and only the second person after Lindbergh, to pilot a plane solo across the Atlantic, and Hazel didn't see why she couldn't do the same.

Hazel didn't care that it was a rich man's sport and that she was neither rich nor a man. Times were changing. There was a new president, Franklin Delano Roosevelt, with a wife who championed women's rights. All Hazel needed was to find a job, any job, to pay for lessons.

That night over dinner, Hazel regaled her mother and siblings with details about the flight, adding drama by making the engine noise and whoosh of the wind that made her little brothers' eyes widen. Sitting at the table surrounded by her family, she told her mother that she was going to learn to fly, and that she was going to get a pilot license.

Hazel's mother was an intelligent woman ahead of her time who had recently become more confident in her ideas, which were far less conservative than her older husband's had been. She reached across the table and took Hazel's left hand. Her mother held to the Chinese belief that left-handedness brought bad luck. Hazel quickly scoffed. "When have I ever been unlucky?" she asked. Ignoring Hazel's question, her mother wanted to know if the airplane was oriented to be flown by a left-handed person.

"Ma, there are other left-handed people who fly planes." Hazel wasn't actually sure about that, but it had to be true; it was logical, and she'd seen the instrument panel and already knew how to use the controls to fly the biplane, and not that it mattered, but the throttle knob and trim cables were on the left side of the cockpit.

So her mother tried another approach. "Nineteen is so young, maybe too young to fly an airplane? And not ladylike. What will people say?" Hazel assured her mother she was old enough and reminded her that she already had a license to drive a car.

Frances, fourteen and wise in the ways of her older sister, reminded her mother, "Ah Ying enjoys danger and doing something that's new to Chinese girls."[5] The words struck a chord with their mother, who had been much the same in her younger years. After all, she'd married a man twenty years older for a chance to leave China and come to the United States, where she knew no one and couldn't speak the language, and she made the journey with two small children in tow. Hazel wasn't the only daring member of the Lee family.

Her mother looked across the table at her daughter, her "little hero," who would do exactly as she wanted and didn't care if her behavior was considered ladylike or not. "Well, it's your decision. If you want to do it, it's up to you."[6]

The H. Liebes and Company Department Store occupied the five-story Broadway Building in downtown Portland, on the corner of Broadway and Morrison. No expense had been spared in its design and construction, with each floor dedicated to a single department. An entire floor held the fur collection, and the basement had been fitted with a refrigerated fur storage vault. The store also offered men's suits and ladies' dresses and frocks. There were recreational facilities for employees and an elevator. H. Liebes catered to the richest and most distinguished citizens of Portland. When the Broadway Building was completed in 1913, Liebes had already been a successful manufacturer and dealer of furs and sealskins from their Alaska trading stations for fifty years.

Hazel applied for a position in the stockroom at H. Liebes. The only occupation open to a Chinese girl or woman outside of Chinatown was as a stockgirl working in the back where she would never be seen by the public. The part-time position wouldn't provide enough money for flying lessons, and so when a position called "Elevator Girl" became available, she applied. Hazel was told that Chinese couldn't apply for the elevator position, because customers didn't want to see Chinese people. Hazel refused to take no for an answer until the man in charge of hiring at the department store, tired of her relentless determination, said he would give her a chance on one condition. She could operate the elevator, he told her, if she could be invisible. Trained by her mother to sink into the background, to be seen and not heard and a threat to no one, Hazel knew how to disappear. He silently handed her a uniform and she turned to hurry from the office before he had time to change his mind.

"Wait!"

Hazel stopped, and her heart sank as she turned back.

"Here," he handed her a hat. "Put this on. It will hide your Chinese hair."

Hazel kept her eyes focused on the floor as customers, often wrapped in voluminous furs, entered the elevator. The clientele did not fraternize with Chinese, and Hazel would find herself out of a job if anyone noticed her enough to be offended by her presence. Although she remained perfectly still, in her mind she rose into the sky in an airplane as the elevator climbed to the top floors. Descending, she imagined gliding the plane back to earth. She passed the time like a statue, while soaring through the clouds in her imagination.

◊ ◊ ◊

In the early morning darkness, Hazel drove across the Willamette River on the Steel Bridge and made her way to the narrow land bridge connecting the east side of the river to Swan Island. Today she would have her first flight lesson toward earning her pilot's license.

Portland's airport sat situated in the middle of the Willamette River, two miles downstream from the city proper on a small piece of land named Swan Island by the pioneers and previously known as Willow Island by native residents. The airport was new, having been built a few years prior, when it had been determined Portland needed its own airport closer than Pearson Airfield in Vancouver, Washington. Charles Lindbergh dedicated the opening in September 1927, four months after completing his solo nonstop flight across the Atlantic. Since then, the dirt runways had been graveled.

Most airports in 1932 were nothing more than open fields with a few hangars and maintenance buildings, and terminals were rare. Swan Island had a stately neoclassical two-story terminal with a front door flanked by columns and Grecian urns, above which were the words "Portland Airport Administration Building." For the challenges provided, it was a good location to learn flying. It was a small piece of land surrounded by water that caused the air to be rough, and the western hills blocked radio-wave landing communication, all factors that contributed to the Portland airport being moved east, adjacent to the Columbia River, in 1940.

The airfield, the buildings and hangars shrouded in darkness, silently waited for the bustle of activity daylight would bring. Hazel's lessons began promptly at sunrise, a concession her instructor made so that she could finish in time to report to work. A pair of Fleet biplanes stood ready and waiting. Fleets, one of the most popular and common planes in the early 1930s, had been created by Consolidated Aircraft Corporation founder Reuben Fleet and specifically designed for civilian flight training. They had staggered fabric-covered wings of equal span, and steel tube frames. An open cockpit with dual controls and tandem seats for a pilot and passenger was best suited for a small person, or someone willing to fly with their knees up to their chest. The plane could be flown from either the front or back seat.

Waiting beside the Fleets stood Hazel's instructor, Al Greenwood. At twenty-three years old, he was only four years older than Hazel. Greenwood possessed a full face and square chin, a mustache, and intense dark eyes under heavy arched brows; he wore his Brylcreem-slicked hair combed straight back with a side part. His five-feet-five height was perfect for negotiating a biplane's tight quarters. Exuding diplomacy, good teaching skills, and a passion for airplanes and his students, Greenwood turned a blind eye to societal beliefs about the inferiority of women and Chinese Americans. Not many flight instructors wanted to teach women, fearing they were temperamental and emotional and would be prone to going "haywire" on solo flights. Greenwood disagreed. He had happily offered Hazel flying lessons and hoped she would help prove his belief that flying had nothing to do with brute strength and everything to do with keen intelligence and skill. Although he had never had a Chinese American woman as a student before, he saw no reason why she shouldn't be as capable as the boys.

◊ ◊ ◊

The eastern sky began to lighten as Greenwood started the propeller and the engine came to life. Hazel sat in the front with Greenwood behind where he would talk her through taxiing and takeoff. Without a radio, instructors communicated through a rubber tube called a gosport, a six-foot-long tube attached to the student's helmet, with a mouthpiece near the instructor's mouth. Hazel could hear Greenwood but not answer or ask questions.

Following Greenwood's instructions, Hazel taxied and lifted into flight. Geese rose from the river and flew beside the plane as they left the ground. Hazel smiled. Taking off was the most exciting thing she'd ever done. The stick controlled the airspeed, and the throttle controlled the altitude—there was nothing to it.

Next, she learned how to use Mount Hood as a reference point on the horizon to determine attitude, or relative position to the earth of the plane. Below her, daylight turned the Willamette River from black to sparkling gray-green. For half an hour she practiced flying straight and level, and then tried climbs and accelerations and decelerations, with Greenwood's steady voice in her ear. It was the first time she'd experienced the sensation of going up and down while flying, like she'd imagined when operating the elevator, and she couldn't get enough. The lesson ended too soon, with Greenwood taking the controls for the landing.

Back at the Swan Island field, Greenwood watched Hazel saunter away and thought he detected a moment of swagger. When she knew she was out of sight behind the hangar, she increased her stride and flipped her hair back. A moment later, her pace slowed. Today had been easy and thrilling. She still had a long way to go, and she was in it for the long haul.

Hazel had been unfazed by her first lesson, something Greenwood had never seen before. She showed promise, a natural, as good as any of his boys. He would soon begin reviewing applications for students to fill his second class. He had his first class in training and they were progressing well. It's likely he considered Hazel for the program from the start; he needed students, and she had the qualities he wanted. He knew that getting approval to allow a girl to join the program would not be easy, and maybe impossible. The Chinese members of the Benevolent Society and their financial supporters held to traditional beliefs about men's and women's roles.

Greenwood saw confidence and fearlessness in Hazel. In fact, he now had a new worry. He wondered if Hazel might not be fearful enough.

4

ELEVATOR GIRL
MASTERS FLYING

*Women are seeking freedom. Freedom in the skies! They
are soaring above temperamental tendencies of their sex
which have kept them earth-bound. Flying is a symbol of
freedom from limitations.*[1]

—**MARGERY BROWN**

HAZEL CIRCLED THE BIPLANE LOOKING for anything suspicious. Missing something on a precheck could cost you
your life. Then she checked the engine, making sure all the nuts were
there; they could sometimes strip. With no oil flow to the tops of the
cylinders in a Kinner engine, they had to be greased by hand every
ten hours or before important flights. Next, she confirmed that no
oil had collected in the lower cylinder.

Starting a Fleet involved choreography. Hazel grasped the propeller with one hand and pulled it backwards. "Just walk it through;
you don't need to use force," Greenwood yelled from the cockpit.
She repeated the process four times; each time she heard the click
that told her she'd done it correctly. Then with both hands on the
prop, she raised her left leg forward, and swinging it behind her for

leverage, she pulled, and the unique thumping that identified the Kinner engine began.

Having climbed onto the wing and into the cockpit, Hazel inspected the instrument panel, starting with the fuel. The tank held close to three hours of fuel when full. If a car ran out of gas or had engine trouble, the driver could pull to the roadside. In flight, the best you could hope for was to find a good field, and quickly. Seated in the confined cockpit, everything was in reach. The control stick was between her knees, with pedals on either side to control the left or right direction. She touched the throttle knob to produce more power. Trim cables were on her left too. Pulling the top trim cable back brought the nose up, and pulling forward took the nose down.

As Hazel performed her preflight check, Greenwood's other training biplane, called *The Student Prince*, taxied down the runway, piloted by one of the Chinese Flying School boys earning solo hours. *The Prince* had been purchased by Greenwood exclusively for the students in his Chinese school. Greenwood was essentially running two businesses simultaneously. With the new Chinese Flying School under his direction, most of his time was spent training the Chinese Americans boys for combat in China, but he continued to give flying lessons as he was doing for Hazel.

Those fifteen boys quickly became idols to Hazel. For as many hours as she could spare, she watched them practice. They treated her like a kid sister, though all of them were about the same age, and good-naturedly tolerated her enthusiastic antics and questions. She was fun to have around, laughing and playing tricks on them, with a wide smile and her deep-voiced wisecracks.

Hazel kept the photo of the first class that had appeared in *The Oregonian* newspaper in January 1931. The boys, looking like a motley crew of street urchins, posed before *The Prince*, uncertain of what they were in for, before Greenwood had begun his process of transforming them into pilots bound for war in China. One of the boys, Moy Gee, was the nephew of Moy Back Hin, the Chinese

Benevolent Society council member who had first visited Greenwood's flying school with the delegates from China asking for help finding fliers in the United States. Other students—Michael Tom, Millard Chung, Hubert Leong, Edward Wong, Ralph Chang, and Sam Chang—all welcomed Hazel as one of their gang.

Hazel had never been among others who shared her passion for aviation. Flying was all they talked about, and they knew as much about airplanes, and sometimes more, than experienced pilots. It was practice that they needed, practice flying. And Al Greenwood would provide it.

The "boys," as Greenwood called them, proved to be able students, a little heavy on the stick at first, but never lacking courage or a willingness to try anything. Training required ten hours of primary work and ten hours of advanced aerobatics from each student, an enormous task for one instructor. Greenwood hired other pilots, like Hanst, to assist. Charles Mears, Morris King, and Dick Rankin also provided instruction to the students.

Greenwood peppered his instruction with stories of his exploits, like one about his narrowest escape, to demonstrate the deadly consequences of fear. While practicing spins with a student, he turned the plane over at seven thousand feet and let it spin for about five thousand feet. The student grabbed the stick, panicking, and as Greenwood described it, began to do all the wrong things while using up nearly every foot of the remaining two thousand feet, before Greenwood could finally regain control from the student—just before the wheels hit the grass tips. Controlling fear was essential no matter what happened in the air.

◊ ◊ ◊

Around that time, Hazel began dressing like a flier, in baggy pants tucked into riding boots. People stared, and pointed, talking behind their hands. "There's the girl who is learning to fly." "So foolish." "Her poor mother."

One evening, Hazel and Elsie Chang sat on the schoolyard grass in the gathering twilight, while Hazel dramatically explained everything about flying to her friend, as if she were taking Elsie along for a ride. Hazel described what she could see while flying and how she steered the airplane and how the air made the plane rock and bounce and all the dangers that needed to be avoided, like stalling on a landing. Power-off landings, and stalls and turns . . . to Elsie it all sounded terrifying.

Hazel was such a good storyteller that Elsie closed her eyes and felt the wind and the weightlessness and heard the engine and smelled the trees in the air aloft. They fell back on the grass and stared up at the darkening sky, waiting for the first star to flicker.

Hazel told Elsie that no other Asian American woman had a pilot's license in the United States. She was going to be the first!

"There!" Hazel said pointing to the first star flickering in the darkening sky.

Hazel counted the minutes until she could get back in an airplane, with the wind in her face and the lulling rumble of the engine to soothe her. She loved the speed, the rhythmic, percussive thump of the engine, the rush of air surrounded by the silent expanse of sky. Hazel experienced a new kind of solitude. Away from her family and the tight quarters of their home filled with younger siblings, and a job where she had to hide her appearance and try to be invisible, she was alone without any expectations or judgments. It didn't matter that she was of Chinese descent. No one could see her race; no one could see her gender. In the sky, she wasn't Chinese or American, man or woman, visible or invisible . . . she was just herself. In the sky, she felt limitless.

◊ ◊ ◊

Hazel's mother expected her to marry and have children, but Hazel wanted a different life. By the time her brother Daniel was born, her mother had been pregnant and having babies for twenty years.

Hazel refused to be tied to a home and children when there were more exciting things to do. She saw how conformity ruled women's lives, offering a suffocating security in return. Women moved from their fathers' homes to their husbands', where their sons would have more power than they ever would. For most women, groomed to deny their own capabilities, to distrust themselves, and to defer to men, the decision to fly was fraught with fears, not only of flying, but of being independent. In an age when women were encouraged to stay grounded, Hazel's wanting to fly was the ultimate expression of individuality.

◊ ◊ ◊

In 1932 there were only about two hundred women in the United States with a private pilot license, representing less than 1 percent of all pilots. That number would continue to grow rapidly thanks to women fliers like Amelia Earhart soaring into towns and showing women what was possible and encouraging them to reach for the sky.

Hazel was not the only Asian American woman in the area pursuing the art and skill of flying. Virginia Wong, a classmate of Hazel's from the High School of Commerce, listened to Hazel's stories about flying and wanted to see for herself what flying was about. They had become friends as members of a Chinese dance troupe. Hazel introduced her to Al Greenwood and she began taking flying lessons. Virginia lived with her family on Everett Street, just a few blocks from Hazel. She had been born on November 15, 1911, to Wong Chock Way and Jung Shee, behind the Hop Chong Store on Chinatown's Pine Street, and her father left for China when she was five and died there soon after. Her five-feet-two-and-a-half-inch frame fit comfortably in the Fleet cockpit, and she wanted nothing more than to travel and see the world.

Leah Hing was another Portland girl who became interested in learning to fly, while watching local stunt pilot Dorothy Hester. Leah didn't live in Chinatown but across the river in Ladd's Addition, one of the few neighborhoods where Chinese citizens with money and a white connection willing to front a house purchase could live. Her father, Lee Hing, had been born in Oregon to Chinese parents, and Leah's mother immigrated from Canton around 1901. The Hings owned a tea and herbal shop called the Chinese Tea Garden, around the corner from the Lees' home.

In comparison to Hazel, Leah's life had already been filled with adventure. After graduating from Portland's Washington High School, she toured the United States with a dance troupe, a contingent of eight girls including Virginia Wong, whose act, called Mr. Wu and His Chinese Showboat Revue, had earned a spot on a vaudeville bill. They performed in New York City at the RKO Orpheum and toured the entire RKO circuit for a year.

In 1927, Hazel, her sister Florence, Leah, and Virginia had been members of a larger dance group that grew into this touring troupe. Eighteen Chinese girls performed the closing spectacular of the Rose Festival Pageant in Portland, and Hazel appeared as a solo dancer. The pageant was a huge extravaganza with a cast of hundreds. Dressed in Chinese headpieces, hair garlands, and silks embroidered with elaborate designs of flowers and birds, they were called by The Oregonian, "the most interesting group in the pageant." But Hazel and her sister would not remain members of the dance troupe and travel across the country with Leah and Virginia.

In Chicago, while performing on the vaudeville circuit, Leah had taken her first airplane ride, at a school for Chinese aviators like Al Greenwood's Flying School. She returned to Portland to work as a cashier in her father's tea house, determined to become a pilot. One day Tex Rankin came into the shop, and Leah recognized him as the famous pilot who had taught Dorothy Hester, the first woman to pull off the difficult maneuver known as the outside loop that Mantz had made famous.

Their conversation resulted in Leah taking lessons with Rankin at his tiny airfield located at Portland's marshy Mock's Bottom, not far from Swan Island. Several national newspapers reported on Leah's plans to earn her pilot's license. New York's *Post Star* called her the "Chinese Miss Lindy," after Charles Lindbergh. On March 6, 1932, *The Oregonian* quoted Leah as saying, "I believe that women can learn to fly as easily as men. . . . Eventually there will be just as many women flying as men."[2]

One warm day, someone new appeared on the airfield standing beside Al Greenwood. "Meet my new student, Clifford Louie," Greenwood said with a smile, already proud of his newest recruit. "He's come from Seattle to learn to fly."

Quick comebacks and witty words had never failed her, but Hazel experienced an unfamiliar shyness under the stranger's smiling gaze. He shook her hand, and she wasn't sure what to make of the unfamiliar gesture. His grin made her wonder what was so funny, and she had to resist the urge to look down to see if she had a cigarette burn on her clothing again.

When she had first seen him from a distance, she had thought he might be a visiting Chinese dignitary because of the way he carried his tall frame, like someone born to privilege, and because he was so meticulously groomed, with thick black hair sleekly side-parted in the style of the day and a thin, neat mustache. When he smiled, his eyebrows arched sharply, accentuating his dark eyes. His expression remained amused as they were introduced, and he told her that Greenwood had already filled him in on her talents. He seemed completely sincere except for that annoying twinkle in his eye, as if he could see through her tough façade. Hazel was confident and used to the company of boys, but this one left her unsure how to stand or what to do with her arms. She hated feeling unnerved and decided she would avoid Greenwood's newest student in the future.

Cliff Louie was staying in Chinatown with friends of his father's.

At a grocery store he asked where Hazel Lee and her family lived. The apron-clad grocer pointed down the street and rattled off the address. He showed up at Hazel's home that evening with his cousin in tow, and her mother invited them to dinner.

Hazel learned that Cliff was eighteen years old. She was nineteen. Cliff and his cousin, Frank Louie, had been in Seattle when they'd read in the local newspaper about the call for flight school cadets in Portland. He had been running a Chinese noodle factory and had no trouble abandoning it to pursue his dream of flying.

He and Hazel had a surprising amount in common. Cliff had been born Louie Yim-Qun in Seattle, and like Hazel he had grown up attending segregated public schools. Parents objected to Chinese students in the classroom with their children, and so to get around the unconstitutionality of excluding anyone from a public education, school districts opened public schools exclusively for Chinese Americans. Cliff's father, like Hazel's, came from Taishan County, Guandong Province, China. They were both second-generation Chinese and spoke Cantonese at home. And they both wanted to fly.

When the meal was half-over, Daniel came through the door, breathing heavily from running. His mother assaulted him with questions about where he'd been and what he'd been doing, and he explained he'd been helping the grocer unload crates. His siblings smiled, knowing the reason he ran home. He didn't like to be outside after dark.

Rumors were repeated in whispered voices among Chinatown's children of young men being offered drinks in a bar or gambling hall and, after they were drunk, taken underground to the tunnels that led to the river, where they'd be sold to ship captains as slave laborers. The tunnels, a labyrinth of narrow passageways with steel trapdoors leading to secret stairways connected to gambling dens, brothels, and opium parlors, were built in the 1800s to move merchandise more efficiently from the river to businesses, but were also used for illegal activities and provided a means of escape from police, or rival gangs collecting debts. Daniel had never seen the tunnels except in his imagination, but the prospect of being "shanghaied" terrified him. He always hurried through the streets of Chinatown wide-eyed, peering into doorways and alleys. Hazel would tell him to slow down, that she would fight off any would-be kidnappers and he was too scrawny to be worth much anyway.

◊ ◊ ◊

Hazel shared a room with her sisters Frances and Florence. Along the sides of her mirror she'd placed photos of the flying school boys posed in front of *The Prince*. Bill Young, who had come all the way from New York to train with Greenwood, signed his photo "Best Wishes!" After the dinner with Cliff, she added his photo, in which his thick black hair was parted and combed back neatly and he wore a smile as if he had just shared a joke with the photographer. His expression and posture exuded confidence and joviality. When Frances teased her about the photo, she scoffed. "Oh, he's too young for me!" Besides, she reminded her sister, she was never going to marry. A husband would insist she give up flying, and that was something she would never do. And anyway, even if she liked him, Cliff would soon be training to go to China to fight a war against the Japanese. His likelihood of surviving was not exactly good.

Before a student was accepted into the program, he had to pledge his life to China, to the interests of China and to Chinese aviation. The pledge to die for China would take precedence over any relationship that might develop.

If Hazel could convince Greenwood and the Benevolent Society to accept her into the next class of students training to go to China, she would sign the pledge without hesitation. To fly against the Japanese invaders would be the ultimate experience and worthy of any sacrifice. She'd die in battle fighting the enemy without any regrets. But the Chinese Flying School, like all the programs across the country, didn't allow women. Hazel decided that needed to change. There were few enough opportunities for a Chinese woman. If she wasn't admitted to Greenwood's flying school, her future options were not just limited, they were unthinkable.

◊ ◊ ◊

In August 1932, Al Greenwood's first class of fifteen students eagerly awaited their departure for China still heady from newspaper interviews and farewell speeches delivered at banquets in their honor. Four of the original nineteen had failed to complete the class due to physical handicaps such as colorblindness. The proud graduates ready to embark on the adventure of a lifetime posed in front of *The Prince* in two rows, wearing tentative smiles and looking like boys not used to being photographed. Most wore ties, a few wore crewneck sweaters over white shirts, and several wore the bomber-style zip-up jackets popular at the time. They had learned more than flying under Greenwood's guidance; they now believed themselves to be confident young men, no longer boys, ready to fight a war and die if necessary for China.

While the men of the Chinese Benevolent Society wondered if these kids would have the toughness required to survive combat in China, Al Greenwood expressed an unwavering faith in his students. In an interview with Webster Jones for *The Oregonian*, Greenwood tried to deflate the accepted belief that people of Chinese descent could not possibly be as capable as white American pilots. "Chinese make rattling good fliers. This myth about Orientals not being able to fly is pure bunk. They are as good as Americans or other occidentals and they are superior in a lot of ways."[3]

After the graduates were photographed, Greenwood invited his flying students to pose for a photo. Hazel sauntered over to stand in front of *The Prince* wearing wide khaki jodhpurs tucked into black riding boots, a polo shirt, and a flight vest. Her goggles had been pushed up onto her flight cap. She took a drag from her cigarette and leaned back on the wing. "Perfect," the photographer told her.

A smile broadened slowly across her face, followed by a wisecrack delivered sotto voce.

Greenwood recognized Hazel's transformation. She moved in a slow, confident stride, with a graceful swagger. Over the summer, she had made rapid progress and would soon fly solo. In a few short months she had come into her own and in doing so had become something completely unique. Greenwood understood her need to be first, to compete with the boys and the girls too. He smiled and nodded toward her as the camera shutter snapped.

Leaving the others, Hazel adopted a pace to keep up with Cliff's long-legged stride. From a distance, dressed in flying clothes, they looked like two young men, one tall and the other short, walking across the field. Having earned his license, Cliff would join the next class of Greenwood's Flying School and go to China after his five months of training. Greenwood had already been planning for his second group of fliers to begin training in October or November. There were plenty of willing students like Cliff, who had already been accepted. Cliff had encouraged Hazel to apply, telling her she was as good as any of the boy fliers, but the Benevolent Society had not yet granted permission. Greenwood's latest argument, that the grant to train thirty-six students had not stipulated they be boys, proved incorrect. The contract called for "young men." He would have to convince them that Hazel was a crack pilot worthy of their financial investment. She had to pass her flying test to receive her license first, but that wasn't going to be any trouble for Hazel.

Virginia Wong wanted to join the flying club too. Her parents, like Hazel's mother, had given their permission. Now the decision was up to the men in the Benevolent Society. Since the Chinese elders and businessmen supporting the school paid all the training expenses for the students, they had to be convinced that two girls were worth the investment. Greenwood became the girls' advocate, telling *The Oregonian* that they had received the same training as the boys and were equally capable, if not more so. He believed Hazel and

Virginia would prove his long-held belief that flying involved more finesse than muscle, and that keen intelligence was more important than brute strength.

Besides helping China defend themselves against the Japanese invasion and having the opportunity to fly, Hazel had another reason for wanting to go to China. Her father's first children—her half siblings—as well as her aunts, uncles, and cousins still lived in the village her father had grown up in. This could be her chance to fulfill her dream of visiting her father's homeland.

On October 24, 1932, Hazel passed the rigorous Department of Commerce pilot examination. Having also accumulated fifty flying hours, half of which were solo, Hazel was granted a private pilot's license. The document described her as five foot three, 117 pounds. On November 1, 1932, the *Oregon Journal* reported on Hazel's achievement, as the first Chinese American woman in Oregon to receive a pilot's license, with the page-two headline, "Portland Elevator Girl Masters Flying And Gets License." The reporter quipped, "The fifth floor of the H. Liebes & Co. was not high enough for Hazel Lee, 20, elevator operator there, so she got up early mornings to learn to fly an airplane. Miss Lee took an airplane ride a year ago, got interested, and now that she can fly, she plans someday to go to China and interest women there in aviation."4

Hazel was, in fact, the first Chinese American woman in the United States, not just in Oregon, to earn a pilot license.

Another Asian woman, named Katherine Sui Fun Cheung, had earned her pilot's license in Los Angeles on March 29, 1932, seven months before Hazel. But unlike Hazel, who had been born in the U.S., Katherine had been born in China and had not yet become a citizen of the United States. It was only after graduating from high school in Canton that she had moved with her family to Los Angeles, where she earned a degree at the Los Angeles Conservatory of Music, playing the piano. She had become fascinated with flying when she saw planes landing and taking off from Dyer Airport in Gardena, where her father was teaching her to drive. Katherine was thirty when she obtained her pilot license, ten years older than Hazel. She would go on to become a well-known aerobatic performer. Wanting to break through the stereotype of quiet Asian girls who obediently stayed at home, she traveled the country hoping to interest Asian American girls in aviation. Unfortunately, her dream to open a school for women aviators in China was denied by the Chinese government.

Meanwhile, Leah Hing would not receive her license until 1934, making her the fourth Asian American female pilot in the United States, after Virginia Wong, who had earned her license in November 1932, a few weeks after Hazel.

Greenwood worked hard to convince the Chinese Benevolent members and other financial supporters that women, exemplified by Hazel and Virginia, were fully capable of piloting planes in battle. After all, he reminded them, China needed pilots to defeat the Japanese invaders, and these two young women were every bit as capable as the young men. Eventually, they reluctantly agreed to allow Hazel and Virginia to join the fifteen young men selected for the second aviation class.

Training for Greenwood's second class began in November 1932, less than a month after Hazel earned her license. Training would last through February, after which the group would depart for China. In December, Hazel told *The Oregonian* that there was a new opportunity to do something for China, and she was going. Her words were vague, but later, when she applied to travel outside the country, her omission of what she was going to China to do suggested that the truth, that she was going to join the Chinese Air Force, might have kept her from being granted permission to leave the United States.

5

FEARLESS FATALISTS

I would rather have a squadron of Chinese pilots, with planes of equal speed and maneuverability, than a squadron of American pilots. Why? Simply because the Chinese has more sheer daring. He is a fatalist with a background of centuries of fatalism. Death means nothing to him. He has all the natural ability that Americans have. And he has the added fervor and spirit which the American does not have. Everything in their temperament helps them to fly well. Never did I encounter fear or nervousness. They seemed to have perfect confidence in the airplane and in themselves. They have a kind of self-assurance that helps them to reach their goals. It is not cockiness, although it may appear to be to persons who do not know them. It is rather the real confidence that comes after hard work and mastery of a difficult art.[1]

—Al Greenwood

BY NOVEMBER 1932, AL GREENWOOD'S Chinese Flying School was the talk of the town. His first group was settled in China, and he was already hearing about their successes, including their commissioning as officers. He was now training a second group of students, including the first two women pilots to train for China, Hazel Lee and Virginia Wong.

Hazel's mother was not happy. Learning to fly an airplane for fun was one thing, but joining a volunteer program to train for war in China was something else entirely. Having made the long ocean voyage from China herself, she understood the enormity of the distance. The war in China had escalated. No reasonable person would head into the fire instead of away from it. Let someone else help China, she thought, not my daughter.

Her wishes and fears were futile and held no weight with her headstrong daughter. Hazel tried to explain to her mother how few choices were available to her, and that times were not much different than the Middle Ages, when a woman was limited to being a wife, a mistress, a nun, or a spinster. Work in a Chinese restaurant, in an elevator, or in a stockroom out of sight offered nothing more than an invisible life, shut inside, quietly wasting away. This was an opportunity to live life out of the shadows, independently and honorably, on her own terms. She reminded her mother that she would be assisting the army under Generalissimo Chiang Kai-shek and his American-educated wife. Madame Chiang Kai-shek was a heroine to Chinese American girls, who saw her and her husband as the spirit behind the New China.

Years later, Hazel's sister Frances remembered, "There was nothing Mother could do. She said, 'You're not afraid of the wind, you're not afraid of the water,' and that was that." Frances added, "I thought it was typical of Hazel."[2]

The Chinese Flying School students came from all over the country and became like a family. Being with other people her age who loved flying, while training together with a singular purpose, was a revelation to Hazel. She had found her tribe.

Bill Young, the oldest at twenty-nine, had left a profitable restaurant business in New York, locking the door and selling out, because he wanted to help China.

Harry Low, twenty, had left the kitchen in Seattle where he was a successful cook.

Thirty-two-year-old Peter Chin had come from Chicago, where he had worked as a mechanic, holding two aircraft mechanic's licenses.

Millard Chung, twenty-seven, had immigrated to Portland from China in 1922 without his parents, on a student visa, and had subsequently graduated from the High School of Commerce. He had worked in a cannery during school vacations. For his application to the Chinese Flying School, one of Chung's teachers called him an A student who didn't smoke or have bad habits. The principal of his high school noted that he'd had a positive attitude and never gave them any trouble. Chung spoke exceptional English and became the flying school's class spokesman.

Mai Euon Lam, twenty-two, had graduated from Portland's Lincoln High School in 1931. To join the flying school, he had quit his training at North Pacific College in Portland where he was taking classes in pharmacy, chemistry, and dentistry.

John Kee Wong was born in China and moved to Portland from Seattle in 1931 to learn to fly.

The class was rounded out by eleven other fliers including Arthur Chin, Clifford Louie, Virginia Wong, and Hazel Lee.

Arthur Chin, another product of Portland's Chinatown, and a year younger than Hazel, had just turned eighteen in October. Hazel knew him from Chinese School, and he was a friend of her younger brother Victor. He was the first of six children born to Chinese American parents Fon and Eva Wong Chin. Art had inherited his soulful, wide-set dark eyes, full lips, and wavy thick hair from his Peruvian mother. He possessed an intelligent, penetrating stare, movie-star good looks, and boundless energy and charm. The girls loved him. Described as physically and mentally compact, he was not tall but powerfully built. A casual personality belied the seriousness of this young man who would go on to greatness. Like the others, without the help of the Chinese Benevolent Society and donations from Portland businesses, he would not have been able to afford the training that would change the direction of his life.

◊ ◊ ◊

Finally, it was Hazel's turn to fly *The Prince*, and even though it was an identical plane to the one she had trained on, she experienced a sacred camaraderie sitting in the same seat as her friends who were now serving in China. Their success meant victory for Greenwood, too, and *The Prince* had become a kind of mascot, a symbol of what they were accomplishing.

Greenwood lit a cigarette and gazed out over the runway toward Hazel coming in for a practice landing. She placed the plane precisely on the circle in the center of the field, executing a perfect three-point landing. Greenwood pushed his flight cap onto the back of his head and strode toward his student, with a reporter in tow running to catch up with the man he'd come to interview, the man who knew more about Chinese flying ability than any instructor in the country. For over a year, Greenwood had been the chief pilot and instructor for the largest and most successful flying club ever formed in the United States for China's Air Force. His name was known across the country and in China. Greenwood's students were "among the best pilots the Chinese have."[3] This would become his legacy and greatest achievement.

Every day Greenwood gave half his students a thirty-minute lesson, and on the next day the other half received the same. The training was intense, and Greenwood pushed them to their limits. Their lives depended on being prepared for battle. He was determined to send China another batch of pilots who were the cream of the crop. Greenwood praised the flying aptitude of his two female students in an interview, saying, "They went through the same training as the men and were equal in flying ability and resourcefulness."[4]

Before graduating, each student would accumulate forty-five hours of flying that included solo hours and ten hours of stunts, spins, loops, vertical rolls, barrel rolls, vertical reversements, wingovers, slow rolls, and Immelmann turns—an aerial combat maneuver from World War I consisting of a sharp turn to reposition for another attack. Most students made their solo flights after six or eight hours of instruction, a shorter time than average flying students. They enjoyed stunts, or acrobatics as they were also called, and couldn't get enough, until they could snap through a half dozen stunts with ease. The maneuvers needed to become second nature, something the pilots could do without thought when they would be too distracted to think about anything other than their opponents and survival during battle.

In February 1933, as the Chinese Flying School training neared completion and the students prepared to graduate, Hazel began the process to request permission to travel to China. All American-born and Chinese nationals were subjected to a complicated process when leaving and reentering the United States. Even though Hazel and Virginia had been born in the United States, their parents were Chinese citizens, making them subject to the Chinese Exclusion Act passed by Congress in 1882, the first federal law to forbid entry to an ethnic working group, which banned Chinese laborers from coming to the United States. Few Chinese entered the country under this law, and it's likely that Hazel's father received permission to enter because he was a merchant and not a laborer. In

1902 the act, renamed the Geary Act, added restrictions including the requirement that Chinese residents register and obtain a certificate of residence or face deportation. When leaving the United States, they were required to obtain certification to reenter the country when returning home. It wasn't until 1943, when China was a member of the Allied Nations during World War II, that Congress repealed the Chinese Exclusion Act.

Hazel's immigration application showed her age as twenty, height five-foot-three, weight 117, and "full and right name" Lee Yut-Ying, alias Hazel Lee. On her birth certificate she is named Hazel Lee, in the common practice of Westernizing a given Chinese name. During her immigration interview, Hazel said that she was going to Canton City to visit and study but didn't have a definite address.

This was not Virginia's first application to leave the country. In 1929, she had applied to visit Vancouver, British Columbia, with the vaudeville group. After returning from British Columbia and finishing high school, Virginia went back east with the group of eight girls that included Leah Hing, to begin their vaudeville circuit.

This time, on February 9, 1933, Virginia's brother George acted as witness, and because white witnesses were thought to be more credible than Chinese, a teacher from Atkinson Elementary School named Nancie Singleton testified that she knew Virginia and her brother as students. Singleton swore in an affidavit that she knew Virginia's family and that Virginia had come to the school when she was seven and "continued to be a regular enrolled pupil at the school for a period of about 8 years at which time she became a graduate thereof and that during all the time I was almost daily in contact with her in my classes."[5] Virginia's mother also testified on her daughter's behalf. Unable to write, she signed her testimony with an X.

The black-and-white photo accompanying Virginia's 430 form

shows a woman looking older than her twenty-one years. Her hair was styled in a marcel wave with a deep side part. The lengthy and demeaning identity confirmation process may have been the reason for her somber expression. Hazel and Virginia must have wondered if, after all their training and the expenses put forth by their supporters, they'd even be allowed to travel to China after all.

Hazel is also unsmiling and looking older than her age on her 430-form photo. She leans forward, her expression almost a challenge, determined, as if to say she would be going to China one way or another and nothing would stop her. Both were asked if they'd ever testified in an immigration office before. Interestingly, they were not asked anything about their pilot training and what the purpose of that training might have been. When an examining inspector asked Virginia why she was going to China, she replied, "I think I am going to fly."[6] There were no further questions, and both Hazel and Virginia had their trips approved.

On Art Chin's application to travel to China, he wrote that the reason for the trip was to visit a sick grandmother. Clearly the fliers were careful not to reveal their real reason for going to China, possibly fearful they wouldn't be allowed to leave to join another country's air force, or that it might raise suspicions that they were not loyal Americans, but possibly working for China.

◊ ◊ ◊

Hazel and Virginia both graduated with honors from Al Greenwood's Chinese Flying School. In early February, the second group of Greenwood's graduates posed in front of *The Student Prince*, but unlike the photo taken of the first group last year, this time the graduates were joined by the leaders in the Portland Chinese community responsible for raising the money to pay for their training. The occasion was one of great honor and pride in making this financial contribution to China. Their goal had been achieved. China would have thirty-two trained fliers at their disposal. In the photo

Hazel, wearing a white short-sleeved blouse and belted jodhpurs, stands in front of Greenwood, both wearing berets and sunglasses.

◊ ◊ ◊

On February 12, 1933, a month before Hazel sailed for China, a photo appeared in *The Oregonian* of her standing in the elevator at H. Liebes and Company, inexplicably wearing not her uniform, but a white satin, mandarin-collared tunic.

"My ambition," she said in the accompanying interview, "is to stimulate interest in aviation and flying among the women in China—just as it has been aroused here in America by a great number of fine women fliers. Perhaps when I go up in an airplane in China and do a couple of loops and wingovers, they will say if one girl can do that, why can't others? Flying, you know, is the most simple and the quickest form of transportation. Women can be of value to flying in China as they can here in America. I have no elaborate plans. I am going over to see what's what, and to do what I can to interest others in aviation. I feel that it is a great opportunity for anyone to be able to fly."[7]

Local celebrity caught Hazel by surprise, and she joked about it with her friends. Featured in another Portland newspaper, the *Oregon Journal*, the reporter ignored the fact that Hazel was born in the U.S. "Twenty, pretty, American in speech and manners Miss Hazel Ying Lee, Chinese, unmarried and an air pilot, recently left Portland to become a military flier in the defense of her country and countrymen against the Japanese."

The article concluded with a jaunty but condescending acknowledgment of the racism prevalent at the time. "Incidentally, what a picture there is in this hurry of Chinese homeward to help defend their native land! It refutes the hackneyed idea of non-intelligence in the Chinese race and shows that when trained in the schools they have thoughts of native land, a love of country and resentment of foreign invasion. If all the Chinese in China would catch the spirit of pretty Hazel Ying Lee and other young Chinese in America now flooding homeward for defense of their homeland, Japan's attempt at forcible conquest of Chinese territory would soon end."[8]

When asked how long she planned to live in China, Hazel replied, "An indefinite stay. Of course, I will come back sometime to see how things are moving in Portland."[9]

6

THE FLYING JOAN D'ARC IN CHINA

I don't see why a Chinese woman can't be as good a pilot as anyone else. . . . We drive automobiles. Why not fly planes?[1]

—KATHERINE SUI FUN CHEUNG

ON MARCH 4, 1933, AL GREENWOOD'S seventeen young fliers boarded the S.S. *President Taft* in Seattle. Ignoring the cold temperature, Hazel and Virginia linked arms and stood at the railing beside Cliff. Joining them on this voyage were Hazel's mother, who had decided to visit her homeland after her extended absence, and four of Hazel's siblings—sixteen-year-old Frances, fourteen-year-old Howard, ten-year-old Daniel, and twenty-one-year-old Florence, all eager to do what they could to help the cause in China.

For the newly graduated pilots, this day was the culmination of intense training and preparation, and now they were finally about to sail to a country they'd never been to before, to do their duty and possibly die for China. Despite or because of that, a celebratory mood prevailed. On deck the group posed for a photo with their families. The handsome young men wore neatly pressed slacks, cardigan sweaters, and freshly shined oxfords. Smoke from cigarettes and pipes drifted around them as they talked in soft, muted voices, perhaps still not quite believing that they were finally embarking on this long-dreamed-of adventure. These were the final moments before they were out on the open water and on their way to Shanghai. With the click of a camera shutter, their brave images were captured and frozen in time.

Wrapped in thick coats, as the ship pulled away from the seawall, they stood at the railing and waved to the crowd below yelling, "Bon Voyage!" A few men from their group collapsed into deck chairs to flip through the pages of the *Seattle Post-Intelligencer*, while the women stood in clusters, laughing nervously, and smoothing their calf-length skirts carefully chosen to wear on this first day of the journey. After weeks of preparation for the voyage, they could finally relax.

The steamship made its way through the Strait of Juan de Fuca dividing Canada and Washington State, where black-and-white orcas bobbed in the frigid water. Someone pointed out an enormous gray whale coming up for a breath and sounding like the swoosh of air escaping a tire, before resubmerging into the dark, choppy water. The young aviators had never seen a whale and were awestruck.

Over the following days most of them suffered seasickness, and photos show the young fliers and their family members slumped into deck chairs in the chilly sunshine.

Most of the fliers' parents had come to the United States from Canton. Shanghai was a long distance from Canton, and they didn't know what to expect of the city other than what they'd seen in the film *Shanghai Express*. In the film, merchants' stalls with patched canvas tents lined a road filled with people wearing every imaginable kind of hat, including straw rice hats on the men pulling rickshaws. One character, who turned out to be the villain, was half-Chinese and half-white. When he said he preferred to be considered Chinese, a British officer asked him incredulously, "You'd rather be a Chinese?"

Hazel and Virginia had been more interested in Anna May Wong, the first Chinese American film star, who, although she wasn't given many lines, turned out to be a pivotal character in the story. Hazel and Virginia copied the pointed fingernails and arched eyebrows worn by both Wong and the film's star Marlene Dietrich.

Someone suggested enthusiastically that being in Shanghai might be like being in a whole city that was Chinatown, not just one small section set aside as it was in Portland. They wondered what it would be like to look like everyone else for a change and not be excluded for being Asian.

The young American aviators and their family members arrived in Shanghai in late March, after a weeks-long journey at sea. They disembarked onto a crowded quay bustling with humanity. People crowded close together and elbowed one another for space as they tried to move along. An old woman said something to Hazel that she couldn't understand. Hazel, like the other American pilots, spoke Cantonese, not Mandarin.

Within days of their arrival, they reported to an air force air base, only to make a disheartening discovery.

The Chinese government was not interested in their services.

Apparently, although China badly needed help from abroad, they had not requested assistance from this particular group, and their status as "overseas Chinese," with possible links to foreign powers, made them highly suspect.

It was a setback, but they had another card to play. They decided they would head to Canton, hoping to have more luck in their ancestral home, where they understood the language.

There, Arthur Chin reported to General Arthur Lim, head of

the Canton Air Force. He and Harold Chinn, a classmate from Greenwood's program, were told they would be paid twenty-five dollars a month, but would have to buy their own uniforms. Frustrated by this icy reception, the young pilots considered turning around and going home.

But General Lim was having none of it. "What do you want to do? Go back to America to be laundrymen?"[2] He stared them all down, as if wondering what kind of spineless weaklings had been produced in the U.S.

They decided to sign up. After all, they were there. They'd been trained. This was what they had dreamed of doing.

But they would have to prove themselves. As a first step they were assigned to take coursework in military aviation. The Republic of China's Air Force had been founded in 1920 and was made up of independent air force bases of varying sizes that would gradually in time unite into the ROCAF. Because of their Cantonese ancestry, and the fact that they spoke Cantonese, the new pilots were accepted for training into the Canton Air Force, one of the largest and best equipped of the provincial air corps. Canton was located northwest of Hong Kong, in the Guangdong Province. Today it is called Guangzhou.

That was for the pilots who were young men.

For Hazel and Virginia, it was a different story.

Women would not be accepted into the Chinese Air Force, period. A commanding officer explained that women were fundamentally unstable and would be erratic in combat. Hazel argued that she and Virginia were trained fliers, not just women off the street, and their training had been paid for by Chinese American citizens commissioned by delegates from China. "We have learned and mastered everything the same as the boys."

Their arguments fell on deaf ears. They would be allowed, however, to go to training, and when the training had been completed, if they succeeded, they would be given jobs—but not flying.

It was a tremendous disappointment. As Hazel described it during an interview in later years, "You can't imagine how downhearted Virginia and I were when they told us they'd allow no girl fliers in the Chinese army. It was terrible. We just couldn't believe it. Heck, here Pacific Coast men had raised $30,000 and formed the Chinese Aeronautical Association to train the group and two of us were to be of no service. We felt as if we had cheated China out of two good fighters."[3]

"Hazel didn't want to talk about it," her friend Elsie said. "She said, 'I was trained to fly. I like to fly.' She was very disappointed but continued with the work that she was assigned to do to help China."[4]

◊ ◊ ◊

In April and May, the Portland pilots remained in Canton, taking classes, training, and learning Mandarin, something Hazel later laughed about. "When we reached China, we had to go to school to learn to speak Chinese—Mandarin, you know—which is the official language of China today. We spoke only the Chinese familiar on the Pacific Coast, Cantonese."[5]

After completing the courses and passing their tests with the highest honors, all of the fledgling Asian American pilots were commissioned as officers. The boys from Portland were scattered to China's four major airfields. Some became flight instructors teaching Greenwood's methods to Chinese pilot trainees, while others trained for air combat. All the boys, except Peter Chin, who developed eye trouble and as a former mechanic became head of an aircraft workshop in interior China, would fly with the Chinese Air Force.

Of the four air bases to which the Americans were assigned, the most elaborate boasted a new air college and was located outside Hangzhou, 171 kilometers (106 miles) southwest of Shanghai. General Chiang Kai-Shek's wife, who headed the Chinese

Commission on Aeronautic Affairs, wielded the power behind the new aviation school. There, eighteen American instructors, most of them ex–World War I fliers, were training the largest and most well-equipped air force in China using the outline of the United States Army Air Corps schools.

The Hangzhou training center included two flying fields and an airplane factory. From this college, four Portland-trained fliers from Greenwood's school graduated best in class: William Young, Mai Euon Lam, Harry Low, and Clifford Louie. Other Americans who graduated in this group included Liao Mack, who had been a waiter at Huber's restaurant in Portland, and Eddie Ho, who had come to Portland from San Francisco.

Hazel visited Cliff in Hangzhou. He encouraged her to never stop trying to fly for China, and she teased him about his new nickname, "Long-Legged Louie." In her photo album, she wrote comments in white pen on the thick black pages. Photographs of Hazel in Hangzhou show temples, peaceful lakes, and pastoral scenes as beautiful as they might have been centuries earlier. Beneath a photo of Hazel in knee-deep snow beside a river she wrote, "Gee, it's cold!" In one photo, Hazel and her mother pose side by side at an airfield, likely Hangzhou. Hazel is wearing a voluminous white coat and stylish high-heeled shoes. An adept chameleon, she looked more like an American film star than an aviator.

The second largest training center after Hangzhou was at Nanking, 300 kilometers (186 miles) north of Shanghai. There Italian instructors taught pilots how to fly Italian and American planes. Portland-trained fliers including Art Chin, John Kee Wong, and Moy Gee, nephew of Portland Chinese council member Moy Bach Hin, were assigned to Nanking.

Some of the Portland pilots were assigned to a third training center located in Canton, as officers of the First Army Air Corps and flight instructors training Chinese pilots. The fourth air base was at Leizhou, 120 kilometers (75 miles) from Canton. Henry

Young, of San Francisco, one of the best pilots in the Portland class, was a captain and an instructor there. He had been turned down at Hangzhou because he was colorblind.

Meanwhile, Hazel and Virginia were commissioned as second lieutenants in the aeronautic division at Leizhou and assigned to work in the Chinese Aeronautical Library.

In June, Hazel achieved her dream of visiting her father's village in Taishan, a small district on the southern coast of China less than a hundred miles from Canton. In the 1800s, Taishan's accessibility to the sea allowed American sailing vessels to recruit cheap labor, beginning a stream of Taishan migrants who became the settlers of American Chinatowns. An estimated 86 percent of Chinese Americans can trace their ancestry to this village. Their ancestors' language was distinctly Taishan, closely related to but different from standard Cantonese.

For the first time, Hazel met her half sister and half brother, as well as their children and other relatives. Clearly this visit had a great impact on Hazel, who began to formulate a plan to open a school there, near her family, to provide the village with better education, including English instruction.

Hazel traveled to other Chinese locales, as well. Her photo album is filled with photographs of historical Swatow, where men posed in Western dress—wide white pants and black-and-white saddle shoes, jackets and ties. As disappointed as Hazel must have been to be barred from joining the Chinese Air Force, she made the most of every opportunity she was given.

Hazel's mother and siblings had now settled in Shanghai. Surviving from this time is a set of professional photos of Daniel at ten years old, smiling serenely, like a beautiful, round-faced cherub.

In other photographs the siblings are dressed like Westerners, but Hazel's mother is wearing the same long skirt and brocade coat she'd worn back home, and her hair is long, in keeping with the old belief that one's hair was inherited from the ancestors and should never be cut. And she wore it severely pulled back, highlighting a high forehead. Hazel's mother was proud of her forehead. A prominent forehead indicated good fortune, power, and wealth.

While Hazel and Virginia toiled at the Aeronautical Library, the others from Greenwood's Flying School were moving up the ranks. On December 1, Arthur Chin was accepted as a warrant probationary pilot. He was popular with the girls in China, just as he had been with the girls in the United States, and developed a reputation as a ladies' man. Handsome, outgoing, sporting a pencil-thin mustache and never without a pipe perched between his teeth, he spoke Cantonese with a distinct American accent that only added to his charm. During this time, Art met Eva Wu, the beautiful daughter of Wu Tingfang, former ambassador to the United States, Peru, and Cuba, and acting premier of China in 1917. Art and Eva became devoted to each other, and it wasn't long before they married.

Although relegated to working in the library at the Bureau of Aeronautics, Hazel hadn't given up on her goals. It occurred to her that with China needing every pilot, including those from other countries, to stop the invading Japanese, there must exist a need for civilian pilots with commercial airlines. Eventually, and undoubtedly through sheer persistence, Hazel and Virginia were both hired to fly on an occasional basis for a company operating out of Nanking.

The two of them immediately moved to Nanking—and became the only female pilots in all of China. They earned no admiration for this distinction, only disapproval and suspicion. The idea of a female pilot was unheard of in China.

Hazel didn't care. While living in Nanking, she began organizing a civilian league to train commercial fliers and encourage women to fly. In addition, Hazel began working with a group of Italian flight instructors, flying a Fleet, the familiar first plane she'd flown, to deliver propaganda materials as part of the war effort.

In the summer of 1934 Virginia became sick with malaria. Suffering from shaking chills, headache, muscle aches, and fatigue, she languished for months in a Nanking hospital without improvement and asking for her mother. Back in Portland, her six siblings were unable to raise the money to travel to China. When Virginia died in the fall, Hazel mourned the loss of her closest friend, the only other woman she'd ever known who understood what it was like to fly an airplane. They had come from the same neighborhood, shared training as the only girls, and traveled across the ocean to do what they loved and to help the country of their parents' birth.

Since it was not financially possible to return Virginia's body home, she was buried without fanfare at the National Cemetery of the Air Force in Nanking.

Virginia's would be the first death among Greenwood's fliers but not the last. Millard Chung, while attempting a dive on a small ground target from several thousand feet, dove too close to the ground and crashed his biplane into a dike. The A student with no bad habits and class spokesman with perfect English had been kind and easygoing. Hazel lamented his loss and would later describe him as the most brilliant and qualified of their group.

On January 12, 1935, Amelia Earhart became the first pilot, male or female, to fly solo from Hawaii to the mainland United States. After being unable to move her knees more than a few inches for eighteen hours in flight, she stumbled out of her Vega to be rushed by a cheering crowd in Oakland, California. "Aviation is the career of the future," Earhart told a young female reporter the following day, when she was asked her advice to high school students. "You and your fellow students have the first chance in history to train yourselves and become a part of it."[6] The reporter, Gene Shaffer, took Earhart's words to heart and six years later would become a pilot. She then went on to graduate with the first class of women service pilots, the WASPs, during World War II.

Stuck in Nanking, unable to fly other than occasionally, Hazel watched aviation history being made back home. She admired and envied Earhart and believed she had as much skill and courage, maybe more; it was luck that seemed to be eluding her.

The Japanese invasion of China continued and intensified, and when it looked like Nanking would fall and it was no longer safe to stay, Hazel returned to Canton. Soon after arriving, she learned that her old friend from Portland Elsie Chang was living in town. Elsie had gone to Shanghai to study and while there had married. Her name was Elsie Lee Soong now, although she had become well known as Elsie Lee for her work helping those fighting on the front lines. An article appeared in a Shanghai daily newspaper about Elsie. In the accompanying photo she sat perched atop packages of medical supplies and bandages for the wounded. The photo was taken before she left with two truckloads of provisions for the front lines near Soochow. Dressed in riding boots, jodhpurs, and a sweater, she smiled demurely for the photographer with hands clasped between her knees, looking the epitome of femininity, belying the courage required to enter battle zones where Japanese aircraft were dropping bombs and strafing the ground, as well as the tenacity and skill she possessed to collect supplies, like fruit, cigarettes, and other comforts, to bolster and sustain the soldiers.

After the tragic loss of Virginia, it must have seemed nothing short of a miraculous turn of events for Hazel to have her child-hood friend back. Hazel's mother and siblings left Shanghai and joined her in Canton, where they all shared a small apartment. In time, Elsie and her brother would move into the apartment as well.

On May 12, 1935, Webster Jones reported for *The Oregonian* on the progress of Portland's Chinese Flying School aviators. A series of photos ran beside the article, including Hazel standing in front of *The Prince*, the boys when they were training in Portland, and one of Greenwood. "Miss Lee is now the flying Joan d'Arc in China," Jones wrote. Hazel laughed at the comparison when others who'd also seen the article teased her, but the reality was the article's misrepresentation of her made her uncomfortable. As much as she wanted to be the flying Joan of Arc in China, she was far from it, because she hadn't been given the chance to do what she knew she could do. Her strengths and skills were being squandered because she was a woman.

While Hazel continued to contribute in any way she was allowed to, it must have been deeply frustrating to see her fellow male classmates continuing to advance. In 1936 Art and four others, including John Kee Wong, who would later become a commanding officer for the Chinese Central Air Force, were selected for advanced flight training in Germany. Despite the Versailles Treaty at the end of World War I that prohibited military aviation in Germany, Hitler had developed an air force that had become the best in the world. His pilots flew the fastest planes that were capable of maneuvers previously unseen. In Bavaria, Art and John learned to fly Me-109s and Me-110s.

Cliff had been appointed chief personal pilot to General Chiang Kai-Shek. By the end of 1936 he had joined the 28th Fighter Squadron of the 5th Fighter Group, becoming their deputy squadron leader and eventually their commander. Hazel must have been exceedingly proud of him, even while she chafed at being left out of the action.

Hazel had been trained to be a combat pilot. Instead, at the Canton Air Base, she was now assigned as a gate guard with the First Army Air Corps. In Nanking she'd been nothing more than a taxi driver and transporter of propaganda materials, and now she was security.

7

REFUGEES

Women, like men, should try to do the impossible. And when they fail, their failure should be a challenge to others.

—Amelia Earhart

On July 2, 1937, Amelia Earhart's disappearance dominated newspaper headlines around the world. Earhart and her navigator, Fred Noonan, had vanished. In order for them to hit a tiny island in the middle of the Pacific Ocean seventeen hundred miles southwest of Honolulu, navigational error could not be greater than a few miles, a difficult feat in the best conditions. And Noonan had missed Los Angeles by two hundred miles on a recent test flight Earhart put him through using only the sun and stars for navigation, as he'd need to do on the planned round-the-world flight. Another incident had occurred that might have caused Earhart to reevaluate her choice of navigator: Noonan caused a serious head-on car collision while driving in the wrong lane. He hoped the flight with Earhart would provide the opportunity to redeem himself after he had been released from his job as a pilot with Pan American Airlines for a drinking problem.

Earhart told her longtime friend and fellow pilot Louise Thaden, who like many tried to dissuade Amelia from the stunt, "If I should bop off, it will be doing the thing I've wanted to do most. The Man with the little black book has a date marked down for all of us— when our work here is finished."[1]

As Earhart's friends had feared, the marker-less flight over the wide expanse of open ocean proved her and Noonan's undoing. Another issue that contributed to their failure was gasoline. The twin-engined Electra carried eleven hundred gallons of fuel, just enough for the eighteen-hour flight to Howland Island, a small speck in the middle of the ocean less than a mile wide, two miles long, and twenty feet high. Without enough fuel to make a mistake, they needed to fly directly to Howland or risk running out of fuel.

Noonan and Earhart never found Howland Island, and no trace of them, or their aircraft, has been conclusively found. Their search for Howland had become further complicated by strong winds, clouds, and poor radio communication. Theories persist, but the official report done by the United States government maintained that Earhart and Noonan, unable to find land, ran out of gas and ditched somewhere in the Pacific Ocean, and their aircraft now lies six thousand meters below the surface. Bones found on a small island atoll called Kikumaroro were lost before modern testing could formulate identification, but some believe Earhart and Noonan may have lived on the island for a time before succumbing to lack of water. One less popular theory proposed that Amelia and Noonan landed in the vicinity of the Japanese-controlled Marshall Islands and were taken prisoner and executed. Whatever became of Amelia Earhart and Fred Noonan, it remains one of the greatest unsolved mysteries of any disappearance.

Eighteen months after her disappearance, Earhart was officially declared dead on January 5, 1939. Although devastated at the loss of their darling, the public turned its attention toward the ominous fascist regimes gaining strength in Europe and Asia.

On July 7, 1937, Japan had launched a full-scale invasion of Peking.

Hazel stood under the guardhouse eaves at the Canton Air Base gate watching the Japanese and Chinese planes diving and twisting around one another to the sounds of revving engines and gunfire. Holding a bag of peanuts, eyes focused on the sky, she rooted for her team and cursed the Japanese pilots. The Chinese planes were outnumbered as usual. The Japanese Zeros were easy to identify with red dots on their fuselages. Hazel watched one spiral toward the earth billowing black smoke. Recounting the experience years later, she said, "When it looked okay for my guys I just chewed on those peanuts, and when it didn't look very good, I never cracked a nut."[2]

The dogfights had been going on for thirty minutes. She kept an eye on one of her guys trailing a Zero with his gunfire blinking. Her hand flexed as if holding the triggers. She wanted to be inside the cockpit of the bi-winged Hawk, feeling the heat, the sweat, her racing heartbeat, and the adrenaline. The Zero, hit, lost part of its wing and spun downward.

"You got him!" Hazel yelled and smiled. Three Zeros came in behind the Hawk, and she warned the pilot, "You got fighters all over your tail!"

A bomber took a hit and smoke poured from its wing as it glided gracefully to the ground. The crash rumbled beneath her feet. When it finally ended and the Zeros flew away, an unnatural silence followed the sound of departing engines.

Hazel ached to fly, but she also missed the comradeship and shared purpose. Flying together with her friends gave her a sense of belonging. Preparing for China had united the small group of misfits, the Chinese Americans who found a place they belonged in the sky. She tried again to join the Chinese Air Force, unsuccessfully. The Japanese had been attacking Canton for months. Hazel would later tell a Portland reporter, "Japanese will not fight unless

they outnumber Chinese planes."³ Shipments of new aircraft from
the United States, Great Britain, Germany, and Italy continued
to arrive in Hong Kong and Canton either by ship, by train from
Indochina, or by flying over the Himalayas.

What didn't arrive was more pilots.

Canton was the third largest city in China. Many of its one million residents lived on small boats called sampans, packed along the
Pearl River. After August 15, 1937, the Japanese residents of Canton
began to evacuate in earnest. Then on August 31, Japan launched
nine bombers across the East China Sea and attacked Canton. One
Hawk was shot down and two were damaged. In September, dogfights caused the largest single loss of Japanese fighters during the
Sino-Japanese War. Hazel began to hope the tide had changed and
China would soon be victorious. But only a few short months later,
in the fall of 1937, the Japanese had managed to eliminate most of the
Chinese Air Force's planes in South China, and their success looked
complete. But the Chinese would not surrender and remained determined to drive out the Japanese—they would fight to the finish.

On December 1, 1937, the Imperial Japanese Army moved into
Nanking, beginning what would become known as the Rape of
Nanking. For two months soldiers destroyed the city. Had Hazel
not returned to Canton, she would have been in the middle of
the massacre. General Kai-Shek ordered the removal of Chinese
troops from Nanking but forbade the evacuation of its citizens.
Many ignored the order and fled, but the rest were left defenseless.
The Japanese soldiers were hungry and tired after the battle for
Shanghai, and they sought revenge for their comrades' deaths. In
six weeks' time, they looted and committed acts of arson while bru-
tally murdering two hundred thousand to three hundred thousand
civilians and sexually assaulting and torturing as many as eighty
thousand women and girls whose only offense was being Chinese.

◊ ◊ ◊

While Hitler annexed Austria in what he called the "Anschluss," and the world braced for where he would go next, the Japanese aerial attacks on Canton launched in July 1937 continued. On Easter Sunday, March 28, 1938, the Japanese Air Force attacked Canton, choosing the date to further insult Chiang Kai-Shek, who had adopted his wife's Christian religion. Twenty-seven bombers in three squadrons of nine made the attack. Anti-aircraft fire kept the bombers at seven thousand to eight thousand feet and scattered them. Still the carnage rained down.

Hazel left their apartment in search of a safe place for her family and friends to hide. They were a large group: her mother, two brothers, two sisters, and Elsie and her brother. Bombs fell randomly and mercilessly. Moving about the city was difficult, like swimming upstream against an onslaught of panicked salmon. Buildings had become piles of smoldering rubble. People jammed the streets running like hunted animals. Screams rose from every direction and mingled with the crack of gunfire, explosions, and collapsing buildings. The crowded streets, littered with demented people stepping over the dead and dying, seemed more dangerous than the toppling buildings or the threat of more bombs raining from the sky. Atop a pile of splintered wood that had been a home, the body of a man sprawled faceup with an arm tossed across his chest. If not for the unnatural angle of his neck, he might have been sleeping. Looking up, Hazel saw that the twin gothic spires of Sacred Heart Cathedral appeared to be unscathed so far. A woman searched through the tangled remains of her home for any possessions she might salvage. People removed bricks by hand searching for their dead. A mother on her knees wept beside the body of her mangled child. Red Cross workers tended to the wounded.

Finally, Hazel returned to their apartment and told her family and friends they had to leave everything and go right away, and if they hurried, they might make the one train leaving for Hong Kong that day. She went to their neighbors and told them the same, urging them to leave immediately and with her if possible. Her calmness caused her mother to question whether it was necessary to try to escape now. Why not wait for people to dissipate? Hazel believed the Japanese intended to flatten Canton as they had Nanking, and she wanted to save her family from the torture the Japanese could inflict.

Hong Kong, in British control, remained neutral and a haven for war refugees. Later Frances would say, "We left everything behind, all the pictures, everything dear to us, family pictures, baby pictures, everything was just gone."[4] Their mother balked at walking, but there was no choice. Smoke blanketed the city and soot made the faces of people crowding the streets look like ghostly apparitions, their expressions confused, as if silently asking, *Why is this happening? We haven't hurt anyone.*

People packed the streets and left little room to move. Some held umbrellas to protect themselves from falling debris. Hundreds pushed their way forward, clutching protectively close to their chests what few belongings hadn't been destroyed. Hazel's group passed a little girl in short pigtails standing alone in the street and looking up at the planes. People determined to save their own lives rushed past the child as if she weren't there. There was no time to stop and ask her if she was lost. Hazel glanced back at her little brothers' expressionless faces. Elsie began to question whether they would make it to the railroad station in time; it seemed an impossible distance and Hazel's mother was slow. At intervals, walking came to a standstill in the crowds. Large groups of Japanese soldiers shouted angry, unintelligible commands, trying to dissipate or hurry the crowd to no effect.

The train to Hong Kong normally took ninety minutes, but crawling past debris and destruction, it stopped and started so often that Elsie complained they'd never make it. It was filled to capacity with more than two thousand terrified people, all worried the

Japanese might bomb the train at any minute. They arrived in Hong Kong six hours after leaving Canton and made their way to a friend of Elsie's husband. Elsie later claimed that Hazel had saved all their lives and the lives of many neighbors as well.

◊ ◊ ◊

In late May, refugees continued to pour into Hong Kong by the thousands daily. Thousands more still waited to get out of Canton. Trains, no longer running daily or even twice a week, arrived sporadically, depositing the destitute and displaced into the crowded city. The newspapers reported on May 30 that the long-anticipated invasion of South China was imminent. The largest concentration of Japanese war ships since the Sino-Japanese conflict began now waited off Hong Kong.

On June 6, 1938, *The New York Times'* front-page headline reported, "CANTON IS BOMBED FOR SEVENTH TIME: 300 MORE KILLED; Japanese Less Indiscriminate in Their Fire and Civilian Casualties Are Fewer THOUSANDS TRY TO FLEE." Hazel's sister, Rose, now living in New York, where her husband had found work, must have been anguished by these headlines, not knowing whether her sisters, little brothers, and mother were safe or even alive. Hazel's family in Portland and New York had seen the newsreels about the bombings of Canton. They scanned the screen for a familiar face among the dead bodies. The monotone narrator reported, "Canton becomes the ghost city of the world."[5]

Little is known about the time Hazel spent in Hong Kong as a refugee, other than a few details she told to friends. Hazel didn't know where Cliff or any of the boys were, but they would have been fighting in the air somewhere over South China—fighting what appeared to be a losing battle. On August 30, when she heard that an airfield near Canton had been attacked, Hazel could only hope that her friends had survived. By October 21, after heavy bombing for several months, most of Canton's inhabitants had fled to Hong Kong. When Japanese ground troops arrived, they seized Canton virtually unopposed. The city fell on October 29, 1938, and the Rising Sun flag was raised on the customs buoy in the harbor.

With so many refugees arriving in Hong Kong and needing help, Hazel worked with the Chinese National Refugee Association to help procure desperately needed supplies. After several months, she grew restless. She wanted to fly in combat, and wondered if while she waited for the opportunity, she could be useful to the war effort in the United States. Through her refugee work, she learned about the Universal Trading Corporation. The corporation, located in New York City and an agency of the Chinese government, had been responsible for the sale of Chinese wood oil to the United States. Now the company was purchasing war equipment and supplies from the U.S. government for shipment to China. Their work proved to be a vital contribution to China's survival during the war. Working at Universal Trading, Hazel wouldn't be flying, but if the U.S. became involved in the war, maybe she would be needed, and she'd be in the country and ready.

With a job secured, Hazel prepared to return to Portland before moving to New York City, where she would live with her sister Rose. When Hazel had visited her family in Taishan in 1934, she received word from Shanghai that a fire had destroyed all her belongings, including her Citizen Return Certificate, Form 430, necessary for her admittance back into the United States. The United States Consulate in Hong Kong advised her to obtain an affidavit, with a current photo, swearing to her citizenship and the loss of her Form 430, in order to be granted permission to return home. On October 27, she applied to the United States Department of Immigration in Seattle, asking that her immigration testimonials be arranged for her arrival on approximately December 12. A handwritten note stapled to the back of her letter reads, "There would seem to be no objection to admitting this applicant directly from the steamer provided identification is satisfactory. Suggest that short statement be taken concerning the loss or destruction of her original F430."[6]

In Hazel's photograph, taken before she left for China in 1933, when she was twenty, her face is fuller, her eyebrows thicker, her hair deeply side parted and pulled back, and her expression one of defiant determination. In the photo taken in China for her readmittance to the United States in 1938, her hair is worn in a popular style of the day, with the sides swept up and back, and her eyes look sad, but the haunted expression on her face is the most arresting. She is no longer the young woman who left Portland to lay down her life for China.

8

A HEROINE
IN CHINATOWN

*A difficult childhood gave me a kind of cocky confi-
dence. . . . I could never have so little that I hadn't had
less. It took away my fear.*[1]

—JACKIE COCHRAN

A N ICY RAIN FELL ON HAZEL'S BARE HEAD as she dodged a produce truck to cross Fourth Street. Even though it was early
in the afternoon, the streetlights cast beams of yellow light onto the
dark pavement. Standing under the dripping eaves, two old men in
traditional long black coats bowed toward her. Hazel gave them a lop-
sided grin they couldn't see because they remained bowing until after
she passed. The attention she'd received since returning from China
caused Hazel some embarrassment. She answered questions from
reporters about the other Portland-trained fliers, her friends, including those who had given their lives for China, as they had promised to
do when they left the United States filled with purpose and hope. Now
the old men who hadn't believed a girl should be allowed to fly bowed
to her. The honor belonged to her friends still fighting and dying and
Virginia, who should be beside her as they walked past the familiar

stores and restaurants, their windows lighted with strings of bright Christmas lights. Virginia had loved Christmas and everything fun.

Six of the Portland fliers from Hazel's class had now lost their lives; five in action and one in an accident. Millard Chung was the first, followed by Mai Euon Lam, who had graduated best in class along with Cliff. And those who survived were still fighting and performing heroic acts. John Wong, promoted to wing commander, had brought down eight planes and was "the best of the lot," according to Hazel. Others who were shot down and captured by Japanese were executed, likely beheaded. Hazel was told those boys stood fearlessly and "gave excellent accounts of themselves before they died." She chose to talk about them whenever she was given the chance and to ask assistance for the refugees in China.

Hazel had left Shanghai November 27, on the *Express of Asia* steamship, and arrived in Seattle December 12. The moment she arrived in Portland, the calls began from the two local newspapers wanting interviews with the returning "aviatrix," as they dubbed her. Articles followed calling her "a heroine in Chinatown," while never missing an opportunity to comment on her looks. "But slender Miss Lee, discounting her own efforts against the invaders of the land of her ancestors, prefers to praise others in a group of Portland-trained fliers whose exploits are becoming legend in the 'old country.' There was a delicate gesture with extremely feminine hands and a flash of red-polished fingernails." When asked about the Chinese American pilots who had been trained in Portland, Hazel responded, "Now, you're really talking up my alley," and beamed. "First of all, their records have been so outstanding it has become a mark of distinction in China to be an overseas aviator from Portland." Asked about the progress of the war and the ability of the Chinese to hold out against the Japanese invaders, Hazel told the reporters, "This war will last until the Japanese say they will stop."[2]

◊ ◊ ◊

After living in a war zone and then as a refugee, life with her sister's family in New York provided a respite, and Hazel enjoyed getting to know her little nephews, who quickly fell in love with their funny auntie. She made up songs for them and told them stories of China and the war and their family members who lived there. Rose had two sons now, ten-year-old Irving and Earl, who was six. They lived in a tenement apartment on East 27th Street in the Kips Bay neighborhood of Manhattan, eight blocks from the Empire State Building. Rose's husband Bowen owned a Chinese curio shop.

Hazel arrived in New York in early 1939, when Europe balanced on the threshold of war. If the United States joined the war, she knew they would need more pilots. While working as a stenographer and buyer of war materials for besieged China at the Universal Trading Corporation, she investigated opportunities to fly. She understood how vital the work they were doing was for China's survival, but she wanted to do what she'd been trained to do—fly.

Working in Manhattan, freed from war and military life and no longer a refugee, she became reacquainted with fun and made Chinese restaurants, of which there were many, her new hobby. She became aquatinted with the flamboyant restaurateur and unofficial mayor of Chinatown known as Shavey Lee, whom she later claimed was a relative. She frequented nightclubs in the Latin Quarter with Shavey. Surrounded by music, theater, movies, and food, she blossomed. After work, she'd gather with friends around tables with heaping plates of Chinese dishes, laughing loudly. Later, she'd smoke cigars, play pool, and gamble; pursuits considered not just unladylike but uncivilized at that time. Hazel didn't care.

World War II began on September 1, 1939, when Hitler invaded Poland. In response, England and France declared war on Germany on September 3. On September 17, Russia invaded Poland from the east, resulting in the division of the country with Germany. At the end of November, the Soviet Union invaded Finland. An armistice agreement ceded the Finnish coastline on the Arctic Sea and the northern shore of Lake Lagoda to the Soviet Union. The Japanese invasion and occupation had crippled China, leaving it virtually cut off from the rest of the world. With the United States allied with China, hostilities between Japan and the U.S. increased.

In the spring of 1940, Hazel received a letter from Cliff about their friend Arthur Chin. Art had been seriously injured. Although he had survived, his life as a pilot was over. On December 27, 1939, during a raid near Kunlun Pass, Art's Gladiator was hit and his fuel tank caught fire. He managed to fly the burning plane back over Chinese lines before bailing out. If he'd not made it across Chinese lines, he would have been executed. His burns were significant. While he was recovering at a house on the Luichow Airfield, the Japanese executed an air attack. Art was in bed, unable to be moved, his face, eyes, and hands completely wrapped in bandages. His wife Eva took their sons, Gilbert and Steve, to an air raid shelter and returned to Art. The sound of bombs exploding grew closer, and the concussions shook the house with increasing intensity. Eva put her body on top of Art's before the next bomb fell on the house. He felt her shudder as the shrapnel hit her body. During an interview years later, Art said, "I held her dead body to mine until help came."[3]

Hazel remembered a carefree, brave, charming boy, loved by everyone. War had turned him into an adult who would never be carefree again. How devastating it must have been to lose his ability to fly, and to lose the mother of his children under such horrific circumstances.

The world watched in horror as Hitler began his relentless march across Europe. On April 9, 1940, Nazi Germany invaded Denmark and the country quickly surrendered. On May 10, Germany marched into France after defeating Belgium, the Netherlands, and Luxembourg. Norway held out until June 9. France signed an armistice agreement on June 22, giving Germany occupation of the northern half of the country and the entire Atlantic coastline, while Southern France would remain officially independent. A collaborationist, authoritarian regime was established there that participated in the deportation of Jewish citizens to death camps in Germany. At about the same time, Italy invaded Southern France.

With Northern France occupied and surrendered and Southern France controlled, Hitler turned toward England. He was determined to show the world that this war, his war, would be fought in the air, and on September 7, 1940, three hundred German bombers attacked London in the first of fifty-seven consecutive night bombings. The "blitzkrieg," lightning war, would continue until May 1941.

In July of 1941 the Battle of Britain began, and it ended in October with Nazi Germany's defeat. Americans cheered their British cousins across the pond. Hazel followed the news closely with an eye to her flying career and wrote letters inquiring about joining the United States Army Air Corps. A branch of the army and not yet a separate entity, the air force would not become separate from the army until after World War II on September 18, 1947. But American pilots were flying to Britain to help, and Hazel wanted to join them. The response from the Army Air Corps was a cordial, but emphatic, no. Women were not allowed. She might consider nursing, the letter suggested.

Hazel was a trained flier, and her skills were going to waste. She longed to be in the air, and she was also frustrated that money had been invested in training her and she was not performing her duty to those benefactors. Such a terrible waste. Whether she flew to help China or the United States made no difference to her. All she wanted was to be allowed to use her skills to help fight back against the enemy.

◊ ◊ ◊

On Sunday, December 7, 1941, the Imperial Japanese Air Force attacked Pearl Harbor. Like most Americans, Hazel heard the news on the radio. Unlike most Americans, she was not shocked. She had witnessed Japan's ruthlessness firsthand in China. A reluctant nation that had clung to its isolationist viewpoint finally realized it would have to join the war. On December 8, the United States declared war on Japan. Hawaii and the West Coast posted lookouts for Japanese submarines and a Japanese air attack. A few days later Nazi Germany and its Axis partners declared war on the United States.

The United States military was dangerously unprepared for war. Overnight, planes were needed, and all pilots were called into service. The draft applied to men between the ages of twenty-one and forty-five. Women were not drafted but could volunteer as nurses and for other noncombat, secretarial positions. They would not be accepted as pilots. Hazel contacted the air corps anyway, again offering her service as a pilot, but waited in vain for a response.

In February of 1942, an executive order issued by President Roosevelt began the forced evacuation of Japanese Americans on the West Coast. They were given a forty-eight-hour notice, told nothing about where they were going, and only allowed to bring with them what few possessions they could carry. They left their businesses, jobs, and homes, to be loaded on trains and sent to internment camps. The United States imprisoned what would become more than over 117,000 Japanese Americans.

Japanese submarines patrolled the West Coast's Pacific shoreline. Out of fear there would be a nighttime bombing raid, nightly blackouts were performed in Washington, Oregon, and California. Hazel wondered what would happen to their Japanese neighbors in Portland, the Senos. She asked her sister Frances in a letter, but the family had moved away and not said where they were going.

Hazel's thoughts turned to her family's livelihood. Chinese restaurants would not be popular when most Americans couldn't tell the difference between a person of Chinese and Japanese descent. In Portland, a button with the American flag and the word "Chinese" below it was produced and worn by Chinese Americans to avoid being mistaken for Japanese. There was a noticeable hatred expressed toward Asian people everywhere in the country. All Asians were assumed to be Japanese and enemies regardless of their actual heritage or whether they had been born in the United States.

Life magazine offered a lesson in how to differentiate Japanese individuals from Chinese in an article titled, "How to Tell Japs from the Chinese." Photos illustrated the supposed physical discrepancies of skin color, nose and face shape, and amount of facial hair, among other characteristics. "*Life* here adduces a rule-of-thumb from the anthropometric conformations that distinguish friendly Chinese from enemy alien Japs."[4]

Immediately after the Pearl Harbor attack, rumors circulated in Oregon that local Japanese had known about the attack and were planning to blow up Bonneville Dam outside of Portland. Fake news stories reported that the dead bodies of Japanese men had washed ashore on Cannon Beach and hidden guns had been found in Japanese homes, all unfounded and intended to cause hysteria. The Japanese, it was reported, were an alien people unable to assimilate. The *Hillsboro Argus* newspaper printed the headline "Officials Feel Japanese May Try Anything." Homes were searched by the FBI, and two thousand men living on the West Coast were arrested during the first week after Pearl Harbor. Japanese assets were frozen, they were not allowed to own firearms, explosives, shortwave radios, or cameras, and an 8 p.m. to 6 a.m. curfew was instated.

The Japanese on the West Coast were forcibly removed and placed in incarceration camps inland. The sixteen West Coast camps were surrounded by barbed wire and watchtowers with machine gun–armed guards. The encampments lacked privacy and basic sanitation, and the prisoners, families with children, were not told when or if they would be freed. The plight of Japanese Americans living in internment camps became more uncertain on September 9, 1942, when a Japanese seaplane launched by catapult from a submarine dropped two incendiary bombs in the coastal forest of Southern Oregon. Trees and vegetation were too wet, and Japan's plan to start a large-scale forest fire was thwarted. Two additional bombs were dropped during a second mission that also failed to ignite a fire, and a third mission was scrapped. The incidents remain the only time during World War II that an enemy plane dropped bombs on the United States mainland.

In the fall of 1942, Cliff was to be sent to Florida to enter Staff and Command College with the United States War Department. After years apart, Hazel and Cliff were finally able to spend some time together.

From Cliff, Hazel learned of the current state of the war in China. With the Japanese in control of all Chinese ports, China was effectively isolated from the outside world. Beginning in 1942, the only routes available to get supplies to China were the Burma Road and a new airlift route called the "Hump" over the Himalayas that was so exceedingly dangerous it was dubbed the "Skyway to Hell" and the "Aluminum Trail" for the five hundred to seven hundred planes that didn't make it. The lives of more than twelve hundred airmen would be lost over a 530-mile stretch of rugged terrain. One-third of the pilots flying the route would perish.

Flying in planes referred to as "flying coffins," pilots dealt with strong winds, ice storms, and thunderstorms at extreme altitudes, while being hunted by Japanese Zeros. As the planes crept along at ground speeds of thirty miles per hour, winds lifted them twenty-eight thousand feet and back to six thousand like a roller coaster through hell. The American pilots were newly trained officers with little flying experience and none whatsoever with the extreme conditions unique to the route. Pilots had to fly the Kali Gandaki River Gorge, wider and deeper than the Grand Canyon, with mountains surrounding the gorge ten thousand feet higher than most planes could fly. The pass to escape the gorge was fifteen thousand feet high, but pilots often could not see it hidden in clouds, fog, or weather. Lack of oxygen caused many to become lost, disoriented, or even unconscious. Cargo planes with heavy engines went into an almost immediate dive when out of fuel. In the rugged terrain, crews would have to bail out and remember to grab their .45-caliber pistols. No search and rescue crew would be coming. Japanese patrols captured American airmen and tortured and killed them. Pilots flying the Hump were trained to save one bullet to use on themselves.

Hazel took in what Cliff told her about the Hump route. This could be her opportunity.

9

OPPORTUNITY

A beauty operator ceased to exist, and an aviator was born.

—JACKIE COCHRAN[1]

ON A DARK AFTERNOON IN LATE DECEMBER 1942, Hazel returned from work to her sister excitedly waving *The Saturday Evening Post*. Opening it, Rose pointed to a full-page advertisement. Next to a photo of a girl smoking a Camel cigarette was an invitation: Jacqueline Cochran was looking for women pilots to relieve men for combat. Hazel read the words several times looking for more information but not caring because here at last was her opportunity to fly.

She knew who Jacqueline Cochran was from regularly seeing her name in the headlines. In the 1930s she had been one of the best racing pilots in the world and had broken countless records for both speed and distance. Before the United States joined the war, as a stunt to publicize the need for pilots in England, Jackie had become the first, and would remain the only, woman during World War II to fly a bomber across the Atlantic. In 1939, Jackie wrote to Eleanor Roosevelt suggesting female pilots be used in noncombat missions, and Mrs. Roosevelt introduced her to General Henry

Arnold, the commanding general of the United States Army Air Corps. Handsome and square-jawed, he was never without a smile, as if the whole world and everything in it provided him pleasure, earning him the nickname "Hap" for happy. Arnold had been taught to fly by Wilbur and Orville Wright in 1911 and held the honor of being one of the first Army Air Corps aviators.

Without enough pilots, General Arnold had a staffing problem, and a pilot shortage would have disastrous consequences if left unresolved. Jackie knew there existed an untapped source of aeronautic talent: the thousands of American women who were licensed pilots. In the United States a significant number of male pilots performed duties such as training cadet pilots, testing aircraft, and ferrying airplanes from factories, air bases, and ports before they went overseas. An enormous number of aircraft required ferrying transport as they rolled off the assembly lines in increasingly greater numbers. Jackie proposed that women could perform all noncombat flying, which would release men for overseas duty.

In her memoir, Jackie wrote, "American industry was producing tens of thousands of airplanes and in the fall of 1942, no one could tell whether we had enough young, qualified men to fly them. All the other services were drawing heavily on available manpower. If a woman could handle a trainer plane, then a man could be released for active duty. That's what I thought, that's what I had seen work in England, and that's exactly what I would prove in the long run. But it was a very long run."[2]

Arnold would later admit that when Jackie first proposed the program, he wasn't convinced that "a slip of a young girl could fight the controls of a B-17 in the heavy weather they would naturally encounter in operational flying." He also later admitted that he had been wrong, and he became one of Jackie's greatest champions. He suggested Jackie study the ATA (Air Transport Auxiliary) in Great Britain, where women had been ferrying airplanes for three years, and come back to create a similar program in the United

States. Jackie recruited women from the United States and Canada and took them with her to England, where she trained female pilots for the British aircraft ferrying service.

Jackie had married one of the richest men in the country. Her husband Floyd Odlum had grown up poor like Jackie. It was his encouragement and financial support that launched both her flying career and her cosmetics company. When she showed up on a British air base in a Rolls-Royce wearing a fur coat, her insensitivity insulted and angered the Brits, who were proud of sacrificing new clothes, food, and other extravagances to defeat Hitler. Still, Jackie's contribution of training women to ferry aircraft, enabling more men to fly with the Royal Air Force, did not go unnoticed, and neither did the fact that while in Great Britain she experienced German bombing raids while hiding in bomb shelters alongside British civilians.

At the outbreak of the war, two women had submitted separate proposals about using women in the Army Air Corps in noncombat roles, to free male pilots for duty overseas, Jackie Cochran and Nancy Harkness Love. Like Jackie, Nancy had been a racing pilot in the thirties. Inspired by seeing Charles Lindbergh land the *Spirit of St. Louis* in Paris when she was thirteen, she had earned her private pilot's license at age sixteen. Unlike Jackie, she was from a wealthy family, a society girl who had attended Vassar, where she earned the nickname "The Flying Freshman," until her family experienced financial trouble brought on by the Great Depression and could no longer afford the tuition.

After dropping out of college, Nancy went to work for Inter-City Aviation in Boston, as a flight instructor and saleswoman, demonstrating to potential customers that planes were so easy to fly even a woman could fly one. Joseph Kennedy Sr. had heard about Nancy's adventurous spirit and beauty and thought she might in time make a good wife for his son, the future president John F. Kennedy, who was a student at Princeton; his transfer to

Harvard would come later. Under the false pretense of buying an airplane, he came to see if Nancy might be interested in a date with John. She wasn't.

Nancy had fallen in love with Robert Love, the owner of the aviation company where she worked, and they married in 1936. In 1940 she became the director of the Women's Auxiliary Ferry Squadrons (WAFS), with twenty-five experienced pilots under her command. Not military members but working for the Army Air Corps, Nancy's pilots transported planes from factories to bases. She became the first woman to fly the B-17 and B-25 bombers and the P-51 Mustang.

Nancy's and Jackie's proposals, although different—Jackie's was on a much larger scale—suggested similar programs. Jackie believed she could convince the country that "it was time for patriotic American women to step up and do their part."[3]

Nancy Love's proposal was accepted. Jackie's was not. Upon hearing the news, Jackie flew back from England, livid that the job that should have been hers had been given to Nancy purposely while she was overseas to leave her out. She wasn't wrong. The "boys" didn't want Jackie because she wasn't part of their set and might not follow their rules, and her ideas were too ambitious, her vision for a larger number of women pilots impractical and expensive. Love had been educated at Vassar and came from established money, and her husband was Air Corps military—in fact he had recently been promoted to deputy chief of staff for the U.S. Army Airforce Transport Command. Most of Nancy Love's "original" girls, like herself, came from upper-class families who could afford to pay for college and an expensive aviation hobby. Possessing the pedigree and polish that Jackie, despite her clothes, makeup, and hairstyle, lacked, Nancy was chosen to direct the women pilots who would be working for the military but without being members of the military.

To appease both women and retain their talents, two stages of the flying experiment were created. Nancy Love would continue to oversee the Women's Auxiliary Ferrying Squadron, the WAFS, and Jackie Cochran would head a ferrying training program which General Arnold named the Women's Flying Training Detachment, or WFTD. Nancy's small troupe of women being used to ferry planes were already experienced pilots. The training under Jackie's command would take less experienced pilots and train them the military way to join the WAFS. Jackie was not exactly appeased but decided to bide her time.

In 1942, the Women's Flying Training Detachment was born. A more distinctive name with a catchy acronym would have to be found. For now, there wasn't time, with male pilots needed overseas and rumors circulating about a bomb to end all wars. With time a critical issue, it was determined that the women pilots would be hired as civil service employees. As Jackie later said, "We were too few in number compared to the armed forces totals and too inexperienced in those early stages to know how it would all turn out. I could wait. A bill to militarize my women pilots was in order, but in the meantime, Arnold and I had to find a way to pay those girls, to organize them without going through the Army's bureaucratic channels, to work fast, to set aside worries about uniforms and chain of command. It backfired later, but at the time, it got us up and flying, off the ground."[4]

On Jackie's insistence, the Women's Flying Training Detachment began as a top-secret project that was not initially publicized, nor would it be submitted for militarization until the point when it was deemed successful. From the beginning it was her intention that the women pilots would become part of the military. Attached to the Army Air Forces, the WAFS and WFTDs, or WASPs as they would become known, were the first women to serve as United States military pilots and the first women ever to fly military aircraft.

Jackie Cochran put forth three objectives in the formation of her training program: "1) To see if women could serve as military pilots, and if so, to form the nucleus of an organization which could be rapidly expanded. 2) To release male pilots for combat. 3) To decrease the Air Forces' total demands for the cream of the manpower pool."[5] With only two months' preparation, the first class of twenty-five women began training November 16, 1942, at Howard Hughes Airport, outside Houston, Texas.

Applicants needed to have a pilot's license and a minimum of two hundred flying hours initially; the required hours would decrease in time. Men entering the air corps to become pilots, whether enlisted or drafted, weren't required to have any flying experience and often didn't. The women applicants had to be over five-feet-two-inches and in good health, and between the ages of eighteen and thirty-five, although Jackie preferred them to be on the younger side of those ages.

Hazel fulfilled all the requirements and had more than enough hours to apply. She sent off a telegram and waited. The only conceivable barrier to her being accepted was her Asian race and heritage.

◊ ◊ ◊

In the New York City office of Jacqueline Cochran Cosmetics, Hazel Ying Lee sat down with its founder for an interview. Hazel possessed all the physical qualities Jackie wanted in her "girls," a radiant smile, natural beauty, and a well-groomed, wholesome appearance. Jackie selected her women pilot trainees with the utmost care, believing the success or failure of her program depended on the girls' looks and behavior as much as on their flying expertise. The bigwigs didn't care if she failed. They had Nancy Love. Jackie would not fail. She required flawless character, excellent flying experience, a good attitude, and feminine, girl-next-door looks. Girls with some college were preferable, but Hazel's experience in China made up for that, and she had an impressive recommendation from none other than Madame Chiang Kai-shek. To

Jackie, Hazel represented the new American girl, who would not be a cookie-cutter, corn-fed, Euro-American girl. As well, it would be good politics, if not a coup, to accept the first Chinese American woman to fly for the United States Army Air Corps. Even though many areas stubbornly clung to anti-Chinese Jim Crow–style laws, the truth was that the Chinese were allies of the U.S. now and both at war with Japan.

Jackie later regretted choosing not to admit black women into the program in the beginning. She was afraid that allowing African American applicants would make it more difficult to militarize her program. She had turned down every black applicant, even graduates from the Tuskegee Institute's pilot training program who had more than enough flying hours and experience, a remarkable accomplishment considering that two decades earlier Bessie Coleman had had to travel to France to get her pilot's license because the United States would not grant a pilot's license to a black woman.

Jackie met with the black women who applied to her program and explained at length that the armed forces remained stubbornly segregated. Of course, the applicants didn't need to be told about discrimination when they lived it every day. Hotels and restaurants refused to serve African Americans, and in some towns they faced arrest after sundown. Ferrying involved flying from place to place, finding a room and meals along the way. That would prove difficult when some airports served only white pilots. Also, Jackie didn't want to provide any excuse for skeptics to stop her program, and she was certain that in the South the integration of housing would pose too many problems. She didn't want to make any more waves than she had to, not yet.

Her voice holding the slightest hint of the Southern accent she tried to hide, Jackie Cochran ended the interview by asking how soon Hazel could get to Texas to begin training. Hazel would be in the fourth class, but Jackie had found a better training location than Houston, and Hazel would be in the first class at Avenger Field outside Sweetwater, Texas.

After Hazel departed, Jackie Cochran leaned back in her chair, lit a cigarette, and gazed out at the muted Manhattan skyline. Hazel Ying Lee was a good find, a girl from humble beginnings like herself, and she exuded a calm and cool confidence. Few professional opportunities existed for women, and even fewer for those without a college education or financial resources. Flying had offered both Jackie and Hazel a route to success and an escape.

Jackie Cochran had already led a remarkable life. An orphaned foster child, she had been forced by hunger to steal chickens for food. She wore a burlap sack for a dress and slept on the floor with rats. At eight years old, she had dropped out of school and remained unable to read into her twenties. By the time she was fourteen, she was pregnant. She married the father of the baby, but her four-year-old son died after accidentally setting himself on fire while in the care of his grandparents. He would be her only child. By the age of twenty she was divorced and determined to build a career as a beautician. She headed for New York, leaving Florida as Bessie Pittman Cochran and arriving at Grand Central Terminal as Jacqueline Cochran, a new identity created to obscure her humble origins.

While working at Saks Fifth Avenue in New York as a beautician, she caught the attention of the owner, who sent her to Miami for the winter season to take care of his clientele there. Jackie grew interested in flying as a way to be noticed, to meet the right people, the elite crowd, and in time, when her cosmetics company was up and running, she could travel the country by airplane selling her products. At a party she met the millionaire tycoon Floyd Odlum, who would become her husband. Odlum, an attorney and industrialist, had built his fortune from nothing. Speculating in utilities and general securities had made him one of the few people to make money during the Depression. He offered to pay the costs of Jackie's flying lessons if she succeeded in earning her license in under six weeks. She accepted the challenge, and when she earned her license in only three weeks, she made the pages of *The New York Times*. Overnight she went from an obscure nobody to appearing in headlines as one of the "girl fliers" the country adored. Her racing records would grace countless newspaper pages around the world. In one legendary incident, she leapt from her burning plane onto the tarmac holding only the cosmetic bag she'd made sure to grab on her way out.

After the disappearance of her friend Amelia Earhart, Jackie became the new first lady of flying. Although she would never have the name recognition granted Earhart, she replaced Earhart as the female representative of women aviators. She and her husband had helped finance Earhart's final flight, although reluctantly, after warning her friend not to make the round-the-world trip and in fact telling her it would be "suicidal." Jackie told Amelia that Noonan would never be able to find Howland Island with the navigational aids available at the time.

Five months after Amelia's disappearance, Jackie Cochran's fame was cemented, when on December 4, 1937, she raced millionaire Howard Hughes to Miami from New York and won. It didn't matter that her engine died as soon as she landed; all that mattered was being first. An observant woman, she likely recognized the same motivation in Hazel, the same fearlessness and drive to be first.

She now owned a cosmetics company, with the slogan "Wings to Beauty" written on the side of her plane. She enjoyed living in a "man's world" and rose to the challenge. Despite being called abrasive, among other things, she was exactly what was needed to advance women into military service. As General Arnold said to her more than once, "Have it your own way, Jackie. You'll do it anyway."[6] Flying, she said, was a highly prized corner of a man's world. Gutsy, intense, with striking blond curls and large brown eyes, Jackie was the ultimate risk-taker in all facets of her life. She claimed to have no fear of dying. The only fear she ever admitted to was that of burning in a fiery plane crash and surviving.

One of Jackie's "girls," who later became Lieutenant General B. J. Williams, said, "You didn't say no to Jackie; if there was an obstacle, Jackie knew how to get around it. That kind of gutsiness and aggressiveness in a woman is not always admired; in a man, it's applauded."[7]

While Jackie Cochran was in for the fight of her life to keep her program and prove its members were capable pilots worthy of the military, Hazel Lee collected her wages and headed for Texas.

10

ENGINEERS, HOUSEWIVES, AND ROCKETTES

I held a moment in my hand, brilliant as a star,
fragile as a flower, a tiny sliver of one hour.
I dripped it carelessly,
Ah! I didn't know,
I held opportunity.

—HAZEL YING LEE

H AZEL STEPPED FROM THE TRAIN at Sweetwater, Texas, in the middle of February 1943. Endless miles of dust and colorless sand stretched to the horizon, broken only by straggly mesquite trees. Named by the Kiowa before settlers and ranchers arrived, Sweetwater, Texas, rested in a flat expanse seventy miles north of San Angelo, forty miles west of Abilene, and seventy miles northeast of Big Spring. The desolate landscape couldn't undermine Hazel's enthusiasm. She looked forward to the upcoming six months of rigorous training she'd been promised and to flying again after a long seven years' absence from the sky.

From the depot, she walked to the Blue Bonnet Hotel. Opened in 1927, the Blue Bonnet was the tallest building in town, dominating the view and a familiar sight to travelers. Hazel and the other train-ees would stay overnight at the hotel then move into the newly fin-ished barracks the following day.

For the past six months, male cadet pilots had been training at Avenger Field, destined for bases in Great Britain upon grad-uation. This was where Jackie Cochran had obtained permission for the women to train. She had chosen Avenger because there was less fog than in Houston, making the flying conditions more reli-able. And the Howard Hughes Municipal Airport where they were training in Houston lacked adequate facilities for women, espe-cially housing. Concerned about men and women working and liv-ing together, Jackie managed to convince General Arnold that once the current cadet class graduated, only women would be trained at Avenger Field, which would then become the first air base in the country to train only women.

When the first class of her pilots had arrived in Houston the previous year, Jackie had been so afraid of negative publicity that she instructed the trainees to tell their hosts or landladies that they were part of a women's basketball team and nothing more. Never mind that the women were small, some barely over five feet tall. Jackie had commandeered one motel, a rat-infested place where one trainee later said she wouldn't have put up her dog. The girls shared double beds. With only one bathroom on the air base, a portable latrine was installed out in the field to accommodate the trainees and their instructors. This may or may not have explained why one of the "society girls" became infected with "crabs." Jackie told her first class that if they behaved like ladies they would be treated like ladies, and if they got out of line, the men were just waiting for them to fail. She made her warning clear: *Don't prove them right.*

Hazel's class would be split in two. Half of the class would train in Houston and the other half at Avenger Field. When Avenger became fully operational in March, the Houston training facility would be closed.

The Blue Bonnet Hotel's lobby echoed with excited female voices from all over the country. Many had already met on the train. One train had collected women beginning on the East Coast, cities like New York and Boston, and then on to Pittsburgh, Columbus, Indianapolis, St. Louis, Kansas City, and Oklahoma City. The women from the East were dressed in drab tweeds, and the girls from California wore brightly colored coats. They teased one another while trying to guess where each was from based on clothing, and sometimes accents, everyone excited to meet different people from fourteen different states and from all walks of life, a first for many, even those who had gone to college.

The trainees came from cities and farms, New York City high rises and North Dakota soddies. Many of the women had never been more than thirty or forty miles from the towns where they'd been born and raised. Some were married with children, and some were engineers. Most had been to college. There was a professional golfer, a professional skier, and a Rockette dancer from New York City. A more varied group of women may never have been assembled. What they all had in common was the desire to fly. They were members of a small, elite group of licensed female pilots who had been chosen to be part of an experimental program that might put the first women pilots in the military.

Some of the women came from money that enabled them to buy an airline ticket or drive their own cars to Sweetwater, while others worked for a living and had scraped together their train fare. One woman brought thirteen pieces of luggage and a steamer trunk, but soon realized her mistake and sent most of it back home.

Many of the women, without financial resources to afford pilot lessons, had been a part of the Civilian Pilot Program. Like the Chinese flying schools, the program trained pilots who otherwise would not be able to afford lessons. The Civilian Pilot Training Program was offered at colleges and paid for by the government, who allowed that one in ten students could be female. Hazel had paid for her own pilot lessons, but the Chinese Benevolent Society had funded the training that allowed her to go to China.

The women beamed at one another with a sense of shared pride and empowerment. Each of them felt that having become a pilot, she could do anything. For the first time in their lives, they were surrounded by other women who could talk about flying and airplanes and who loved flying with an equal passion.

The women met in one another's rooms that first night at the hotel, like girls at a sleepover, sizing one another up and trying to determine who among them was the hottest pilot. Hazel had clout right from the start. Her experiences in China, flying commercial aircraft and witnessing bombings and dogfights, mesmerized the others, and her extroverted personality, outgoing sense of humor, and confident style drew people to her. She delivered deep-voiced playful comments that sent the others into fits of laughter. They had never met anyone like Hazel, who looked so different from the rest of them and yet made friends so easily.

The following morning, wrapped in a white winter coat and wine-colored dress with boxy shoulders and slim-belted waistline, Hazel stepped outside and found a cattle truck parked in front of the hotel where she had been told transportation to the air base would be waiting. She looked around before approaching the driver, and he assured her in a charming drawl that "Yes, ma'am, this will take you to the air base." The truck bed had been fitted with benches on either side to accommodate the women, who good-humoredly complained that they were being herded like cattle.

The trip was not long. Avenger Field had been built on the outskirts of town, four miles from the hotel. At the sound of plane engines overhead, Hazel twisted in her seat to see the base come into view. Through a veil of wind-scattered dust, tidy rows of gleaming planes lined up waiting for their pilots to materialize. Hazel remembered well the bitter disappointment of her years in

China, waiting to be given a chance. She had been waiting eleven years for this opportunity.

Avenger Field appeared as a series of long, gray buildings huddled at the edge of two crisscrossing gravel runways. Another longer building with windows across the front sat parallel to one of the runways and opened onto the flight line. On the edge of the runway, a control tower was being built. At the far end of the rows of barracks, a large hangar was also under construction.

Hazel checked in at the administration building before being directed to the rec hall, a large open room equipped with desks, couches, Ping-Pong tables, and a radio making an indistinguishable noise drowned out by women's voices. Clusters of women sat on the floor enveloped in clouds of cigarette smoke. Hazel joined the nearest group, introduced herself, and accepted an offered cigarette.

Major Landon E. McConnell, the commanding officer at Avenger Field, switched off the radio and tried to quiet everyone. "Ladies!" he finally shouted. "Welcome to the class of 43-W-4 of the 319th Army Air Forces Flying Training Detachment."[1] The young women beamed at him and one another. He reminded them that they were the first class to occupy this base, and to treat it accordingly. Then, arranging his face into a more serious expression, he looked over the crowd of women staring up at him. "Look on each side of you," he said. "Only one of the three of you will graduate."[2]

The energy in the room deflated; this was not going to be a cakewalk. They were civilians, not in the army, and yet they were at the mercy of military commanders. They had relinquished their freedom, and gladly, for a chance to fly, but none of them was accustomed to strict military discipline.

Despite being civilians and not military personnel, the women would be disciplined using the same thirty-three-page "delinquency list" as male cadets. Starting the following day, demerits would be given for infringements such as lint on their clothing, playing the radio when not authorized, and crying, to name only a few.

The girls gave each other incredulous *What the hell?* looks. They weren't children. As if reading their expressions, Major McConnell told them he did not want to hear any profane language; they were ladies, he reminded them, and expected to act as such. Any unseemly or immodest behavior would be grounds for immediate dismissal. This remark was met with eye rolling by some who turned around so the major couldn't see.

Leoti "Dedie" Deaton also spoke to the women at the initial orientation meeting. Dedie oversaw the women at Avenger Field and functioned as housemother, disciplinarian, and Jackie's eyes and ears. There were more than a hundred women in Hazel's class. Dedie, a thirty-nine-year-old housewife and mother, had been recommended to Jackie based on her administrative skills with the Camp Fire Girls of America. When she first agreed to help Jackie with her top-secret wartime experiment, she had no idea what she was getting herself into. The first class in Houston had been uncontrollable. Jackie's program had been put up so quickly that those in charge were making it up as they went along. Slowly Dedie found a way to rein in the women trainees while assuming a completely new role for herself. No longer a housewife and volunteer, she became a working woman with responsibilities that required she answer to the United States Army Air Corps and the more formidable force that was Jackie Cochran.

The first Avenger Field meeting left the women convinced that they wouldn't last long. Learning to fly the "army way" would be like learning to fly all over again, and the rules seemed impossible to follow, let alone the daunting prospect of classes, room inspections, and flight checks they would need to pass. Hazel took it in stride and bolstered the others, telling them they had to remain positive and not let anyone make them think they didn't deserve to be there. She had been told more than once she wasn't worthy to do what she knew she could do—narrow-minded ideas were challenges, not sentences to life in prison.

After dinner the women went to their "bays," as their living quarters were called. From the outside, the rows of barracks looked like a motel with screened front doors and a covered porch. In front of the barracks, a sandy walkway, where they would line up each morning, opened directly onto the flight line. Each bay consisted of two rooms housing six women in each and a bathroom in the middle. Two sinks, one mirror, two toilets, and two dual-headed showers would all be shared by twelve women getting ready at the same time. The new rooms were clean and freshly painted white with dark green molding. A study table and chairs ran down the middle of the room. Each girl had a gym locker–style closet, with hanging space and half shelves, and a narrow cot so small that Madge Rutherford, who was tall, asked where she would put her legs. Hazel had met Madge at the Blue Bonnet Hotel. Both were outgoing extroverts and became friends immediately.

Hazel's bay mates were all college graduates and, like everyone in the program besides Hazel, white. At thirty, Hazel was the oldest. Being Asian American and having been to China gave her an air of mystique. The women enjoyed getting to know one another while sharing the details of the lives they'd left behind and treats left over from their travel.

They weren't allowed to keep photos, or "pix" as they called them, on their desks. Hazel tucked her photo of Cliff in her locker. One of her bay mates asked if Hazel had a boyfriend, and she told her she did and shared Cliff's photo. She could no longer dismiss her feelings for Cliff. He had been her closest friend for eleven years. They shared the same love of flying and had come through their training together as well as their time in China. Their shared experiences and respect for each other's talents had created a strong bond. The last time they were together they had expressed their love for each other, but they had no idea when they would ever be together again.

Hazel had other photos to put away, including a recent photo of Art Chin. The previous year, Art had visited New York to receive additional treatment for his burns. Meeting him in Central Park on a chilly afternoon, Hazel found Art leaning against a lamppost waiting for her with his pipe tucked in his mouth. He still looked like the boy she'd known in Portland. The extensive scarring he'd received from his burns made his skin appear unnaturally smooth. Only his eyes, protected by his goggles, had been left unscathed. To reconstruct his face, skin grafts had been taken from his calves, upper arms, and thighs, causing wide swaths of scarring. Eyebrows were created using hair from other parts of his body. The scars hadn't diminished his good looks. He was still handsome and confident, his familiar smile and personality unchanged. In an early photo Hazel had kept, he looked every bit the flying ace, wearing jodhpurs, helmet, and boots, and a white scarf to warm his neck and wipe his goggles.

Art had been shot down three times, and would become known as the first American to become an ace in World War II. An ace was a title given to the best pilot, the top of the pack. Unable to return to flying, he had retired as a major from the Chinese Air Force and now spoke at war rallies and on radio broadcasts supporting war bonds in the United States. He had recently written telling Hazel he planned to marry again, and she was happy for him.

In addition to not being allowed to display photos, they weren't allowed to have cameras either. The rule would eventually be abolished, but in the beginning Jackie wanted everything kept secret. For now cameras would have to be sent home or be confiscated. Madge took this especially hard. A blue-eyed, fresh-faced blond with a huge smile, she wore her hair pulled up high on her head and falling in curls. She looked young and was in fact the youngest. The women weren't supposed to write in their letters about life at Avenger. But they did anyway. Madge didn't like all the rules and regulations and hated the idea of earning demerits. No nail polish, minimal makeup, no full-length mirrors.

As they talked, sitting cross-legged on their beds in their

pajamas, something slunk out from underneath one of the cots. Someone screamed, and everyone flew onto a bed. The startled snake stopped and raised its tail, and its rattles made a dry sound like cicadas on a summer evening. Hazel grabbed a broom and, jumping from cot to cot, used long, determined strokes to sweep the rattler toward the door and outside. Madge had studied reptiles in college and planned to make a career of her passion if flying didn't work out. She enthused about the Crotalus and promised they would see lots of them at Avenger Field. Sweetwater was the rattlesnake capital of the world; this was their kind of climate. "Oh, goodie," one of the bay mates muttered sarcastically.

Madge, from Greensburg, Indiana, had earned her pilot license in 1940, the only woman to complete the first class of the Civilian Pilot Training Program at Butler University, Indianapolis, where she worked as an assistant in the English Department to pay for her tuition. The following semester the CPTP offered an advanced class of aerobatic and cross-country flying to the top ten students in the first class. Being third in her class, Madge applied. Her application was rejected on the grounds that she was a woman. She wrote a letter of protest to Eleanor Roosevelt, who responded through the chief of the Private Flying Development Division that no regulation excluded women from the course and "no discrimination will be made against pilots of your sex." In reapplying, Madge was told that although there was no rule to exclude women, no specific institution had been designated to give advanced training to women pilots and therefore she could not be accepted. After graduating from Butler in June 1941, she served in the Indianapolis Civil Air Patrol before coming to Texas.

The bay mates became the best of friends on the first night. Alice Jean May, whom they called AJ, had dark hair and movie-star beauty. Joanne Trebtoske came from Minnesota and liked to break the rules. Hazel nicknamed her "Trouble" because it sounded like her last name and she had a penchant for fun at any cost, but most everyone called her "Treb." Betty Haas, a professional skier from New York, had long eyelashes, dark eyebrows, and a big smile. Her father was the vice president of Random House publishing company, Robert Haas, who had earned the Distinguished Service Cross for rescuing a wounded soldier under fire in France during World War I. Grace Clark, Mary Amanda Bowles, and Virgie Lee Jowell completed the group. It was decided that Hazel would be called "Ah Ying." Everyone agreed it fit her, and as that was what her family called her, the name seemed right here with her new family.

Madge complained that of the more than one hundred girls, she seemed to have the least hours and experience. Her parents had already managed to get her in trouble and nearly thrown out of the program before she started. They had called the local newspapers to tell them about Madge coming to Sweetwater. She had told her parents the program was top secret, but they either forgot or got carried away with pride in their daughter.

Madge's fiancé, Sherman "Shay" Minton, had joined the navy after completing medical school. They had been planning a wedding for April 26, when Madge got a telegram inviting her to come to Chicago to be interviewed for the ferrying training program. When she was accepted, Shay was not pleased. Now she wasn't sure what to do. Shay still wanted to go through with the wedding as planned.

The first full day of training flew by in endless responsibilities and marching. The women filled out Civil Service Commission forms in quadruplicate, had their fingerprints taken, and took their oaths of office. Officially "Civilian Student Pilots, Unclassified," the women stood in line again to get their supplies, including the mechanic's jumpsuits the women dubbed "zoot suits" after the full-legged, narrow-ankled suits men were wearing in Harlem, a leather flight jacket if they were lucky (the army ran out and so not everyone got one), and a heavy sweater that smelled like mothballs. They were issued parachutes, which strapped uncomfortably between their legs, flight caps, and goggles.

To welcome the women to Avenger Field at the end of their first day, the male cadets presented a musical vaudeville-style show. The evening helped at least somewhat to dispel the uneasy feeling the women had been given when they heard in town that the cadets and instructors didn't want women at Avenger Field. Instead of resenting them, the cadets went out of their way to welcome the women. The "burbling bartenders," with aprons and handlebar mustaches, sang a familiar barbershop tune, "How Can I Leave Thee?" The meaning was not lost on anyone, as the women were essentially kicking the men out. As the cadets sang, the women joined in on the chorus. After the show, the men and women mingled and talked about where they were from and their favorite topic, flying. For the men, this was an entirely new experience, talking to women who enjoyed airplanes and knew as much about flying as they did.

The women had to be in their bays no later than nine, and lights out came with taps being played at 10 p.m. Madge returned to the bay at eight to find her bay mates studying, showering, or talking. She'd been playing Ping Pong with a cadet named Marion Culver and she confided that she was thinking of going out with him. Shay was getting too demanding about the wedding, she told her bay mates.

The women talked about home and boyfriends and being homesick. Unlike the others, there was nowhere Hazel would rather be, but she certainly remembered what it was like to be away from home for the first time.

As they got ready for bed, every one of them was anxious, praying that their first day of training would not be their last. Although the cadets had been nice to them, the commanding officers seemed like they might enjoy seeing a girl wash out on the first day, proving men were the stronger sex and better suited for flying. Even the cadets assumed the girls would want to give up flying once they were married and had children to raise. A few looked incredulous when one of the girls said she'd never give up flying. Would he? she had asked, and he laughed as if that was a ridiculous question. It was a decision he would never have to make.

Hazel went to sleep thinking about Cliff, far away in China after completing the courses in the United States. She had last seen him in the fall, months ago. Would she ever see him again? The Allies were making progress in the Pacific, but the loss of life still mounted daily. If she was kicked out of training on the first day, she knew exactly where she would be heading.

11

PROSTITUTES OR LESBIANS

I always wanted to learn to fly. . . . I got that fearlessness from my family. . . . Back in the days when it just wasn't the thing for young ladies to ride a motorcycle, my mother was riding a motorcycle. If she'd known about airplanes, she would have wanted to fly.[1]

—MILDRED "MICKEY" TUTTLE AXTON,
WASP, CLASS 43-W-7

WHEN REVEILLE BROKE THE PREDAWN silence at 6 a.m. on February 27, 1943, the bay mates quickly dressed and began scrounging for mirror space to apply their red lipstick. The reflection of eight faces pressing their lips together made them laugh. The United States government had decided that women, especially those working for the war effort, needed to maintain their femininity, and lipstick kept up morale and was therefore too important to ration.

By the time Hazel and her bay mates lined up in front of the barracks, the cloudless Texas sky glowed a brilliant blue and the planes waiting on the flight line beckoned invitingly. From the barracks, they marched gracelessly to breakfast, the process of lining up and marching being something completely new.

For breakfast they were given an hour, shortened by a fifteen-minute wait in the cafeteria-style line. "Mom," a smiling, gray-haired woman wearing wire-rimmed glasses, spooned eggs and bacon from steaming service troughs, and then placed toast, jam, and real butter onto their stainless-steel trays. Eyes widened. Real butter had been rationed for civilians, and most of the new arrivals hadn't eaten it for months. Endless coffee, pink lemonade, and milk were also available. The women wrote home about the delicious Texas grapefruit. Before they knew anything about their training, they knew they would be well fed.

They again lined up after breakfast and, to the shout of "Hut, two, three, four," were hustled to calisthenics. Lieutenant Albert Fleishman had developed a fitness program emphasizing building upper body and arm strength and including head-rolling exercises to prepare the pilots for spins. In a spin the little primary trainer plane whipped around so fast the pilots thought their heads would fly off. Strong necks avoided injuries. From where he stood atop a table outside in the parade yard, Fleishman led the trainees through exercises for an hour. He was tall, tan, born military, and possessed a good sense of humor, helpful under the circumstances. At thirty-eight years old, he was too old for combat. He had been with the women's training program from the beginning, first at Houston before moving to Avenger Field when it opened.

Hazel had been sitting at a desk for years. Attempting push-ups, she managed several before crashing face-first into the ground. Reestablishing her plank position, she completed twenty-five push-ups while spitting sand. The physical training classes were necessary, the air corps had determined, not only for discipline and preparedness for the physical demands of flying, but also to provide a release of sexual energy. Tire the girls out and they wouldn't get into trouble.

After calisthenics they changed into their coveralls—the "zoots." A motley crew made their appearance that first morning on the flight line, with rolled up cuffs and sleeves and waistbands ripped off and tightened with a belt. One trainee cinched her belt buckle so tightly that she claimed to have cracked two ribs climbing into a plane. They stood in line still adjusting their ill-fitting zoot suits. Madge's didn't cover her ankles, and she complained it was the least attractive outfit she'd ever worn and the drab beige beyond ugly. Previously worn by male cadets, the coveralls came in men's sizes. When the smallest size, a 40, ran out, the next girl in line received a 42. Hazel's five-foot-three, 115-pound frame was overwhelmed by the size she was issued. Violet "Vi" Thurn, who was five feet tall, wore a 44 for the duration of her training. Madge was nearly a foot taller than Vi, who, like many, would have to strap wooden blocks to her feet to reach the rudder pedals and stack three cushions on her seat to be able to see out of the airplane.

Most of the training instructors were civilian employees with not much more experience than the students. Testing would be done by army personnel. Hazel had more flying hours and experience, including those as a commercial pilot in China, than her instructor, Lieutenant LaRue, who was not a civilian but a commissioned officer. Tall and blond, he wore cowboy boots, and Hazel imagined him wearing a white Stetson when he wasn't wearing his flight cap. He stressed that although Hazel knew how to fly, she had yet to learn the *army way*, and many girls would wash out because they couldn't learn a new way to fly. Hazel was tempted to smirk but didn't want to be rude. And despite his heavy-handed approach, she liked him.

The instructors at Avenger Field were not always objective with female trainees. Until recently, air bases had been male territory, and some preferred it stay that way. Others said they just didn't know how to teach women, as if they were a different species. Some instructors, resentful over the addition of female students and believing they would be more difficult to teach, decided to treat the women exactly like men, in other words to yell directions and insults and limit praise. The women trainees, unused to aggressive behavior from a teacher, adapted and learned to take whatever their instructors dished out. A symbiotic relationship developed between instructors and their female students, and that sometimes led to romance despite a rule against instructors dating students. Sharing the cockpit for many intense hours created a unique intimacy.

Still, there were times when instructors intentionally failed to provide information. For example, when asked about the questionable-looking tube in front of the pilot's seat, instructors refused to explain its purpose. The men were too embarrassed to explain relief tubes, because it would involve mentioning a part of the male anatomy not discussed in front of women. Women were unable to use the relief tubes, lacking the male anatomy they were designed for, and therefore instructors deemed it unnecessary to explain. After speculation and discussion, the women figured out the purpose of the tubes and passed on the information to one another.

Hazel had never flown a Fairchild PT-19 primary trainer. The cute little monoplane with an open tandem-seated cockpit looked like a toy that had been blown up to life size. Hazel taxied into position. With fifty of her classmates and the male cadets also preparing to take off, the field was a flurry of airplanes. After pausing for incoming traffic, she took her foot off the brake and pushed in the throttle. The tail went up and the plane increased speed until it lifted off the ground.

Until now, most of the trainees' flying experience had been limited to 40- and 60-horsepower Cubs, but by their second day, they would be climbing in and out of the 175-horsepower PT-19s with confidence, thrilled to be flying the powerful planes. Since most of the women were used to flying Cubs, her instructor thought Hazel would be impressed. But in fact, she had flown bigger planes in China.

The fifty women trainees took off three at a time with their instructors. From the air, they saw that West Texas was perfectly laid out for flying, with roads running north to south and east to west as convenient navigational aids. LaRue pointed south and warned Hazel that when she started flying cross-country to never make a forced landing in Mexico, where she would be put in jail and never let out.

A wide blanket of blue stretched in all directions and enhanced the feeling of expansiveness and freedom that Hazel loved about flying. The earth had a dried, barren appearance, and the airport and surrounding land were devoid of even one blade of grass. She could see no water or shade, until she spotted a trough surrounded by cattle.

Hazel caught on quickly. Using flaps on landings was new to her and difficult at first. When the flaps dropped, so did the nose, and at what seemed like only five feet from the ground. If the flaps were lowered too soon, the plane stalled, and that was the worst thing that could happen. Her second time up, she worked on spins and stalls and learned that the little blue-and-yellow Fairfield, with its tail switching back and forth like a good bird dog, spun like a champ.

One of the Avenger runways was still under construction, so from the first day of training every landing was with a crosswind, or perpendicular to the wind. They learned to dodge tiny cyclones filled with dust the locals called dust devils that blew across the runways, which could tip up a wing in a second. Also hazardous on landings were meandering flocks of tumbleweeds that could become entangled in landing gear or entwined in the propeller.

In the afternoon, Hazel changed from her zoot suit to tan pants and white shirt and attended ground school while the morning group reported to the flight line. There would be physics classes, which Hazel had never taken and hoped wouldn't be her undoing. Most of the girls had college degrees or at least college experience, and a few were engineers. Before graduation the women would receive more than four hundred class hours, the equivalent of a college aeronautics degree. In addition to physics, they studied aerodynamics, electronics and instruments, engine operations and maintenance, meteorology, Morse code, navigation, military and civilian air regulations, and mathematics.

Today's classes would be math and navigation. Class began with a math test, "just to see if you girls can do any of this stuff,"[2] the instructor said. The women kept their heads bent to their papers, wanting to impress him. The test would be used to group students according to ability. The women were used to having to prove themselves, and this wouldn't be the last time. To be accepted into the program, they had passed the same intelligence tests given to the male cadets, yet men continued to question whether women could master the technical requirements of flying. In the end, not a single woman during the entire program failed ground school.

The first day ended with the women exhausted and hungry at dinnertime. For dinner they changed into civilian slacks or dresses and arrived at the mess hall ravenous. In the chow line, someone asked how they would keep their weight over one hundred pounds marching and sweating all day. A sign instructing them to take as much as they wanted as long as they ate everything they took provided a clue, and so did the thick, marbled steaks smothered in butter. Mashed potatoes, gravy, and string beans made their mouths water. There had been beef in some form at all three meals that day. Rationing meant most of them had not eaten beef for more than a year. For dessert they chose between ice cream, cake, and pie, or had all three if they wanted, while sipping cups of hot coffee to keep them awake for studying.

Hazel met Vi Thurn at dinner. Although not one of Hazel's bay mates, Vi became a good friend. She had grown up in a sod house in Bowdle, South Dakota, where she'd watch hawks swoop over the family farm and yearned to fly. "If I could be like that hawk, wouldn't it be nice if I could just be up there floating around," she said.[3] After earning a teaching certificate, she had taught first grade in Spearfish, earning one hundred dollars a month. She had ridden her bicycle six miles to a local airfield for flying lessons. Like most women she didn't have a driver's license. "Growing up on a farm, I thought women were just as important as men. I never had the feeling that I was different than the guys because I loved to play basketball and do all the things they did. I almost always felt equal."[4]

As well as sitting with the women in classes, in the beginning the male Army Air Corps cadets ate alongside the new ferrying trainees and enjoyed the novelty of female company. Meals were going to be more fun.

On the way back to their bay after dinner, the sun was setting, and Hazel and her bay mates stopped to watch the purples and oranges dance across the sky. The dust in the air created the effect of a fire burning on the horizon and the most beautiful sunset Hazel had ever seen. After dinner they were so full and sleepy it was difficult to study. Madge collapsed onto her cot to sort her mail and told her bay mates she'd been asked to lead the drill commands and believed it was based on her experience in the Civil Air Patrol. Madge's mother had sent candy, and it was passed around. Nobody was too full for candy.

◊ ◊ ◊

The first days of training were cold, and the women were happy to be wearing pounds of bulky GI clothing. They marched to lunch at a faster pace, inspired by hunger and the temperature. Half of the class flew in the morning, while the other half attended ground school. In the afternoon, they reversed. There were swarms of male army cadets already on the field strapping on parachutes and adjusting goggles and helmets. Some waved enthusiastically, and for a moment, Hazel missed the boys from Al Greenwood's Flying School.

One evening after dinner, Inez "Woodie" Woods waltzed into Hazel's bay ready for a date with cadet Bill Burkett. She was twenty-six years old and from St. Louis, Missouri, and already one of Hazel's closest friends. As she loosened the dark blond curls she'd pinned on top of her head, she complained about the mail not going out every day, which disrupted their connection to family and more importantly boyfriends. And, she added, abruptly changing the subject, she couldn't understand why all Texans seemed mildly profane, although she liked their accents.

Woodie had beautiful blue eyes slightly slanting downward so that she looked innocent and a bit sad. Tonight, her lips were perfection. With a pencil she'd made an outline outside her natural lip line and added Vaseline on top of her lipstick to make her lips appear larger, to great effect.

They discussed a new rule that made them roll their eyes: Jackie Cochran had decided that henceforth, the girls would go to a beauty parlor once a week—and at their own expense. She wanted them to maintain a certain image to keep her program running. But it was one thing to make a rule, and another for the girls to comply. Gusty winds would destroy their styled hair before they even got back to the base. And the cost was unreasonable for most of them. They were paid $144 per month minus $12.15 for room and board. Most sent some money home and tried to save what they could for the future.

Woodie took one more look in the bathroom mirror and ran a finger along her lower lip line to erase any errant lipstick that had escaped her careful ministration. Pleased, she returned to the girls. "Au revoir," she said, blowing them a kiss, "don't wait up," at which everyone laughed because curfew was strictly enforced at ten.

Hazel and her bay mates had survived the first few days of training with more to write home about than they had time to fit in their letters. Anxious about what lay ahead and whether or not they were up to the task, Hazel committed herself entirely to the program, determined to not only succeed but excel.

Leaving the church on Sunday morning and stepping into the bright sunlight, Hazel took a deep breath of fresh air. The church had been suffocatingly warm inside. Her damp dress clung to her legs and back in a most unladylike fashion and the thought brought up a laugh she quickly stifled, but not before others turned and stared. The church had been crowded and the pews tightly packed because so many women from Avenger Field were in attendance. The cool air reenergized Hazel after being plastered to AJ and Madge throughout the long and boring service. Taking the pastor's hand, she heard him say, "Good morning, thank you for coming." As he mopped his drenched bald head with a handkerchief, she smiled at the man who looked so exactly what a pastor should look like that he might have stepped from a Hollywood film.

Attendance had not been optional. Jackie insisted her girls attend church to boost their image. The townspeople of Sweetwater, Texas, population ten thousand give or take a few souls, had been none too happy about the arrival of women to Avenger Field. They'd accepted the male cadets after some initial concerns for their daughters, but in fact soon realized the young men gave the local economy a much-needed boost, and the young women of Sweetwater enthusiastically welcomed new young men to date and attend dances with. Men from all over the country gave rural Sweetwater what they imagined to be the cosmopolitan atmosphere of a big city, or at the very least a small city. But after the women trainees arrived, the male cadets didn't go into town as often. Now women were available at every meal, on the flight line, and in their classes, and they possessed knowledge and passion about airplanes and flying.

Not only in Sweetwater were women wanting to serve in the military considered the worst kind of woman. People across the country believed that women stationed on army bases must be prostitutes or lesbians. At the very least, they were looking for husbands, and no one's husband would be safe.

Soon after Hazel's class had arrived, a group of prostitutes set up shop in the Blue Bonnet Hotel. They said they were pilots from Avenger Field, confirming the townspeople's suspicions that the women arriving and saying they were pilots couldn't possibly be telling the truth; after all, people said to one another, "normal" women wouldn't want to live on an air base with men. Overnight stays in town or anywhere off base were not allowed unless a woman trainee could prove her mother or husband was visiting. An announcement of this policy was published in the Sweetwater newspaper to further make clear that Avenger's female ferrying trainees were not engaging in prostitution.

Jackie, determined to clear her girls and their reputations, suggested they visit the local churches to convince locals they were upstanding young women. Although only a few streets wide, the little town of Sweetwater boasted twelve churches. Young women in this era were expected to behave as ladies, including, but not limited to, wearing hats, stockings, and gloves to town, attending church services, and exhibiting a long list of behaviors defined as feminine, to prove they were moral and well-behaved. Jackie flew into Sweetwater and called upon the mayor. He heartily agreed with her proposal to improve relations and planned a day of events designed to better acquaint the community with the trainees. After the Avenger women entertained the crowd with songs, they were invited to a nearby ranch to enjoy a rodeo and barbecue.

Following the day of introduction arranged by the mayor, the Sweetwater townspeople hosted a Hospitality Day during which each of the trainees signed up to attend the church of their choice and a home-cooked dinner that would be provided by a church member. The women groaned when they were told, and the requirement included the Jewish trainees despite there being no synagogues in Sweetwater. Jackie allowed no exceptions. Not all Sweetwater citizens embraced the purpose of the meals. Some, not so easily swayed, served the trainees their meals while they sat alone in the kitchen. The meal provided, they must have believed they'd fulfilled their obligation as best they could considering the women's dubious character.

In the end, Jackie's mission was a success. The Sweetwater

newspaper reported, "They're civilians, but men of the flying fraternity think they're the greatest little sisters that a group of Army fighting airmen ever possessed."[5] Sweetwater accepted the "lady pilots" from Avenger Field with open arms after seeing they were churchgoing, God-fearing, barbecue-loving women with impeccable manners and graces. They certainly weren't prostitutes and would be brusquely defended to anyone who dared to speak otherwise. The losers were the "Blue Bonnet Girls," who were run out of town, and their patrons.

◊ ◊ ◊

A few days after training began, Hazel reported to the flight line to find snow blowing horizontally across the field. The anchored planes groaned and heaved in the wind, and the temperature gauge showed eight degrees. There would be no flying today. Disappointed, she removed her chamois leather mask intended to protect her face from frostbite and made her way back inside the ready room.

Madge looked up from her letter writing when Hazel entered with a gust of wind and snow. "I'm telling the folks about my stunt yesterday." Madge had stalled during a power-on spin, and her instructor yelled, "Rutherford! Your stalls stink!"[6] She had had a nightmare about the incident last night. Stalling, especially on landing, could be fatal. It wasn't good during a spin either.

The trainees remained grounded and unable to fly for two days due to the wind and freezing temperatures. With radar still a decade in the future, ground visibility was essential for flying navigation. Under a blanket of white, highways, rivers, and roads disappeared. Maps proved difficult to hold on to while wearing heavy gloves, and sometimes blew out of cockpits, leaving pilots with only a compass and a watch. In addition to all of the other issues of flying in low visibility, it didn't help that the names of towns that had been painted on roofs, barns, and railroad stations in the 1930s had been painted over at the start of the war. Al Greenwood had instigated the marking of buildings to orient pilots in Oregon in the 1930s. But now what had once been a useful navigational tool could help Japanese bombers find their targets.

Unable to fly, the women practiced marching and close-order drills used for military parades, led by Madge. She had been chosen for this dubious honor partly because of her experience in the Civil Air Patrol, an air force auxiliary that provided emergency air response services, and partly because she was loud and a natural leader. When the wind swept the tarmac free of snow, a group of instructors and army personnel with cigarettes and coffee in hand gathered to watch the women attempt coordinated marching. Coordination wasn't their problem. Some were not much over five feet tall and had to take long strides to keep up with the line. Watching the shorter women trying to take big enough steps brought muffled laughter from the men. Madge yelled at them, "Not helping!"— with little effect. Her troupe members tried to suppress smiles when she got twisted on the commands. They loved Madge and enjoyed being her guinea pigs.

After being told by her commanding officer that she was too lenient, Madge drilled her section for a solid hour one morning. After that a tidy and disciplined unit marched to drill exercises, the flight line, classes, and the mess three times a day. Everywhere the trainees went, they marched. Talking while marching was forbidden, so instead they sang. Some of the songs from the WASP songbook were suggestive enough that Jackie Cochran decided to ban them for the women.

I just called up to tell you that I'm rugged but right

A rambling woman, a gambling woman, drunk every night.

I order porterhouse steak three times a day for my board

And that is more than any decent gal in town can afford!

I've got a big electric fan to keep me cool while I eat,

A tall and handsome man to keep me warm while I sleep,

We may be browned-skinned lassies but what do we care,

We've got those well-built chassis

And that take it or leave it air.

We've got the hips that sank the ships

In England, France, and Peru,

And if you're like Napoleon, then it's your Waterloo.

I just called up to tell you

That I'm rugged but right[7]

Hazel and her bay mates had cleaned and double-checked every inch of their bay prior to their first inspection. Inspections occurred on Saturday mornings. Beds had been made army style with square corners and rulers used to smooth the bedcovers. Lying on the floor underneath their cots, sheets and blankets were pulled tight and bedsprings were washed. Dust on the bedsprings earned one demerit. Everything in their bay must be kept uniform and clean, and there was a specific manner for how shoes were polished, the order clothes hung in the lockers, and how towels hung on the bathroom rack.

When the lieutenant entered the room and put on his white gloves, they stood at attention beside their bunks. As he searched lockers for infractions, he suddenly stopped, cleared his throat, and turned away, blushing. The women managed to control smiles. Was it the first time he'd been confronted with female undergarments? He showed no embarrassment as he examined each girl's waist, looking for a shirt uneven with a slack seam. This intimate duty performed, he looked under the beds to see that blankets were laced underneath, and no dust could be found. No demerits were given. As soon as the lieutenant left, the women fell from their stance and burst out laughing. They jumped onto their beds and threw their

The Lee family in 1927, Portland, Oregon.
Back row (left to right): Hazel, Florence,
Big Sister, Rose, Harry, Victor.
Front row (left to right): Frances, Mother,
Daniel, Father, Howard.
*Courtesy of Museum of Chinese in America,
New York City.*

Hazel stands in front of *The Student Prince*,
Swan Island, Portland, Oregon, 1932.
Public domain, 960th Cyberspace Wing website.

Lee Yuet/Yut Ying (Hazel Lee) affidavit photo, 19
Chinese Exclusion Act case files, RG 85,
National Archives—Seattle, Lee Yuet Ying
(Hazel Lee) case file, Seattle, Box 582, 7030/5149
and Box 710, 7030/10411.

Major Clifford Louie in the 194
Released to public dome
by Clifford Louie's granddaught

Chin Suey Tin (Arthur Chin), Form 430 photo, 1932.
Chinese Exclusion Act case files, RG 85, National
Archives—Seattle, Chin Suey Tin (Arthur Chin) case file,
Portland, Box 102, 1209/614.

Wong Quai Yin (Virginia Wong), Form 430 photo, 1933.
Chinese Exclusion Act case files, RG 85,
National Archives—Seattle, Wong Quai Yin (Virginia Wong)
case file, Portland, Box 96, 5017/723.

Arthur Chin in China, 1933 or 1934.
Courtesy of John Wong.

ginia Wong and Hazel on Swan Island
ing their training, 1933–1934.
urtesy of Museum of Chinese in America,
w York City.

an air show in Shanghai, 1936. Hazel stands in front
aring white. Behind her is Mayor Wu Tiecheng.
blic domain.

Hazel and Clifford Louie, 1943.
Courtesy of Texas Woman's University Woman's Collection.

From newspaper wedding announcement
for Hazel and Cliff Louie, 1943.
Courtesy of New York Daily News.

Hazel during training at Avenger Field, Sweetwater, Texas, 1943. *Courtesy of Texas Woman's University Woman's Collection.*

ie Cochran in the early 1940s. *Courtesy of Florida ographic Collection, State Archives of Florida.*

Ferrying trainees being briefed in the ready room, 1943. Front row, left to right: Group Commander Charles M. Sproul, Irma Cleveland, Faith Buchner, Martha Lundy, Mary Jane Stevens, Anabelle Kekic. Back row, left to right: Ruby Mullins, Hazel Lee, Virginia Harris Mullins. *Courtesy of Texas Woman's University Woman's Collection.*

Hazel with Geneva Slack, 1943.
*Courtesy of Texas Woman's University
Woman's Collection.*

Faith Buchner, Hazel Lee (standing on whee
and Grace Clark, wearing "zoot suits."
Avenger Field, Sweetwater, Texas, 1943.
*Courtesy of Texas Woman's University
Woman's Collection.*

...el, AJ, Virgie Jowell, Alice Lovejoy,
Sylvia Dahmes Clayton, 1944.
...rtesy of Texas Woman's University
...nan's Collection.

November 1944. In one of her last photos,
Hazel stands in front of AJ and Fran,
who are on the wing of a P-63 at the
Bell Factory, Niagara, New York,
the night before they left
on the mission to Great Falls.
Courtesy of Texas Woman's University
Woman's Collection.

The aftermath of the crash in Great Falls, Montana on November 23, 1944.
Public domain, Malmstrom Air Force Base.

President Barack Obama signs bill to award the Congressional Gold Medal, the highest award
a civilian can receive from Congress, to the WASPs, recognizing their contribution to World War II.
From left to right and closest are WASPs Bernice Falk Haydu, Elaine Danforth Harmon,
and Lorraine Rogers. *Photo by Pete Souza, public domain, U.S. Department of Defense.*

pillows at one another. They had passed their first inspection. Flying might be the easy part of this new military life.

◊ ◊ ◊

On Sunday, March 7, 1943, Margaret "Margy" Burrows Sanford Oldenburg was beginning her second week of training in Houston. Although a member of Hazel's class, she was in the half of 43-W-4 training at Houston's Howard Hughes Municipal Airport instead of at Avenger Field in Sweetwater. Margy had graduated from the University of California at Berkeley and took up flying after meeting Amelia Earhart. She had clocked about three and a half hours' time in the PT-19, and her instructor, Norris Morgan, was introducing her to spins, how to get into and out of them.

Approximately six miles south of the Houston airfield, Margy failed to recover from a spin. Both she and her instructor were killed when the plane crashed nose-first into the ground. Two witnesses said it looked like they were practicing a forced landing, until the plane continued spinning into the ground.

After the accident, all instructors were checked and some were dismissed. Since Margy was not a part of the military, none of her funeral or burial expenses would be paid for by the government. Jackie Cochran paid for them out of her own pocket. Margy's was the first death in the Women's Flying Training Detachment program. Fearful of bad publicity, Jackie decided the accident should be kept quiet. The girls on the Houston base were told not to tell anyone or write about it in their letters. It's possible that Hazel never even knew about Margy's death. None of the archived letters from Hazel's classmates at Avenger Field mention the accident.

12

RACING THE BOYS

As a matter of fact, I know a great many boys who should be making pies—and a great many girls who would be better off in manual training. There is no reason why a woman can't hold any position in aviation providing she can overcome prejudices and show ability.[1]

—**AMELIA EARHART**

AFTER TWO DAYS OF NO FLYING due to weather, the blue sky returned and two figures raced toward the flight line dodging the tumbleweeds that skated across the tarmac. Hazel tagged her plane with a palm and whistled for LaRue to hurry up. The race was not won until she took off. Every day the male cadets and the women trainees raced each other to be first off the ground. Whichever group took off last had to taxi out through the dust created by the first and begin their training period with a windshield covered in a grungy film obstructing their view.

The previous day, Hazel had trundled half-blind to the takeoff line while eight other pilots tried taking off at the same time. During flight sessions there were around one hundred planes competing for a piece of sky to practice maneuvers. Like a frenzy of bees in a hive, there were planes taking off and landing, planes above, behind, and on all sides. The tower had not yet been completed to regulate air traffic, so the trainees developed eyes like hawks. They flew a traffic pattern stacked four or five levels high, beginning at the top, circling, and then dropping down to the next level until it was their turn to land. LaRue had Hazel perform coordination exercises while three planes were spinning within a half mile's distance of her plane. One cut under her within a hundred feet of her wing.

In one of Madge's letters, she wrote, "You couldn't stir the sky down here with a spoon— planes, planes everywhere, all the time, just one continuous roar, day and night. I wouldn't have missed this for anything."[2]

One afternoon, LaRue had Hazel practicing the difficult outside loop that made Paul Mantz famous when he performed it forty-six times consecutively. His record still held. During the maneuver, unlike the easier inside loop, the pilot was inverted for most of the stunt. It required more control and more stress on the plane, as the outside loop is done against wing lift. Beginning the outside loop required more speed than the inside loop and was executed with the pilot's head on the outside instead of inside the loop. Better than any amusement park roller coaster, the loop required strong neck muscles and a fearless temperament. Hazel loved performing it.

After their lessons, Hazel and AJ watched Madge head over to her plane and fold herself into the cockpit with her legs up to her chest—she was still having a hard time finding the right rudder adjustment because of her long legs, and her classmates were amazed that she was able to fly in that position.

They turned their attention to some of the cadet upperclassmen on the far side of the field taking off to fly solo for the first time. AJ and Hazel couldn't wait until it was their turn to go up alone without their instructors. In order to solo, they had to pass their first check ride. A primary trainer landed and taxied to a stop. The instructor scrambled out across the wing and leapt to the ground, and the plane staggered erratically back into the sky again. The instructor left standing on the runway kept his eyes fixed on his student. AJ and Hazel turned toward another PT coming in to land. The cadet put her down too hard, and the plane bounced twenty feet and settled back hard, bounced again, and landed on its nose and left wing. Fortunately, the cadet was unhurt.

The male cadets and the women ferrying trainees worked and trained in the same spaces. They took the same classes and had flight instruction at the same time. The only difference between the training of the two sexes was that the women did not receive gunnery training or learn to fly in formation. Some of the men had been drafted, unlike the women, who all came for the love of flying. The "girls," as the boys called them, learned that the cadets had the same fears as women about flying, and maybe more so coming in with no flying experience, but for them, it was less socially acceptable to show it, especially in the military.

For Hazel, fear was never a problem. As she once said to her sister Frances when she asked if Hazel was ever afraid, "No, if everybody else is afraid, there has to be somebody to take over."[3]

With men and women working and living so closely together, romances were inevitable. The male cadets and officers and the women trainees were an elite group of carefully selected individuals with a shared love of flying, and they were all in top physical condition. The women were between the ages of twenty-two and thirty-five, had been chosen based in part on their looks, and most, although not all, were unmarried. Away from their families and gossiping neighbors, they embraced a new freedom and a more uninhibited attitude toward relationships than other American women. Empowered by their independence and living and succeeding in what was considered a "man's world," most believed a sexual relationship with a man they intended to marry was acceptable. They were liberated adult women, serving their country to help win a world war. Conventions once held dear by their mothers weren't practical in wartime. There wasn't time for weddings with everyone pouring themselves into winning the war. Add to that the prevalent attitude of "eat, drink, and be merry, for tomorrow we die." The war scattered people and kept them separated for months and even years. Death seemed imminent, if not inevitable, especially to women who had said goodbye to husbands and boyfriends heading overseas to combat. No one knew what the future would bring.

In 1943 unmarried men and women who weren't related to each other were still being segregated. Colleges required female students live in women-only dorms. Single-sex hotels still existed, and landlords did not allow single female tenants to entertain male visitors in their rooms, or even in public rooms after hours. The trainees at Avenger knew to be careful of appearances while working around men. The consequence of stepping outside cultural norms was no longer neighbors' gossip but a real threat to the women's ferrying program, and if a scandal wasn't enough, then a pregnancy was sure to end their flying careers.

Even before the women arrived, Jackie had expressed to Dedie her concern about the male cadets fraternizing with the new female trainees, and had asked her to keep an eye on the situation. Should a scandal appear in the newspapers, Jackie knew that public support would plummet and the experiment would fail. She suggested Dedie try to keep the men and women apart as much as possible.

That would prove challenging. Their living bays were so close, only a few feet apart, that the men passed hamburgers they'd squirreled away from the canteen across the space to the girls after curfew to appease their limitless appetites after long hours and strenuous work. Because the men's barracks were so close, the women's windows had been painted black to provide privacy. On the first warm day, windows were thrown open in favor of fresh air. Initially, the women sank close to the ground from the showers to their lockers to avoid being seen, but eventually even that was abandoned by all but a few.

Each group worked hard to make certain the other didn't achieve a better flying record, and the competition between the sexes created a playful atmosphere in the mess hall at the end of the day. Dedie first tried to separate the men and women at mealtimes, requiring them to eat at opposite ends of the mess hall to avoid conversations. The men and women still stood together in line, and everyone arrived for dinner looking their best.

Keeping the men and women separated had become Dedie's full-time job, and it soon became obvious there was no way to keep them apart. No precedent existed, as men and women had never shared an air base before. To head off any scandal, Major McConnell came up with the somewhat draconian rule that men and women were forbidden to talk to each other at any time except in the canteen between 7 and 8 p.m. and at Sunday middays.

This didn't go over well. Madge wrote in a letter home, "Some of the girls are very attractive and all of them are normal and they find it very hard not to be friendly and casual with the boys just as they were on their college campuses before this began. . . . We are here to fly, not date cadets."[4] This lofty statement came from Madge, who had recently decided to date a persistent cadet despite being engaged.

During the war, with husbands and boyfriends overseas and couples separated for months or even years, a different attitude about loyalty within committed relationships existed. Dating was accepted and not considered cheating, even for those who were married.

Dating did not pose a problem for Hazel. White men did not date Chinese women, or Chinese American women either.

Major McConnell's rule intended to restrict fraternizing between the men and women, and made entirely Dedie's responsibility, proved impossible to enforce and within a week was abandoned. Dating was again allowed, and even deemed important for morale, as long as curfews were observed. Dedie allowed Friday night movies on the base and dates on Saturday and Sunday, with an extended curfew on those nights. Jackie trusted Dedie but wasn't happy about the failure of the separation rule and grew more and more concerned about the reputation of her girls and the future of her program. Even with the cadets' upcoming graduation, the problem would not be solved. Officers and instructors were dating the women as well, ignoring the rule forbidding them to date their students.

◊ ◊ ◊

One night in March, spring arrived in Sweetwater, Texas. A thunderstorm brought the first rain since November. Hazel and her bay mates woke up, threw open the doors and windows, and breathed in the scent of damp earth. In the morning the sunrise was green. The following days were either freezing cold or blazing hot with episodes of intense heat lightning. One of Hazel's classmates, a spunky red-haired Texan, told them Texas weather could be wild and extreme with "sandstorms so heavy that you can look up and see prairie dogs burrowing 20 feet up in the air."[5]

The northerly wind blew at a constant twenty-five miles an hour, whipping up dust storms that appeared from out of nowhere like a solid red wall. Sand blew through doors and windows into their rooms. Madge wrote in a letter, "I wake up every morning with Texas between my teeth."[6] Every day their zoot suits collected a thick layer of dirt and sand. Nevertheless, they'd receive a demerit if they showed up in dirty coveralls in the morning. They decided to wear them into the shower and then hang them outside to dry in the strong Texas wind while they ate breakfast. It worked perfectly and became part of their routine.

As Hazel and the rest of class 43-W-4 staggered exhausted and aching through their second week, the war raged on around the world. The United States and British armies labored across the sands of Tunisia hoping to push Nazi forces back and out of Africa. In Russia, the siege of Stalingrad had been broken a month before, and the Russian Army was advancing south and west to recapture Kursk, Kharkov, and Vyasma. Meanwhile, the Allied assault on Japan continued in the Pacific. And in Europe, the British Royal Air Force and the United States Eighth Army Air Corps continued their round-the-clock-offensive bombing of German manufacturing sites and submarine pens, with mounting losses for the Allies that resulted in pilot and aircraft shortages. In Sweetwater, Texas, one hundred women training to fly for their country would soon free up a hundred pilots for combat.

Unlike their first days, when the bay mates woke early and clamored for mirror space to pull curlers from their hair and put on lipstick, by now they had mastered shortcuts to catch an extra half hour of sleep. Lipstick fit in pockets and could be applied in the airplane. When the flight lieutenant called, "Fall in! Two minutes!," they were just waking up and splashing water on their sunburned faces. Beds were made in seconds, and they lined up outside still buttoning their shirts.

With only two sinks, two toilets, and two dual-headed showers, the bathroom was crowded after flying, when they were hot and dirty and wanted to clean up for dinner. Any modesty experienced on the first night had evaporated. Privacy didn't matter anymore. AJ drew a cartoon of three naked women, all crammed together into one shower stall, scowling at the drill leader telling them to "fall in for drill in two minutes!"[7] At the end of each sixteen-hour day, Hazel fell into bed exhausted and happy.

One day the blue sky beckoned soft and welcoming, and Hazel couldn't wait to get in the air. The southeast wind would create some chop, but the warm air swept across her face like silk, and she looked forward to the cooler temperature waiting in the air aloft. Sitting on the bench in front of the flight line, she fidgeted, unable to keep still. For the length of three city blocks to her right and left extended two rows of swirling propellers on blue-and-gold-winged trainers. Madge sat beside her chewing her nails. She'd been having trouble with stalls and spins and confessed to Hazel her fear of "going upstairs," as they called flying. She complained of being rusty after days "downstairs." She didn't have much choice. Madge was scheduled for a check ride tomorrow with her instructor. It was best to get back up there, Hazel reminded her.

Before her first check ride, Hazel carried out the tradition established by her class of tossing a coin in the wishing well with a prayer for an "up-check." The wishing well was a twenty-foot round reflecting pool filled with about three feet of water, centrally located near the administration building and not far from the flight line. At about two weeks into training, depending on when each student was deemed ready, they had their first check rides with their instructors. After passing the test, an official army test check followed, given by a commissioned army officer who flew in from a nearby air base. If the first army check was unsatisfactory, a trainee was given a pink slip with the ominous letter "U" as a warning. The test was repeated after a few more hours of training, and if the pilot still did not pass, she washed out.

The Avenger wishing well became the site for many traditions. Women tossed in a coin when they graduated, for luck before a primary check ride and again after passing, or just to make a more conventional wish, and sometimes the instructors found themselves thrown in just for fun. Following a trainee's first solo flight, she was dumped into the wishing well to emerge drenched and laughing.

After less than two weeks flying primary trainers with their instructors, Hazel and her classmates began one by one to solo. Soloing the primary trainer was the first milestone of training. Ferrying trainees were required to have eight to ten hours of instruction before being allowed to fly alone. Flying forty-five minutes a day and recording every minute in her logbook, Hazel was close to eight hours when LaRue decided she was ready.

Alone at last in an airplane, Hazel checked and double-checked everything and managed to take off in a straight line. She performed loops, snap rolls, vertical reverse, slow rolls, and then shot landings on the field. A first solo flight was about fifteen to twenty minutes, but LaRue kept waving her around every time she landed, so she ended up flying forty minutes. No one wanted to stop flying alone. It was what they'd been waiting for. After her final landing, LaRue told her she'd done well.

Hazel began earning solo hours now that she was allowed to take the PTs up by herself to practice areas surrounding Avenger Field. Flying alone across Texas, Hazel saw women hanging out wash, kids playing baseball, and farmers working their fields. She experienced a surge of empowerment when flying solo. No one could tell her what to do or how to do it. It didn't matter whether she was man or woman, white or Asian. She was in control of her fate.

On one solo flight, the wind whipped up a wall of sand that obscured visibility. Hazel could see the other airplanes around her and the ground below, but she couldn't locate the airfield. Her compass told her the direction, and she flew toward the railroad and followed the tracks east until she saw the field.

Hazel learned to recognize the sound unique to each aircraft and thought of it like music or a song that each plane sang. Each motor had its own roar, drone, purr, or growl. Buzzing, the name given to a pilot making a fast pass close to a target or the ground, often to startle someone or something, was dangerous and technically not allowed, but when flying solo, it sometimes just couldn't be resisted. Hazel and Madge enjoyed buzzing cows to see them run. Swooping downward at a high speed, they'd come as close to the herd as they felt was safe before pulling up, sending the frightened animals scurrying in all directions and bellowing in fear.

They learned not to buzz sheep, because the unintelligent animals would pile on top of one another, getting hurt in the process. That wasn't fun for anyone, and it would earn demerits if reported by an angry farmer.

On the night of March 11, 1943, the women trainees went to the cadets' graduation celebration dance after going out for steaks. The cadets had sent corsages they pinned on the women's dresses. Upon graduating, the final class of young men, now commissioned officers, would leave Avenger Field for additional training before their assignments overseas. There would be no more racing the boys to the flight line, and the competition and friendships would be missed, and so would the flirting. Because the cadets did not leave Avenger Field all at once, but one by one over the following weeks, a cartoon drawn by AJ and published in *The Avenger* newspaper, called "The Last Cadet," showed three smiling women trainees chasing the last worried-looking cadet.

Three more girls were excused from the program and sent home. Stress was beginning to get to all of them. More than a few suffered stress-related physical symptoms of varying severity. No one went to the doctor unless absolutely necessary, as any health issue might be grounds for dismissal. One of Hazel's bay mates, the skier Betty Haas, was afraid that she would be eliminated because of problems with her ears. Losing altitude rapidly made her ears hurt. After one flight, she couldn't hide the pain she was in any longer, and her instructor transported her directly to the doctor, where she was diagnosed with an ambiguous throat infection. With medication, she recovered and was allowed to remain in training.

The threat loomed that they could be sent packing for any illness or physical issue, including the entirely new phenomenon to army doctors of women menstruating. Until now doctors on air bases had treated only men and not been confronted with female menses, about which they'd had no training.

Before being admitted to the ferrying training program, the women were required to pass a physical, which included meeting a height and weight requirement. Male cadets took a rigorous physical exam before entering the Army Air Corps, and Jackie Cochran wanted her girls to pass the same physical to further prove that the women compared favorably to the most highly selective combat squadron in the war, while setting them up for militarization in the future. For most, the physicals were conducted at army bases near their homes and were the final step in their application process.

Minimum weights had been set for each age and height, roughly corresponding to charts for male cadets, and assuming that weight inferred strength. A twenty-six-year-old woman pilot who was five-foot-seven had to weigh at least 125 pounds and not over 175 to be accepted and to remain in the program. One applicant had lived for a week on a diet rich in bananas and malted milk to raise her weight from 92 pounds to 100, the required minimum for her height. Another from San Francisco ate a nine-course meal at Fisherman's Wharf before driving with her mother, who would not let her go alone to an air base, to Marin County for her physical. In the car she ate bananas and a quart of milk. Her weight was still three pounds too light. She told the flight surgeon that she had been on a diet. "Well, you're overdoing it,"[8] he told her and passed her. For weigh-ins at Avenger Field she wore a bandana full of buckshot, easily obtained in Texas.

Military personnel, including the Army Air Corps cadets at Avenger Field, were required to have regular physical examinations. The women, even though civilians, would be subjected to the same. Jackie hoped that regular checkups would help prove women could handle the demands of the military, but it led to the trainees being treated as guinea pigs by the army flight surgeon at Avenger Field, Dr. Nels Monsrud. With Jackie's approval, he monitored their every move. He found that the arbitrary height-weight charts adapted for female trainees were overweight by four pounds, and he created a more realistic height-weight requirement.

The women were weighed regularly and their menstrual cycles monitored. Menstruation had been used since the late nineteenth and early twentieth century as a reason to keep women from entering the workforce. Monsrud would conduct a pioneering medical study to determine if women could take the physical demands required of professional pilots. Women were required to report details of their menstrual cycles. Many had never spoken about such intimate details and balked, especially considering they were not told for what purpose the information was being collected.

By the end of the war, Dr. Monsrud wrote a report on his collected data that was billed as "revolutionary." He concluded no correlation existed between menses and elimination from training or with high or low flying grades. Women pilots lost less time on duty for physiological reasons than men pilots. Dr. Monsrud reported that "menstruation, in properly selected women is not a handicap to flying or dependable performance of duty."[9]

Betty Gillies, one of the first female pilots to ferry as a civilian for the Army Air Corps and president of the Ninety-Nines, a national organization founded by Amelia Earhart for women pilots, led a successful fight against a proposed ban on women flying during their menstrual cycles by the Air Commerce Department. The ban would ground women pilots during their menstruation periods and for a few days before and after, based on the belief that they were physically weak and less efficient mentally and emotionally at those times, despite no supportive proof. Betty argued that women had been flying while on their periods and while pregnant, without incident, for years. In fact, one pregnant ferrying pilot had flown until she could no longer fit in the plane. When the ban was adopted at some air fields, one general noted that none of his female ferrying pilots menstruated. What he didn't know was that the women had adopted a "Don't Tell" policy regarding their cycles. As one WASP said, "The plane didn't care whether or not the person at the controls had a uterus or not."[10]

13

KILLED IN THE SERVICE
OF HER COUNTRY

*We realized the spot we were in. We had to deliver the
goods, or else there wouldn't ever be another chance for
women pilots in any part of the service.*[1]

—**CORNELIA FORT**

INNERTIME WAS HIGHLY ANTICIPATED, and for Hazel it was
her favorite time of the day after flying. She never apologized
for her love of food, especially fried chicken. And it was obvious
what a sweet tooth she had by the fact that she always ate her dessert
first. When asked why she did this by someone thinking it might be
a Chinese custom, she replied simply, "I always eat my sweet things
first,"[2] as if it were her mantra for life.

As the only Asian American at Avenger Field, for the first time
in her life Hazel represented all Asian people. Many of the others
had never seen an Asian person before. And as the only non-
white woman or man, she immediately stood out from everyone
else. The women were kind and well meaning but were the product
of the racial stereotypes they'd been raised with and the prevailing attitudes about Chinese Americans at that time. One of her

friends referred to Hazel in a letter home as "the little Chinese girl."[3] Another marveled in an interview that she'd "never known a Chinese person."

In an oral history interview, Hazel's friend and Avenger classmate Virginia "Ginny" Luttrell Kahn, said, "Hazel was not what you would call the epitome of the Chinese woman. She was tall, slender and she had her hair cropped very short. She spoke very abruptly, very quickly, more masculine than feminine. She was hysterical."[4] Hazel wasn't tall at five-feet-four-inches. Ginny is likely referring to a common belief that people of Chinese descent were short.

Faith Buckner said in an interview, "She had the American name of Hazel, but Ah Ying did so much better than Hazel. Anybody can have the name of Hazel . . . she was just something else."[5]

Hazel's classmate Marty Lawson remembered her in an oral interview as "well-liked by everyone in her class. I don't think there was a person in her class who didn't love her. She was full of energy, fun, you know, just a good time."[6]

Hazel was universally described as happy, friendly, animated, intelligent, and confident, someone who was always "wanting to try something new and adventurous," and "a bubbly optimist with a mischievous streak and a taste for fried chicken."[7] Classmates said she was compassionate, smart, always willing to help a classmate in need, and possessed an infectious, uninhibited laugh. She was also a highly experienced pilot, which made the training course fairly easy for her.

Despite being older than most of the other girls, Hazel made friends quickly and became a favorite. And yet, she was different. The product of a life no one had lived or read about, she had experiences, both in China and as an Asian American woman, that her new friends could never understand. Hazel had experienced war firsthand, whereas the closest the other women had gotten was watching newsreel footage at the cinema. Her self-reliant nature made her a lone wolf, but she was also an extrovert who loved people. Hazel emerged as a leader, maybe because she was older but also because of her personality and charisma.

Dinner conversations were lively, like sitting down with a huge family who loved to discuss the same topics, and Hazel's storytelling often took center stage. Being the only Asian American was a new experience for Hazel. She made fun of herself, her Chinese-ness, playing it up to make others laugh, and found that playing the clown came easily to her. Sometimes she adopted her mother's Chinese accent, exaggerating it to humorous effect. But she was also aware of a new sense of belonging. It reminded her of her friendship with Virginia but on a larger scale. Now she belonged to a group. She was more than accepted, she was one of them, and she liked it.

One night Hazel talked about her youngest brother Daniel— "Little Brother" she called him. Hunching her shoulders down and arranging her face into a childlike determined expression, she pumped her arms to show how fast he'd walk through Chinatown in Portland trying not to be seen, terrified he would get smuggled into the tunnels that ran beneath the streets and shanghaied, never to be seen or heard of again. Daniel also believed their apartment was haunted, and who knew, Hazel told her friends with a languid shrug, maybe he saw something the rest of them couldn't see. Her audience loved Hazel's cavalier attitude about ghosts; believing in the supernatural was not something their Christian mothers allowed.

Hazel knew how to keep everyone entertained.

◊ ◊ ◊

Charlotte Mitchell, a six-foot-tall blond from the San Joaquin Valley in California and a class behind Hazel, waited for her turn to practice flying. Watching the other planes go through their maneuvers she noticed a small white speck in the distance. As she watched it, a PT landed and skidded erratically up to the flight line. Lieutenant

LaRue vaulted out of the cockpit. His eyes were wide, and he shouted, "Lost my girl! She fell out!" The back seat of the PT was empty and the gosports hung over the side. "She took us into a spin and suddenly she wasn't there anymore!"[8]

He was talking about Hazel.

A jeep roared off, dispatched to retrieve her. Thirty minutes later the jeep returned with Hazel in the back seat. The twenty-five-knot wind had carried her four miles, and her parachute dragged her fifty feet, ripping off her shoes along the way, before she could spill the billowing chute. Her feet were bare, her face scratched, but she grinned and waved her rip-cord D ring. Lieutenant LaRue took her immediately to another PT-19 and made her fly for half an hour so she wouldn't be spooked by the incident. Hazel wasn't scared in the least.

In the mess hall that night, she was hailed as Avenger Field's first bona fide member of the Caterpillar Club, the prestigious group of men and women who had safely bailed out of an airplane during an emergency and had their parachute D ring as proof. Founded in 1922, the name referred to the silk threads that had been used to make parachutes before the supply was cut off from Japan and parachutes began to be made of nylon.

Hazel joked about her mishap and explained that she popped the stick and before she knew it was soaring out over the windscreen. "My seatbelt latch came unfastened."[9] Her friend Barbara said, "Everything happens to Hazel." It wasn't because Hazel was careless or even prone to mistakes; she was a crack pilot. Maybe it was her storytelling, her willingness to expose herself and keep nothing hidden, and her eagerness to try anything, that made it seem like everything happened to her.

The anticipated reprimand came the next day. Major McConnell yelled while Hazel stood and listened. He did not want Hazel to wash out. She was too good a pilot to lose, he told her. Instead, he issued a demerit and a warning to *be more afraid* (one can imagine his glare as he spoke those words). McConnell didn't mention the lipstick-monogrammed plane.

On Monday evening, March 21, every member of the ferrying training class gathered in the ready room for an announcement. Sipping Cokes and smoking cigarettes, they were told there had been an accident. The midair collision and subsequent crash occurred ten miles south of Merkel, Texas, in Mulberry Canyon. Cornelia Fort, a ferrying pilot stationed at Long Beach, California, was flying in formation delivering Vultee B-13 Valiants from Long Beach to Love Field in Dallas. With eleven hundred hours of flying time, Cornelia's delivery mission should have been routine. Pilot Frank Stamme Jr. had been flying too close to Fort's plane, showing off, approaching her and then pulling back. He was slow rolling over her aircraft when his landing gear struck her left wingtip and then the cockpit. Stamme maintained control of his plane, but Fort's plane went into a dive and crashed. Witnesses said she made no attempt to recover from the spin. She was likely killed instantly when Stamme's plane hit her cockpit. The nose of her plane hit the ground vertically with enough force to bury the engine two feet under.

The news took the oxygen from the room. The first death of a ferrying pilot that they knew about, having not been told about Margy Sanford Oldenburg, brought the significance of what they were training to do into perspective. Jackie Cochran had been able to keep Margy's death a secret because she was in her training program, but Cornelia was not, and therefore Jackie had no jurisdiction over the announcement of her death. Some cried, some stood with blank expressions in disbelief, most reached out to be comforted and held. Going forward, it would be more difficult to disregard the danger, the ever-present but ignored possibility of death.

At the time of her death, Cornelia Fort, a twenty-three-year-old Nashville debutante who had left a pampered life to pursue her dream of becoming a flight instructor, was regarded as one of the most accomplished ferrying pilots. When the possibility of the United States joining the war began to loom on the horizon, Cornelia's father made her three brothers swear they would never join the Army Air Corps. Airplanes were new enough that their father didn't trust the machines and believed in better odds of safety on the ground or even on the water when his boys enlisted or were drafted. He never made his daughter swear; he didn't think he had to.

When her father died, Fort took her first flying lesson. Less than a year later, she was working as a flight instructor, the first female flight instructor in Nashville. From there she went to Fort Collins, Colorado, as a flight instructor in the Civilian Pilot Training Program created by President Roosevelt. Soon after, she was hired to teach flying at Hickam Field, Oahu, for the U.S. government.

Cornelia never trained at Avenger Field. In 1942 she had been recruited into Nancy Love's program as one of the original WAFS (Women's Auxiliary Ferrying Squadron) without any training necessary because of her prior experience as a pilot instructor in Hawaii. In fact, Cornelia had been the first United States pilot to encounter the Japanese air fleet just before their attack on Pearl Harbor. Early on the morning of December 7, 1941, she was flying a Cub with a student at the controls when she encountered a Japanese Zero fighter aircraft. Grabbing the controls, she took over as pilot and narrowly escaped a midair collision. The Japanese pilot fired on her, but she managed to escape being hit. Less than a quarter mile away, smoke filled the sky over Pearl Harbor. After landing, she jumped from her plane and ran, dodging bullets as a Zero strafed the field. Her initial confrontation in the air and subsequent harrowing escape was portrayed in the 1970 movie *Tora! Tora! Tora!* by actress Jeff Donnell.

The news of Cornelia's narrow escape during the infamous attack on Pearl Harbor would not have reached her mother for days. The news of her death came within hours of the accident. Cornelia's mother had just recently lost her husband and their home in a fire. She managed to pay her daughter's funeral and transportation expenses after receiving a two-hundred-dollar Civil Service Commission death benefit because Cornelia had listed her mother as a dependent. Mrs. Fort received no burial flag or gold star to display honorably in the front window. Some might assume she hadn't earned the gold star, having not flown in combat; however, the families of *men* killed in accidents during the war, even those on American soil, were certainly entitled to and received gold stars.

Cornelia was the first female pilot in American history to die in active duty. The distinction of active duty pertains to everyone working in service of United States, whether domestically or overseas, and not just to those in theaters of war. The footstone of Cornelia's grave is inscribed, "Killed in the Service of Her Country." Stamme was not charged for the accident, and it was dismissed with a "boys will be boys" attitude.

The trainees carried on, undeterred by this tragedy. Not one woman quit. The commanders at Avenger made sure the women were back in the air as soon as possible. Meanwhile, it must have been agonizing for the parents of the trainees. Despite a flippant attitude toward insurance among the women, Madge's mother and many others convinced their daughters to purchase insurance policies after Cornelia's death.

The Texas rainy season kicked into full gear at the end of March. The women reported to meals and classes soaked, and marched through ankle-deep mud. Sidewalks would not be installed until the end of the year. The rain maintained a steady, heavy onslaught for five hours at a time, and when there came a break, the ceiling and visibility remained too low for flying. Everyone remained grounded for a week. Coordinated flight maneuvers of any kind were impossible in forty- to sixty-mile-per-hour wind. Sudden gusts blew a few women off their feet, inciting shrieks of laughter.

Madge led her troupe through drills, singing enthusiastically. They decided to call themselves the Hut, 2-3-4 Glamour Gals. Friday night sing-alongs were parodies they called "shows," and provided the opportunity to perfect the songs they knew and invent new ones.

(Sung to the tune of "Loch Lomond")

You take the runway,

And I'll take the mud-hole

And I'll hit Avenger a' fore ye,

For me and my PT are standing on our nose,

In the muddy, muddy field of Sweetwater.[10]

Hazel used the time they were grounded accumulating hours in the Link trainer. The Link, also called the Blue Box, was a rotating boxlike device on a pedestal that moved around to simulate flight. Based on technology pioneered by Edwin Albert Link in 1929, the flight simulator taught pilots how to fly on instruments without reference to the ground. The pilot inside the Link, unable to see out, was given instructions by radio from outside the box, by an instructor who controlled conditions like wind. Stubby wings had been affixed to the outside so that the Link weakly resembled an amusement park ride. The Link made it possible to practice aerial maneuvers while still on the ground instead of thousands of feet in the air, where the consequences were less forgiving.

Hazel found the Link difficult in the beginning. It demanded more effort than flying. After five minutes watching the turn-and-bank indicator and the airspeed and clock, she forgot she was anchored to the floor. The controls were the same as those in a training airplane. The instructor, usually a corporal or sergeant, made a flight path record and screamed out directions on the radio like "make a two-turn spin to the right," or "make a 90° turn to the right."[11] Spins were enjoyable once she became comfortable in the box. As Madge described the Link experience, "You really feel like you're spinning. The airspeed drops to 80, you kick rudder, pull the stick back, turn twice, kick opposite rudder, shove the stick (wheel) forward, neutralizing rudders and pull her on up."[12]

◊ ◊ ◊

By the end of March, one hundred new girls had arrived, and the class of 43-W-5 was installed. To train the most women possible in the least amount of time, a new class would begin every month, with a graduation taking place every six weeks. Madge was charged with visiting all the new girls and answering questions. Hazel plotted how to initiate the new recruits, whom they nicknamed "Dodos." Throwing them in the wishing well was the obvious choice, but short sheeting deserved consideration too. The final decision was a cold dousing in the showers.

Air traffic became more congested after the new class arrived, even with three flying periods; there were still one hundred planes in the air at once. As many as five planes would be landing and taking off at the same time. When trying to land, all the pilot could do was try to find a hole or gun it and go around to try again.

One day Hazel and a group of trainees waiting for their turn to fly watched two torpedo bombers called Grumman Avengers take off. A rugged ship that could absorb significant damage, the Avenger was primarily used by the navy as a glide bomber. At takeoff, the wings folded back slowly and smoothly like a swallow's, then the pilot spun her around, and the wings swung back into place, locked, and off the pilot went. Hazel stood in openmouthed amazement as the pilot buzzed the field at about a twenty-foot altitude going almost three hundred miles per hour. The speed of the aircraft took her breath away.

The final check rides between primary and basic training were like an air show as the trainees went through the complicated aerial maneuvers designed to save lives in an emergency. The difference was that the air show spectators at Avenger Field knew their name might be called next to perform. Hazel graduated from primary training to basic training and from flying primary trainers to basic trainers, or BTs as they were called. The BT-13, called the Vultee Valiant, was the plane Cornelia Fort was flying when she crashed. Students called it the Vultee "Vibrator" because it shuddered like it would shake apart when put into a spin. To pull it out of a spin took two thousand feet of altitude before it would fly level again. Its 450-horsepower engine was powerful, and the plane seemed enormous. Unlike the primary trainers, the BT-13 had a radio. They also flew BT-15s they dubbed the "Basic Bitch." Being inside an enclosed canopy was a novelty to most, although Hazel had flown that way in China with the commercial airline.

Everyone looked forward to soloing in a basic trainer as a significant rite of passage. The BTs were much faster than primary trainers. Flying at speeds of up to 120 miles per hour required constant attentiveness. Each flight began with a complicated cockpit checklist to complete before contacting the tower for permission to take off. "Flaps at twenty degrees, rudder three degrees right, trim for climb—trim for level—trim for glide. Propellor in high pitch, propellor in low pitch. Open the hatch, close the hatch. Switch gas tanks and change the mixture. Hit the wobble pump—check cylinder head temperature, check carbonator heat, and last but not least, call the tower."[13]

The newly constructed tower was now operational, and the women who had not flown at major airports before the war had to learn a new language. "FF eighty-one from fifty-six on the ramp requesting taxi instructions . . . over . . ." they said into the microphone attached to their earphones. "Fifty-six in number one position, ready for takeoff . . . over . . ." Instead of depending on their eyes, ears, and instincts, they would be given instructions from the control tower operator.

Since they were training to become ferry pilots, who often flew alone, the women received more instrument training than the male cadets. When Hazel's class advanced from primary to basic training, they learned to fly "under the hood." Under the hood meant flying under a black curtain in the back of the tandem cockpit seat to reduce visibility outside the aircraft and force the student to fly using only instruments. Someone sat in the front seat to watch for air traffic. The amount of concentration required with their eyes riveted to the airspeed and altimeter to see if they were climbing or descending, or the needle ball to tell them if they were slipping to the left or right, was exhausting.

On a typical evening, after dinner Hazel bounded into her friends' rooms, laughing, and asking, "What's what?" "Jolly" is how her friends described her. Everyone was always happy to see her. She would have the latest information, or a joke, and she'd raise everyone's spirits. "Everything A-okay," she would tell anyone who needed reassurance, and she was so optimistic it was impossible not to believe her.

Then they'd sit together on the beds with their cigarettes to discuss the day. AJ drew in her sketch book while they talked. There never existed any bitterness or jealousy between them. "We weren't competitive, we wanted to do better. Lots of laughs."[14] They hugged often and talked flying and rarely gossiped unless it was too good to avoid. Like the Saturday night one trainee had come home drunk. She threw her watch across the room and fell onto her bed dead asleep. The next morning, she was told to pack up, and a lieutenant escorted her from her bay. Drunkenness was grounds for immediate dismissal. Another trainee made it back to base on time, but not to her bed. In the morning, she was found sound asleep in a ditch behind the building. She was also excused from the program. Many of the women drank alcohol but understood it was imperative to know your limit.

Having paid her own way to Sweetwater, the newly dismissed trainee would pay her way back home again. Washing out meant they had lost the biggest, likely the only, opportunity of their lives to do something of importance and to be part of something extraordinary while flying. Often, the women were not even given a chance to say goodbye, leaving friends to learn by returning to find an empty cot.

◊ ◊ ◊

It became clear that the rules needed to be changed after a trainee with more flying hours and experience than most failed her check ride and was dismissed. She had rejected her army check pilot's advances. He claimed she had made mistakes that she hadn't made. Sometimes all the check pilot had to write down was that the student wasn't a good pilot or was too frail to handle an airplane, without giving any more specific reason. One became known as Captain Maytag for washing out so many. In time, a review board was created for students who believed they'd been unfairly given an unsatisfactory grade from a check pilot. The new rule allowed that after receiving a pink slip, trainees could have five extra hours with a different instructor.

They knew their odds: about 20 percent washed out, whether it was for sinus trouble or because they weren't up to army standards. In the end 756 women left the program due to dismissal, out of the 1,830 initially accepted. They were all terrified of this—it meant the end of flying for them, which felt like a fate worse than death.

14

COCHRAN'S CONVENT

They were a fine bunch of ladies. Maybe 1 or 2 percent of them were a little on the wild side but you can expect that of any group. These girls realized that they were guinea pigs, that it was a trial deal. Jackie Cochran impressed on them that it was necessary for them to conduct themselves in a manner that everybody'd be proud of—and they did a good job of it.[1]

— INSTRUCTOR RIG EDWARDS

AFTER THE FINAL CLASS OF MALE CADETS graduated, Avenger Field became the first all-women air base training facility, and is still the only one in United States history. Without the cadets, and with dating instructors and officers off-limits, the plan from top command, mostly Jackie, was to keep the women exhausted and too tired to get into trouble. In the late afternoon heat, they were called onto the playing fields for baseball or volleyball, after spending five hours in ground school classes and four hours on the flight line. They grumbled that their downtime had disappeared, but they were in better physical condition than ever. A few complained that there were no men to see them, still lamenting the loss of the cadets.

Pilots from training schools around West Texas wanted to

see the rumored women pilots for themselves. About one hundred pilots experienced aircraft trouble that required an emergency landing at Avenger Field, forcing base command to close the field except for authorized flights. Consequently, the field became known as "Cochran's Convent."

One night three cadets doing a cross-country flight got caught in a lightning storm. They circled Avenger Field for thirty minutes before getting a clear enough view of the runway to land. Climbing from their planes, sagging with exhaustion, they were greeted by a large group of grinning women who had heard the planes circling, thrown on their zoot suits, and dashed to the flight line. The three young men smiled at the warm welcome and chatted with the women after being rushed in out of the weather. It wasn't long before Dedie appeared and told the women to get back to their bays. The fun was over. They turned to leave, muttering a chorus of protests.

Ever resourceful, they found other outlets for fun. None of the bay mates wanted to go to the show or swimming at the Sweetwater pool one Saturday night. Without the cadets, life had become boring. Throwing the new recruits in a cold shower had been forbidden after someone suffered a splintered tailbone. They discussed possibilities. Short-sheeting had already been done, Treb reminded them, sprawled across her bed reading *Esquire*. At her desk, AJ drew cartoons satirizing everyone from their instructors to Major McConnell.

Grace complained that she didn't have the energy for pranks, but Hazel would not give up. It was decided to go visiting. Since most of the women were at the rec hall or on a night flight, it proved to be a simple stealth operation. Later that night, at 3 a.m., every alarm clock went off in all the bays except Bay 3.

◊ ◊ ◊

One day, the cooler air temperature aloft and the warm sunshine provided the ideal opportunity for a sunbath. Holding the stick between her knees, Hazel looked around for other aircraft. Men from other training fields in the area learned of the women's tendency to go topless and would sneak up on them. If Avenger Field was off-limits to men, the skies above and around it were not. Finding herself alone, she carefully wiggled out of her shirt, leaned back, and sighed as the sunlight fell across her bare skin.

The growl of plane engines caused her to slink down in her seat. On both sides of her appeared four primary trainers piloted by men wearing broad smiles and waving appreciatively. Hazel grabbed her shirt and nearly lost hold of it in the windy cockpit, which was met with cheering. Her plane wobbled and dipped as she slipped her arms into the shirt. Waving to the disappointed onlookers, she turned back toward Avenger Field.

◊ ◊ ◊

While Jackie Cochran worked on a new name for her program, still being called the Women's Flying Training Detachment, she searched for a mascot and found what she was looking for in Walt Disney and author Roald Dahl. Disney was making an animated film of Dahl's book *The Gremlins*, although the project would later be scrapped. Dahl, a former Royal Air Force pilot, had crafted a children's story about gremlins, the mythological imps the RAF pilots blamed for mechanical problems and other mischief. Disney designed and gave the women their mascot, Fifinella, a shapely female gremlin nicknamed FiFi, wearing a short red dress, giant red boots, gold tights, a yellow flight cap, large blue goggles, and red lipstick. Atop the administration building's roof, a ten-foot wooden disc was erected of Fifinella in flight, her two bright blue wings spread behind her as if poised to touch down.

◊ ◊ ◊

On April 24, 1943, the first class of Jackie's training program prepared for their graduation in Houston. The "Famous First," the class of twenty-three women who had endured so much as the initial guinea pigs and were given so much to prove, had been told they would graduate to Ferry Command in February, and then March, until finally the day came in April. Dedie couldn't wait for the rebellious, wild class to be gone for good. In their final months they grew even more delinquent. Refusing to march to class, they skipped or hopped, and they buzzed tourists while practicing night flying maneuvers.

Jackie was determined to be at the graduation despite the fact that she'd been in the hospital with a serious health issue. In March Jackie had been diagnosed with abdominal adhesions and warned to slow down. She did not. Her hospitalization meant that someone else would have to obtain silver wings to be pinned on the women at the ceremony. Jackie would pay. Lieutenant Fleishman took on the responsibility. He purchased the silver pilot wings given to cadets at Ellington Field and had a jeweler engrave W-1 in the center to signify their class.

Jackie would have her way. Just days out of the hospital and still in pain and unable to sit up, she arranged for a mortuary's "meat wagon" to transport her from her home in Indio, California, to the airport in Phoenix. Calling her girls to the podium, no one would have guessed that she was in pain or anything other than proud. She had showed the world that women could not only fly but stand up to the same rigorous training as men in the United States Army Air Corps. Her program was a success.

The day after graduation, Hazel wanted a few minutes of solitude, to think, to write a letter to Cliff, and to just be alone. Cliff had been injured in battle and needed surgery. With paper and pen, she climbed into the front cockpit of a PT and made herself comfortable in the well-cushioned seat. She pulled out the latest copy of *The Avenger* newspaper. Its subline aptly read, "We live in the wind and sand . . . and our eyes are on the stars." There had been no flying today and would be none tonight due to wind. Hazel had enjoyed an enormous dinner of not one but two large T-bone steaks, potatoes, salad, and chocolate pie. She began her letter describing a solo flight of two hundred miles over a rocky landscape dotted with blue lakes and carpeted in purple verbena and yellow wildflowers. Flying over plateau-topped mountain ranges swathed in green-black scrub cedar and mesquite, she had felt the sensation of never wanting to come back to earth, and she described it for Cliff knowing he would understand.

The following day, six thousand feet above Texas, Hazel practiced slow rolls, snap rolls, and loops. The lower air stratus had proven too bumpy, and so she flew above the scattered cottony blobs of cumulus clouds to find her own bit of sky. Having mastered lazy eights and chandelles, she needed more work on rolls and loops. After landing and picking up LaRue for some work on vertical snap rolls, high-speed 360-degree rotations on the plane's yaw axis, the line perpendicular to the wings, they played in the clouds, going over and down like a roller-coaster ride. Flying into clouds was against the rules. Hazel smiled in contentment. This was her favorite kind of flying, flipping and spinning and turning in the air like a bird going through all the motions her body couldn't do without an airplane.

Next, LaRue had her fly "downstairs," where they chased tornado-like columns of dust. It was fun, but with a purpose behind the exercise. Hitting a whirlwind during takeoff could upturn an airplane, and a pilot needed to know the sensation of being caught in one. LaRue told her they were harmless creatures if you knew how to handle them and didn't panic, and Hazel reminded him that she never panicked. Hazel had flown more than forty different primary trainers and had become familiar with the idiosyncrasies of each aircraft.

◊ ◊ ◊

In later April, Cliff came to Sweetwater. The Chinese Air Force had sent him to the United States for the dual purpose of recuperation and to take air force officer classes in Washington, D.C. He had been decorated for distinguished war service and received his commission as a major in the Chinese Air Force. Now he was Major Clifford Louie, and to Hazel he looked more handsome than ever in his decorated uniform and radiating pride from his accomplishment.

The Avenger newspaper reported on Cliff's visit and that he had met Hazel's bay mates and other classmates before returning to China.

The *Houston Chronicle* ran an announcement of the engagement of Major Louie and Hazel Lee. "Shortly he will return to China while Hazel remains here flying for the United States." The article said that their romance, disrupted by the war, "has covered half the world."[2]

15

SCANDAL

No more dates with flight instructors. I haven't had one for two weeks now and can't afford to have another one under the present circumstance, even if I wanted to. Fortunately I don't."[1]

—MADGE RUTHERFORD

THE WEATHER IN SWEETWATER, TEXAS, turned unforgivably hot. On Sunday afternoons, when not making up flying hours, the women would pile into someone's car and head to Lake Sweetwater five miles south of town. Hazel dove off the dock into the cool water and swam toward the middle of the lake. On the beach the others sunbathed on blankets wearing sunglasses and two-piece swimming suits, writing letters, flipping through magazines, and braiding each other's hair. Later the wind would pick up, tossing the bushy mesquite trees, and the first flash of lightning would send them packing up and back to Avenger Field.

Swimsuits and warm sunshine helped to create a perfect storm. Instructors and officers from Camp Barkeley, eleven miles southwest of Abilene, came to the lake on weekends, bringing with them contraband moonshine. Prohibition had ended officially in 1933 in the United States, but Texas allowed counties to choose whether they would remain "dry," although a statewide anti-saloon law prohibited hard liquor in bars open to the public. Sweetwater voted to remain a "dry" town except for 3.2 beer. However, the gray-haired proprietress of the town gift shop kept a stash in a room upstairs, where from underneath a checkered tablecloth she would produce a bottle of clear liquid for two dollars. And at their private club, the Avengerette, in Sweetwater, the women from Avenger Field drank spiked Coca-Cola until curfew sent them back to base.

Dates became a regular occurrence, with many girls going out every night. On Saturday nights, they'd go into town. Ten o'clock curfew had been extended on weekends to twelve, at which time the gate was closed and locked. Those who returned late had to be boosted over the cyclone fence by their date.

Rules employed by Dedie at Jackie's request proved as impossible to enforce as the separation from the cadets had been, and problems of varying degrees of severity occurred regularly. Dedie's job was to ensure the women held to military regulations and to Jackie's increasingly higher standards for behavior, while tempering what she could, understanding that the young women, many of them unmarried, and even those with husbands serving overseas, would want to have fun, and she believed they deserved a reward for the hard work and mental mindset required during wartime.

There could be no scandals. A pregnancy or an affair with a married officer in the hands of the press would jeopardize everything Jackie had striven to achieve and likely put an end to her program. Officers' wives complained about women trainees working with their husbands, who apparently could not be expected to resist temptation. Eventually, women who dated officers were sent home with harsh letters of reprimand addressed to their parents, hoping shame might keep the women in line. Whether a woman had been the victim of harassment didn't matter, she was still sent packing.

Jackie of course worried about all this. Drinking on base had never been allowed, but would be more firmly enforced with added demerits. The one sure way to save the girls from any perceived impropriety was to remove the men who were pursing the women. Before the final male cadets had shipped out, Jackie had already begun to make plans to replace any officers who had solicited the women trainees and carefully screen instructors, making sure that those who had dated or made advances on their students were reassigned elsewhere or, if they were civilian, simply fired. Now she believed she'd have to remove them all. First, she would have to convince the big brass to implement her plan, and it would take time.

By mid-May, Jackie Cochran had moved to Avenger Field for an indefinite stay, or until the problem with the army personnel was sorted. Staff at the air base now included 40 commissioned officers, 81 enlisted men, and 744 civilians. Base command officers who believed they were above the rules continued to pursue trainees regardless of rules or the consequences to the women. After rumors circulated about a shouting match between Jackie and Major McConnell, the women crept around base on their best behavior, not wanting to give Miss Cochran a target.

Some of the women were not happy about this development. But others were relieved. "We got word that the entire Army personnel up here is going to be shoved out and it is a good thing too for they couldn't get in anything that could be much worse no matter what so at least our class is satisfied. Most of the women felt good riddance."[2] "It seems Miss Cochran thinks we have too many privileges, that the present personnel has been too lenient with us in matters of weekends and dates," Madge wrote. While unhappy with the loss of instructors and command that she liked, Madge admitted, "unfortunately it's true."[3]

Classmate Caro Bayley understood why the men needed to go, and wrote home, "They are too susceptible to the girls."[4]

Still, it would take until the end of May for Jackie to finally gain permission and enact the removal of the entire army command at Avenger Field.

◊ ◊ ◊

Around that time, Hazel, Madge, and AJ went into Sweetwater to see Deanna Durbin in *The Amazing Mrs. Holliday*. After the movie, Madge wanted to go shopping. The ground floor of the Blue Bonnet Hotel had a drugstore selling incidentals like soap, stationery, and cold cream. The shop was cozy and friendlier than the USO, and the owners had adopted the girls as their own. They sent each girl a decorated cake on her birthday, and they would do their laundry if they missed the truck from the field. When the post office was closed, they'd help send mail and refused to take money for postage. To show their gratitude, the women took to hanging out there and loyally gave them their business. Leaving the store, Madge held up a pair of turquoise bracelets she had purchased for eight dollars and showed off her new hand-tooled Texas belt with a heavy silver buckle. She'd *had* to buy them, she said; they were so beautiful they made her mouth water.

They talked about rumors that a member of their class had gone home because she was pregnant, but decided rather than speculate it was best to know nothing and wish the best for her, whoever she was. Several girls had left recently, which wasn't unusual with the high rate of dismissals. Reliable, affordable birth control was not available. The diaphragm was unpopular due to the expense and the need to see a physician, who would likely turn down an unmarried woman or a married one without a medical excuse to avoid pregnancy. At Harvard, doctors were forbidden by Massachusetts law to teach medical students about birth control.

Dedie, in a 1982 interview with Doris Brinker Tanner, said that several women became pregnant while in the WFTD program, and two children were fathered by officers. One pregnant trainee left to get an abortion. Although abortions were illegal, they were still performed, behind closed doors or in private homes. Doctors charged a large fee, and women without financial resources resorted to desperate and sometimes deadly procedures like knitting needles, coat hangers, drinking chemicals, or douching with lye. Dedie had the woman's references checked when she found out about the pregnancy, and finding her to be a "nice girl," she decided the woman could return after a sixty-day leave, but would have to be "washed back" to a later class due to missed flying time. Her classmates never knew about the pregnancy or the abortion, or if anyone did, the secret was well kept.

If Dedie sometimes looked the other way when men and women dated, she drew a hard line at lesbian relationships, or what she called "indecent" behavior between two women. When she learned that two trainees were sleeping together after lights-out, they were immediately dismissed. Dedie refused to listen when one of the women tried to take the blame for initiating the relationship and asked that her girlfriend be allowed to stay in the program. Lesbian relationships were not unusual, and although they had to be shrouded in secrecy, they were tolerated and protected by the other women.

As they walked back to Avenger Field from town, Madge and Hazel talked about marriage. Madge had been writing to a cadet named Jim Baker although he had graduated and would soon be sent overseas. She still hadn't made up her mind about Shay. He had made his position clear: he didn't want her flying after they were married. "I'm as happy here as I've ever been," Madge told her mother in a letter. "Shay's being as desperate and screaming as much via mail, via phone, has caused me to dislike the idea of being tied down so I counteracted this to a certain extent by childishly wearing my ring on my right hand. I can't see further than the nose of my airplane."[5] She had already postponed the wedding twice, once after the announcements had been printed. "Shay took it pretty well," Madge had written, "but seemed resigned that I would never marry him. He said I had no business loving a guy like him, etc. I wish he'd get rid of that inferiority complex. He is getting a potent letter from me, written this morning, which is designed to either snap him out of his melancholia or else. I love him, but I won't spend my life molly-coddling his complexes. I wish I could do more for him, but this is his and my chance to see how he stands up under fire before the all-important step is taken. I hope I'm not expecting too much."[6]

Hazel and Madge agreed that they were living the life of their dreams, free to do just as they wanted and to pursue their own desires with no concern for anyone else. To give that up, to stay home and cook and raise children, was unthinkable. Hazel knew Cliff would encourage her to go on flying after they were married, even if it meant being separated. He understood at a bone-deep level how important flying was to Hazel because it meant just as much to him. But Shay, like most American men in 1943, objected to Madge's flying. Madge told her mother, "I don't write much to Shay about flying because he's so peculiar about it. I guess I'm a little disgusted with him."[7]

◊ ◊ ◊

Due to the temperature that climbed to one hundred degrees daily, the trainees were working and flying in cruel conditions that left them exhausted and depleted. One trainee was put in the infirmary for a breakdown caused by "perpetual hot wind." The Link trainer was called the sweatbox, and after an hour in it, pilots wobbled out drenched in sweat. The best place to be was in the air, where the temperature dropped three to five degrees with each thousand feet climbed.

One day someone rigged a hose into the slats of a straight-back chair. Putting boards on the dirt, which soon became mud, and donning bathing suits, the women took turns running through the nozzle spray squealing like children. As the bays ran the same direction as the prevailing wind, there was no cross-ventilation and never a breeze through the front door or back window.

Hazel and the bay mates studied after dinner wearing only their underwear. They secretly squirreled ice from the mess back to their bays and hid it in the shower for water fights. Standing on their beds they threw ice at each other until they and their beds were drenched. When lying on top of wet sheets or covered in wet towels didn't produce sleep, they received permission to drag their cots outside at night, into the walkways between the bays where they lined up each morning. They tucked the blankets in tightly so no scorpions or tarantulas could crawl under the covers and slept under the stars with a cool breeze, forced to admit there were some advantages to the cadets' departure.

A week of no flying due to fog and rain left the bay mates bored and lethargic. Wanting only to get "upstairs," Madge wrote, "At this rate (fog) we won't be thru until September. None of us feel very happy just now."[8] Time off would make them rusty and possibly delay their graduation, which they'd been told would take place sometime in early August. They had received no information about what they'd be doing after that or where they'd be stationed. All they knew was they would be ferrying planes. The weather allowed Hazel more practice time in the Link and what had at first been a miserable punishment became fun. Now when the instructor turned on the roughest air, she relaxed on the rudder stick as the Link pitched and rolled and moved in unison with the box like she was riding a bucking bronco.

They played bridge and slunk around like the grounded pilots that they were. Hazel and Madge commiserated about the temperaments of propellers and their pitches while in the theater waiting to watch another training film. They found the films difficult, and wished they could watch them more than once. Movies had only been for entertainment, not education, and they needed to pay attention differently. After a week the flight commander, who had been "chewing his nails down to bloody stubs," decided they would fly if the clouds remained at six hundred feet and didn't drop another ten.

On a foggy morning in May, four pursuit planes arrived at Avenger Field. A group of women watched them land easily despite the lack of visibility. Pursuit aircraft, or fighter planes as they would soon be called, were the fastest planes in the world. The P-40 pilot took Hazel into the cockpit and let her examine the confusing and unfamiliar gadgets. She studied the gunsight in fascination. Would she fire a gun from a fighter plane someday? Why not? Next, she sat in the single-seat cockpit of the P-51. This was the cream of the crop of fighter aircraft, luxurious, with a bombsight, and speed. The North American P-51 Mustang flew at top speeds of more than four hundred miles per hour.

From the cockpit of the P-40 Hazel watched a B-25 bomber come in for a landing. The North American B-25 Mitchell was a relatively new medium bomber with a wingspan of sixty-seven feet that extended far beyond the edge of Avenger's little runway. The copilot jumped onto the tarmac and fell into the arms of his wife, a ferrying trainee. The sight reminded the onlookers of better times and several women cried watching the reunited lovers.

Hazel and LaRue climbed into the bomber and ran cockpit checks. To fly a bomber, Hazel thought, would be a dream, but to fly at four hundred miles per hour would surpass everything she'd ever done. Hazel had a new goal.

16

"ARE YOU CHINA GAL OR JAPANESE GAL?"

We think, talk, live, and sometimes dream flying.[1]

—ADALINE BLANK,
WASP, CLASS 43-W-8

O N MAY 27, A FORMATION OF ADVANCED trainers descended on Avenger Field. Hazel and her classmates watched the AT-6s and AT-17s land one after another and come to a halt in front of the hangar. When the pilots jumped from the ships, they removed their flight caps, shook their hair out in the wind, and waved to the trainees watching from the flight line. Press scurried up to the women alighting from their planes. At the end of May, graduation ceremonies would take place at Avenger Field for the second class, 43-W-2. They had flown in from Houston, having completed their training there. Their mass dramatic exit from Houston marked the closing of that facility. From here on out, all women pilots would be trained at Avenger Field. To enhance the spectacle, Jackie flew in from her Fort Worth residence, with her French-speaking maid in tow. The Houston graduates gathered around her. While this was going on, an observant mechanic discovered five bottles of liquor hidden behind the seat of one AT-17. The pilot groaned at the loss.

The following day, the graduates, still feeling the effects of a party at the Blue Bonnet the night before, leaned against one another for support during the ceremony. Hazel stood at parade rest on the flight line under an unforgiving sun for almost an hour alongside her classmates and the classes of 43-5 and 43-3, who had recently arrived from Houston to complete their training at Avenger. Her tailored beige whipcord slacks and white shirt clung to her body as wet as if she'd stepped from a shower. From her boat-shaped "general's" hat sweat dripped into her eyes. As her shoes began sinking into the melting asphalt, she cursed silently at the thought of paying for another pair. The thermometer read 130 degrees. The band from the bombardier school at Big Spring, Texas, played on, no doubt suffering inside their heavy uniforms. Cameras rolled, documenting everything for upcoming newsreels. Through all of it, Jackie glowed.

Few family members of the women pilots were able to make it to the ceremony, because of the rationing of tires and gasoline and the limited availability of train travel for personal purposes. Instead, the people of Sweetwater showed up en masse, having laid to rest their initial feelings and adopted the Avenger women as their own surrogate daughters. They applauded with pride the smartly dressed women standing at attention who, without uniforms, had bought their own clothes, and told one another these women were true patriots doing their part to win the war. One by one, the women received from Jackie Cochran their silver wings and a leather Fifinella emblem for their jackets.

◊ ◊ ◊

Life, the magazine that captured American life in photographs, wanted to publish a story about the women ferrying trainees at Avenger Field. Photographers arrived in late May and stayed for a week. Most of the women were excited and hoped their photo would end up in the article. Peter Stackpole, the globe-traveling photographer of the elite and famous, was thirty-one years old, fit, blond, and blue-eyed. In the beginning the women loved being models for him, posing in front of a camera and feeling glamorous, but the novelty soon wore off. They didn't like standing still, they would rather fly, and Stackpole arranged them in unlikely poses like using an airplane as a mirror to put on their lipstick, something they would never do. They began to make excuses, or disappear, when asked to go outside in the heat to pretend to exercise or sunbathe, to show they were just ordinary girls who also happened to be pilots.

"Look busy," Madge whispered to Treb while they waited on the flight line writing letters. Both sat on the ground leaning against a building where they'd found a small patch of shade to escape the sun. She wrote, "Here comes that man again. The photographer from the *Life Magazine*. He has taken 6 pictures of me already and now into eight. Poor chap, he likes my grin. I hope that at least one of these is used. The newsreel cameraman had me climbing into BTs and grinning for them last Friday."[2]

The sun glowed in a cloudless sky on June 1 when Hazel took off in a BT to earn some solo hours. By the end of May, she knew every little cow town in West Texas from the air, especially those along the cross-county practice triangle of Odessa, Big Spring, and Sweetwater. The new soloists sometimes became lost in storms or fog that came up quickly, forcing them to land at air bases where they received a chilly reception, if they received any welcome at all, due to their gender. Only yesterday bad weather had caused trouble with most of the cross-country flights, sending pilots off course and scrambling to find their way back home from distant airfields. One trainee landed at an air base in Oklahoma, a hundred miles off course. She received a cold shoulder from an officer who refused to give her directions back to Sweetwater. She got back in the air and figured it out herself. Hazel's bay mate Treb also got blown away by the storm and landed at a bombardier school in southern Oklahoma.

Not long after Hazel took off, the winds picked up and a dust storm developed and, as quickly as it appeared, engulfed her plane. Hazel took a deep breath and focused on her BT. She didn't dare look out the windscreen or she'd become disoriented in the muck that produced the effect of flying in the shadowy depths of the ocean. Instead, she used the compass and airspeed indicator. The wind had blown her off course. Flying on instruments, she reminded herself that there was no need to be afraid. The little BT didn't have a lot of horsepower and faltered in the gusty wind. Her eyes darted to the gas gauge nearing empty. She would have to find somewhere to land and try not to damage the aircraft or herself. If only she could see the ground. She dipped down gradually until finally a break in the dust showed her a field that appeared long enough for a landing. It would have to do.

The landing was not her best, bumpy but adequate. Easing on the brakes, she came to a stop in a furrowed cotton field and climbed out to look for damage. The plane thankfully appeared fine. Looking down at herself, she decided she did too. She was circling the BT one more time when a green Chevy truck pulled up and from it stepped a farmer and a young woman carrying a baby. The man reached into the bed of his truck, pulled out a pitchfork, and yelled, "Are you China gal or Japanese gal?"

Hazel stopped and considered the man. He was big and heavy, and Hazel knew she could outrun him, if necessary, but first she'd try diplomacy. "I'm a China gal, sir." He stepped closer, holding the pitchfork forward. She decided it was time to put some distance between herself and the farmer and ran to the back of the plane. As the farmer chased Hazel around the BT, she ducked under a wing and yelled, "I'm an American flying for the Army Air Corps."

"Women don't fly in the Air Corps."

Hazel pointed to her regulation name tag with Hazel Ying Lee printed on it. "See?" He inched forward, still holding the pitchfork toward her, and squinted at the name tag. "Please sir, if you'll call Avenger Field, someone will be able to confirm my identity." He scratched his chin and seemed to consider this, still looking Hazel over.

Finally, in what Hazel hoped was agreement, he said, "Wall, dag gum it, girl. You sho made a purty landing."

The couple's name was Doty, and they didn't have a phone but drove Hazel to the nearest one ten miles away. Hazel later described the trip: "The Chevy acted as old as the proverbial gray mare and the radiator boiled like the first steam engine." When they finally arrived, and Hazel called Avenger, the connection was bad enough that she had to shout. She told them she would stay with the plane per army regulations until someone arrived, which she hoped would be sooner than later.

At the Doty farm, Hazel was served "fried eggs and colorful conversation" before being led to the couple's guest room. In the morning, after a fitful night of tossing and turning, Mrs. Doty made bacon and eggs for breakfast. While eating, Hazel heard a plane circling and knew they would spot the BT and her rescue would follow.

Lunchtime came and still no rescue. Again Mrs. Doty served fried eggs and bacon, while Mr. Doty sang cowboy songs to his baby son at the top of his lungs, rocking him furiously in a rickety old chair. Hazel watched the clock and every once in a while stepped outside to check on the plane. Still there. In the evening Mrs. Doty "labored over the hot stove cooking bacon and eggs for supper."[3]

At the sound of a car pulling up outside, Hazel sprang from the house and ran toward her saviors shouting, "Boy am I glad to see you!" Four men and a lieutenant climbed from the vehicle. The lieutenant told her they'd been to every ranch in West Texas and opened and closed at least two hundred gates. She assumed they were kidding, but clearly they'd spent some time in their rescue operation, and she could only be grateful.

A guard was left to watch the BT and Hazel departed. "I made my adieus to the Dotys who despite their quaint way had certainly shown me the best their house could afford. As we drove off Mr. Doty's final puzzled remark was, 'Miss Lee, I'd sho' like to know what they all goin' t' do to you: put you in the cooler or wot. Lemme hear from you, dag gum it.'"[4]

The next morning in the chow line Hazel eyed the eggs and said, "I think I'll pass." Everyone laughed, knowing how much Hazel appreciated what the Dotys had so generously provided for her, and not least of all for not killing her. Madge told her that while they waited anxiously for news of her, they had hoped she was being served fried chicken.

On Monday, June 28, the *Avenger* newspaper printed Hazel's story in her own words under the title, "Dad gum it! Why Don't I Watch the Weather?"[5]

◊ ◊ ◊

A week after Hazel's adventure, she rushed to shower the day's dust off and wake up before what might be a long evening. If her name was called, she might get to fly until 2 a.m. A ferry pilot would fly between sunup and sundown, but part of their training included night flying in case they ever ran out of daylight and needed to land after dark. Avenger Field had no lights, so burning oil pots were placed along both sides of one runway to make the edges of the landing strip visible.

The women enjoyed night flying and liked to pretend they were RAF pilots flying night bombing raids over Germany. Hazel waited to hear her name. Standing on the flight line directly outside the barracks, hundreds of planes waited in the dust under a darkening sky. Flight Leader Oates screamed the names of those who would fly tonight. Finally, "Lee! Hazel Ah Ying Lee!"

Takeoff was exhilarating. In the dark there was no sensation of speed. The airspeed indicator would tell her when to break ground, and when she did, the plane lifted into a dark void. She had to trust the indicator to tell her she was climbing fast enough. Night flying brought to mind Peter Pan and Wendy soaring out the nursery window over twinkling fairy lights into an ocean of black under a canopy of winking stars. Hazel's Link training hours helped, but when she lost the horizon, she wasn't sure she could trust her instruments.

Practicing landings on the gravel runway, Hazel couldn't keep from dropping with a heavy thump. The ground wasn't where it seemed it should be. The oil pots flashed past, and the BT's landing headlight offered little assistance. After a series of landings, Hazel and LaRue took off to practice navigation by radio beam.

For those on the flight line waiting their turn, Mom had set out sandwiches and coffee. One night swarms of locusts had descended on the field like a biblical plague. Hazel found her cockpit, opened for only a few minutes, already filled with crawling insects that she had to scoop out using her hands. Locusts covered the sandwiches and even managed to climb into the coffeepots.

Two of those waiting tonight were bay mates Jennie Hrestu and Jane Champlin. Like Hazel, Jennie was from Portland, Oregon. She had left two daughters in the care of her husband, who had been unable to get out of his war-essential job. Having recently emigrated from Greece, Jennie and her husband had family who had been captured and killed by the Nazis. They decided together that since Jennie had a pilot license, she should be the one to go and fight fascism by freeing pilots for combat. Jennie wanted nothing more than to serve her new country. Her bay mate, Jane, came from St. Louis. When she heard about Jackie Cochran's flying school, she quit her job as secretary in the Railway Express Agency and flew full-time to earn the required hours to be accepted. Then she invested all her savings on two expensive operations to correct a sinus and breathing condition so that she could pass the physical. When Jennie and

Jane's names were called, they waved to each other and followed their instructors to their planes.

With her instructor, Jennie practiced landing and taking off and hypothetical navigational problems until finally at one in the morning she came staggering back to her bay. Jane's cot was still empty. But Jane's instructor, Henry Aubrey, had the reputation of occasionally getting off course, and Jennie sighed for her friend. He probably got lost, Jennie thought. Like several instructors, he was only a couple of weeks ahead of the trainees in learning to fly the planes in which he was teaching.

In the morning, Jane's bunk was still empty and undisturbed. In the chow line at breakfast, everyone spoke in low, worried whispers, asking if anyone knew what had happened to Jane and wondering if she'd become lost, as her instructor was known to do. Maybe they had been able to land somewhere else and would return soon in the daylight. After breakfast, in the ready room, the announcement was made. The bodies of Jane Champlin and her instructor had been found with the charred wreckage of their BT-13 on a ranch near Westbrook, Texas.

The trainees wrapped their arms around one another and cried. Avenger Field's first fatal air crash sank deep. It could have been any of them. One of the instructors said, "There's a war on, girls, and we've got to get flying."[6] Those flying in the morning wiped their eyes and followed their instructors out to the flight line.

There had been no witnesses to the crash that occurred about forty miles west of Sweetwater. Mr. Aubrey's watch had stopped at 11:15. The investigation determined the BT-13 Vultee Valiant had been in a turn before the accident, and that both instructor and student lost the horizon and allowed the ship to spiral. Aubrey failed to go on instruments in time to prevent the crash. Jane had asked to be assigned a different instructor after he had fallen asleep during several flights. She also reported that his screaming didn't inspire a calm flying experience. Aubrey tended to scream irrationally at his students for every error. Her request was not granted.

After Jane's death, the mood became less casual on the flight line. Everyone took their missions and one another and the work they were doing more seriously. They had to tell their parents about Jane, because it was in all the newspapers, but they gave no details, as they'd likely been instructed.

Jackie Cochran had informed her girls when they began the program that they were not in the army and would not be covered by the ten-thousand-dollar death benefit awarded to cadet families. Molly Merryman, in her book *Clipped Wings: The Rise and Fall of the Women Airforce Service Pilots*, wrote, "When I spoke to the veterans featured in this book . . . the pain was still visible when they spoke of collecting money at their bases (from female and male pilots alike) so that bodies could be returned to families, because the military didn't provide their standard military benefit to the 'volunteers.' They were haunted by the fact that the families of the dead weren't permitted to display gold stars in their windows, the Service Flag marker denoting the ultimate sacrifice."[7]

On June 28 *The Avenger* printed a small square that was headed "Jane Champlin, In Memoriam" and read: "We'll miss you, Jane, but we won't forget you—the way you made us laugh, the many friends you found among all our classes, or the cause for which you made your sacrifice." Jane was twenty-six years old.

The weather kept them grounded, which was probably just as well. A storm descended that caused four planes to circle for an hour before being able to land. A deluge of rain came in through the bay windows and a lake formed under their beds. The mood among the women remained subdued.

One day, the sky cleared and an unexpected announcement was made on the flight line. They were to choose a buddy with whom to practice instrument flying under the hood. The women in Hazel's class had all soloed the BT-13, the Vultee "Vibrator," and flown many hours under the hood with an instructor. They had never flown with one another. Knowing their life was in the other woman's hands, and that they were responsible for their partner, made them uneasy. In the tandem cockpit, the pilot sitting in the backseat would pull a black hood over her seat and fly the airplane on instruments while the other pilot, sitting in the front, scanned for other aircraft so they would not collide with anyone, ready to take control of the plane in an emergency while also acting as instructor and making practice suggestions. The pilot under the hood practiced banking, climbing, and descending, and then the two would land and switch seats.

The women wrote home that flying under the hood with a buddy was "too awful to contemplate."[8] But once they became accustomed to the exercise, they enjoyed going "upstairs" with a friend, away from their instructors like freed children. Their confidence grew, and as they laughed and owned their piece of sky, they forgot about the danger of flying and wondered if that's why their instructors had suggested the crazy idea in the first place.

17

CELEBRITIES

I feel like I belong in the air. I have no fear at all. The worst thing is coming back to earth.[1]

—VI THURN,
WASP, CLASS 43-W-4

THE WEATHER HAD FINALLY TURNED DRY and Hazel and her friends were no longer forced to sunbathe between thunderstorms. As the torrential rains of June abated, temperatures became so hot the dust stuck to their clothes and exposed skin. Sand blew in their faces, and not just when they were facedown doing push-ups, but all the time and everywhere. Hot, windy, sandy, and without air-conditioning, no one complained, much; they were just happy to be flying.

They had flung blankets and turned chairs upside down to lean against on the sandy patch between the barracks where they lined up in the mornings. Sunburned noses were covered in a white, zinc-based protective sun cream they used while flying, and on the rest of their bodies they drizzled olive oil. The Ping-Pong table had been moved outside, and with her eyes closed Hazel heard the balls hitting the paddles and remembered playing tennis years ago, so long ago that it seemed like a dream or a memory belonging to someone

171

else. She stretched like a cat, feeling the sun on her skin, and when one of the girls asked if she was able to tan, she good-naturedly told them she came with a tan. Of course her skin tanned, but she wasn't offended, knowing the girls meant nothing beyond curiosity. Later, to satisfy them, she demonstrated a tan line. They had become a family, more like sisters than any sisters Hazel had, and she would miss them all when next month they graduated and were assigned to bases scattered across the country.

Caro flipped through a flying magazine and announced she might cut her hair like Amelia Earhart's. That would solve the hair problem. Because their hair got in their eyes and instructors claimed they couldn't see around a mass of flying hair, the women were ordered to wear turbans that covered most of the hair, and they hated them. Madge had come up with the idea of braided pigtails to avoid wearing a turban.

Caro had put peroxide in the front of her hair, and it turned white, and everyone loved the look. Treb kneeled behind Grace to braid her hair, and Madge, who had just gotten a permanent wave, was writing a letter home and adding a request from her bay mates to please send more cinnamon rolls. AJ talked about the Bob Hope movie called *My Favorite Blond*, which she'd seen last weekend. Sweetwater had two theaters, but rarely got newly released films.

Someone mentioned the famous pilot who had recently arrived at Avenger Field to train. In England, Helen Richey had been flying Spitfires and was considered one of the best pilots in the world. There was surprise that a woman of her experience would be required to undergo training. As one of the most experienced trainees, Hazel understood. No woman pilot could enter the Ferrying Division of the Air Transport Command without training at Avenger Field and learning to fly the army way.

Madge put down her letter and told her friends about Shay's recent phone call. He still wanted their wedding to take place in August. She said that unless she was assigned to Long Beach, near

Shay, she wouldn't consider it. "I guess I'd really like to get married. But, on the other hand, I'm not at all sure that it would be an intelligent thing to do."[2] Tiring of the subject, they changed it to talk about maintenance class, where they'd recently rebuilt an engine. Madge said there was nothing better than sticking her nose and hands into an engine, and everyone agreed.

Seventeen girls had washed out that week, mostly from Hazel's class. No one felt safe. Maybe due to anxiety, the trainees had become increasingly unruly. Dedie created a board to act as judge and jury for girls who got into trouble. Women appeared before the board, terrified they'd be dismissed, based on concerns about their flying ability, and were assessed by the all-male board for their flying mistakes as well as their looks and general demeanor. Dedie and the board went easy on women who had a "nice attitude" and a neat appearance and usually gave these women a second chance with more time or an additional check ride. But a poor attitude, unkempt appearance, or tears would cause the woman to be described in the board's notes as "mentally unstable." No second chance would be granted, and dismissal from the program was immediate.

For two weeks, Hazel had been practicing the final task of her advanced training, soloing on the twin-engine AT-17. Only two sets of students were selected to fly the Bobcat. Taxiing was done entirely by throttle, and pilots were surprised to find two of everything; two throttles, two mixture controls, two prop pitch controls. Cessna had developed the five-seated plane to be the air-car of the future, with gray mohair upholstery and chromium fittings like a Pontiac, further demonstrating the hope that airplanes would in time replace cars. Pilots nicknamed it the "Bamboo Bomber" or the "Bunson Burner" due to its plywood fuselage that looked like it might go up in flames at any minute. In September an AT-17 would blow apart midair, killing two trainees and their instructor.

◊ ◊ ◊

In July of 1943, Jackie told her women pilots that they would be in the Army Air Corps within the next ninety days and be issued uniforms, shoulder insignia, and wings. They would be officers in every sense except they would not wear bars. While most of the women wanted the benefits associated with becoming officers, some preferred to remain civilians and independent. Woodie wrote home, "I neither know nor care what Cochran considers us a part of—I'm not in any army—I'm not in any government clutches."[3]

On July 5, General Arnold issued a press release announcing Jackie Cochran as the director of women pilots assigned to the assistant chief of staff, Office of Commitments and Recruitment. Nancy Love would continue to direct the women of the Air Transport Command. Finally, Jackie was getting what she wanted. She moved from Fort Worth to her new office at the Pentagon. Her first official order of business was to give her pilots a new name. General Arnold suggested a name and Jackie approved. They would no longer be WFTDs. Because the women would perform more than ferrying duties, the "F" would be dropped and they would be called Women Airforce Service Pilots—WASPs.

◊ ◊ ◊

Hazel's class began practicing acrobatics. After doing spins for a couple of months, they were used to inverted flying. Woodie's mother worried she'd lose the coins in her pocket, and possibly her life, while inverted. Woodie told her, "Flying upside down does not encourage you to keep anything in your pockets."[4] Parents worried. Flying seemed dangerous, especially when they'd never been in a plane. The accidents and deaths that had occurred fueled the concerns. Some mothers and fathers were more supportive than others. One set of parents, who had been vehemently opposed to their daughter flying, didn't attend their daughter's funeral when she was killed in an accident.

The article in *Life* magazine appeared on newsstands Tuesday, July 19, 1943. Madge squealed to find her photo on page 79. The article devoted six pages of photographs to the women who would become officially known as WASPs in August. Many of the trainees appeared in the *Life* article and, to their disappointment, many did not. Rebecca Edwards, a twenty-two-year-old widow whose young husband had been killed in action, posed with her nose and cheeks covered in white zinc cream against sunburn. Flight caps, baseball caps, turbans, and exercising in the hot wind were all displayed in photographs. A whole page of photographs was dedicated to their various hairstyles or lack thereof. Eyes rolled. They were disappointed at being objectified and that the article missed what was most important about their work and what they were accomplishing.

The article reported that the "girls are very serious about their chance to fly for the Army, even when it means giving up nail polish, beauty parlors, and dates for a regimented 22½ weeks." And "these girls, who so joyously scramble into the silver airplanes of Women's Flying Training Detachment each day, fly with skill, precision and zest, their hearts set on piloting with an unfeminine purpose that might well be a threat to Hitler."[5]

Jackie didn't like it that the *Life* photographs showed the girls exercising in a hodgepodge of mismatched shorts and tops and in everything from strappy, open-toed sandals to tennis shoes to leather oxfords. Navy-blue rompers were ordered immediately, and a newsreel from later in the summer showed the women exercising in matching outfits and shoes that they of course had purchased with their own money.

Next Jackie renewed her quest for official uniforms. Sometimes as women pilots ferried planes across the country, they had trouble proving their identity. Uniforms would help keep the women safe and, as in one case, out of jail. Four women pilots on a ferrying mission had found all the hotels in Lebanon, Tennessee, booked. They ended up at run-down motel in a bad part of town. A group of army men spotted the women as they were going into their room for the night and proceeded to rattle their doorknob and yell for them to come out. The MPs were called, and despite the women trying to prove they were not in fact prostitutes, they were taken to jail. In another instance, in Americus, Georgia, two WASPs were forced to land when darkness fell. When they tried to explain who they were, no one would believe them, and they were put in jail for impersonating Army Air Corps officers.

The *Life* article misled its readers in portraying the women as girls having a good time while leading a glamorous life as pilots. Long, strenuous hours, little independence, heat and sand, primitive conditions, rattlesnakes, cockroaches, scorpions, locusts, military rules, a strict routine, very little time off, and danger added up to a life that was anything but glamorous. There was a cost to flying in the face of convention. Some even paid with their lives, and the rest lived with uncertainty about their safety and their futures.

But there was no denying that *Life* fueled the public's interest in the "Glamour Girls" or "Lipstick Pilots," as they were being called in newspapers and magazines. The Army Air Corps men were upset about all the attention the women were getting. They were doing the same job and being sent overseas to fight and die in combat. Which is one of the reasons the women never said no to a dangerous job. They didn't want to be treated differently or given special treatment because they were women, and wouldn't be accused of cowardice or using their gender to do less than the men.

Not all the media attention on the women ferrying pilots was positive or accurate. A movie called *Ladies Courageous* starring Loretta Young was meant to portray a fictionalized story based on the women's ferrying squadron, but it was filled with inaccuracies despite the claim they'd had a WASP as a consultant. The WASPs were embarrassed by their portrayal and found the film's negative effect on the program disheartening.

At the theater in Sweetwater, Hazel and her bay mates watched the newsreel in which they were the stars. They laughed and groaned. There they were facedown in the sand doing push-ups as the male narrator said, "Right away the Air Force wants to get a little muscle on those pretty little arms." A shot at Lake Sweetwater that they remembered well showed them slipping off their zoot suits to reveal swimsuits underneath. They never wore their zoots to the lake, but the cameraman had liked the idea. After stepping out of the suits, they ran into the lake to swim as the narrator quipped, "Yes, they talk Army talk and wear G.I. clothes, but a very small change of clothes can remind her that she's still the softer, fairer sex worried to death she's going to get her hair wet."[6]

Later Hazel mimicked the film's narrator: "Gone into a man's world because the men needed her. Gone in just a girl and came out a girl pilot."[7] How was it, they wondered, that boys went into training and came out men? They couldn't even graduate from girls to women. They were seen as little girls playing at the boys' games, adorable, but not in any way on the same level.

◊ ◊ ◊

Before graduating, each pilot had to make a successful dual and then solo cross-country flight. Long-distance navigation would be required of them as ferrying pilots. These flights would be done in the North American AT-6 Texan, a 600-horsepower advanced trainer with a cruising speed of 145 miles per hour, a big step up from the 175-horsepower PT-19. It was called the best fighter training aircraft of all time, and most World War II pilots trained on the Texan. Jackie wanted her girls trained on the AT-6 because she believed they would become combat pilots.

The long cross-country flights could be stressful. The women learned, among other things, the importance of a sufficient gas supply. It was embarrassing and dangerous to come to a midair standstill and have to glide into the nearest field or pasture. One trainee returned after an eleven-hour flight nearly hysterical from fatigue.

After the graduation of class 43-W-3 in July and too much standing in the hot sun, Hazel, AJ, and Madge went into town to see the new Disney movie, *Bambi*. Madge had recently been granted leave to go to Long Beach to visit Shay, but since he was now a doctor, he had been busy delivering babies most of the time she was there. He still hoped they could marry in the fall, but he had come to the realization that to Madge marriage came second to flying and might not happen until after the war.

Finally, Hazel's class graduation date was set for August 7, and she and her classmates were tremendously excited. Cooped up for so many months, working long hours in extreme heat, the women had become manic for entertainment. Each morning a colored flag raised on the Avenger flagpole indicated what attire would be required for the day. A green flag meant flying gear; red indicated civilian clothes, as on Sundays. One day both red and green waved from the flagpole. The trainees lined up that morning wearing hats with veils, high heels, fox furs, and dresses over their zoot suits.

Amid the excitement and pride about their impending graduation, another sobering accident occurred at Avenger Field. This time the pilot was Kathryn "Kay" Lawrence, who had only arrived a month earlier as a member of class 43-W-8. No one saw the plane go down, but it was guessed that she couldn't recover from a spin and, when she bailed out, was unable to pull her parachute rip cord, maybe due to having blacked out. Her body was recovered one hundred yards from her crashed PT-19. Her memorial service took place the next day at the Sweetwater Methodist Church.

Devastated, shocked, and more resolved than ever to continue their training and honor those who had died in service, most of the women adopted the attitude of Amelia Earhart. If their number was up, that was it, there was nothing to be done about it, and they'd rather die flying than live a life not flying. Another prevalent attitude was denial. "In order to keep on flying when your classmate, your best friend was killed, you had to believe that fate would spare you and you said to yourself, 'It can never happen to me.'"[8]

Kay Lawrence's family could only afford a plain wooden casket, and while it was being loaded on the train to be brought home, a WASP who had escorted the casket to the train station saw that they were handling it roughly, like a piece of luggage. To ensure that Kay's remains were treated respectfully, she decided to escort Kay home to Grand Forks, North Dakota. Kay's death wouldn't be the only wartime loss for the Lawrence family. Her brother William, a member of the U.S. Marine Corps, was killed on September 15, 1944, in combat on Palau island.

On August 5, 1943, Women Airforce Service Pilots, WASPs, became the official name of the Air Transport Command Ferrying Service. The WAFS and WFTD would be incorporated as members of the WASPs. Loyal to their name, the WAFS were not enthusiastic about the change, but understood that the divisions did the same work and had always been part of a whole. And they accepted it as a sign of the Army Air Corps's determination to bring the women pilots into the military along the same route as male civilian pilots, who were brought in as service pilots and then commissioned after ninety days. The WASPs would remain civilians but would be granted army officer privileges and the use of officers' clubs.

Hazel and the class of 43-W-4 received their ferrying assignments the day before graduation. They could submit a request as to where they wanted to go, although many did not get their first, second, or even third choice. Most wanted to be close to home or close to a husband or boyfriend's station. Their choices were the 6th Ferrying Group of the Air Transport Command in Long Beach, California, the oldest and most prominent of the ferrying groups, near dozens of important airplane manufacturers; Romulus, Michigan; Love Field at Dallas, Texas; Kansas City, Missouri; and Wilmington, Delaware.

Hazel was assigned to the 3rd Ferrying Group in Romulus, Michigan. Close enough to her sister in New York, and she'd be flying all over the country, so it was as good as any other location. Her other siblings, except for Victor, were in Portland. Cliff was in China. The WASPs were her family now. Her bay mates AJ and Treb would be going to Romulus too. Madge got her first choice and was assigned to the 6th at Long Beach, where she would be near Shay.

◊ ◊ ◊

The graduation of the class of 43-W-4 took place on August 7, 1943. Hazel stood beside her classmates in formation and marched past the line of AT-6s and the five other classes standing at attention, to the reviewing stand where Jackie Cochran waited. She heard her name called and stepped onto the platform to meet Miss Cochran, who spoke a few congratulatory words and pinned her silver WASP wings over her heart. The wings were a symbol of an enormous accomplishment and pride; as one WASP said, "No one can take this away."[9] Most WASPs would describe the pinning on of their wings as the proudest moment of their lives.

While the Big Spring Bombardier School Band played the air corps song, Hazel stood at attention and knew she had proven something to herself. Her silver wings proved she could do a "man's job." And it wouldn't be called a "man's job" any longer. Hers was more than a personal accomplishment. She was part of a triumphant experiment. One hundred and fifty-two women had made up the class when they began in February; one hundred and twelve made it through the months of rigorous flight training to graduation; thirty-nine washed out, and one, Jane Champlin, had died in service.

Attending the graduation was a member of class 43-W-9 named Maggie Gee. She and Hazel would be the only Asian American WASPs. Gee was a third-generation Chinese American born in Berkeley, California, on August 5, 1923. Her grandfather, upon arriving from China in the 1870s, had settled south of San Francisco, on the Monterey Peninsula, and become a pioneer in the abalone business. The family moved to San Francisco's Chinatown in 1906 and then to Berkeley. After the stock market crashed in 1929, Maggie's father suffered a heart attack on a street in San Francisco and died soon after, leaving behind a wife and six children.

Negative attitudes about Chinese prevailed during Maggie's childhood, like Hazel's, and she found an escape at the Oakland airport where her family would go on Sunday afternoons to watch planes. Maggie would scan the skies for Amelia Earhart, who often flew into Oakland. Once she spotted her and waved, and Earhart waved back. When the United States entered World War II, Gee was studying physics at the University of California, Berkeley. She dropped out to work in the drafting department at the Mare Island Naval Shipyard in Vallejo, California, where her mother was a welder. Maggie and two coworkers pooled their funds, bought a car, and drove to Nevada to learn to fly. In June 1944, Maggie left her home in Berkeley and boarded a troop train filled with soldiers. For the entire two-day journey to Sweetwater, Texas, she either sat on her suitcase or stood up.

There wasn't much to pack up; goodbyes would be the most difficult task. Last night's sandstorm and accompanying forty-mile-per-hour winds had deposited enough dirt on the floor to grow a crop. With the toe of her worn-out shoe, Hazel wrote her name, *Ah Ying*. The class of 43-W-9's eager new recruits had arrived two weeks ago; another bunch of new pilots would arrive soon, and they would keep coming until the war ended and maybe after. The war showed no signs of ending. Air Corps crews were being rushed through training with fewer required flight hours, to get more planes and pilots overseas and into the Allied offensive. The women wondered when women would be needed overseas in combat or in other capacities, whether people liked the idea or not. Hazel wanted to fly in battle—this had been her dream since she had earned her pilot license eleven years ago. She was needed, and, just as in China, limiting beliefs that people clung to about women meant more lives would be lost. For what purpose? What really lurked behind their fear? That women would no longer be satisfied to stay home and raise children? The WASPs had already proved they could do what male pilots were doing, and in fact with a better safety record. If she wanted to die in a plane battling the Luftwaffe, why did someone else get to decide that she couldn't? Was she more valuable as a baby maker? Or did men fear sharing their power as much as having no one home to fix their dinner?

18

PICNICS IN THE SKY

I can cure your men of walking off the [flight] program.
Let's put on the girls.[1]

—Jackie Cochran

THE SUBURB OF DETROIT CALLED ROMULUS was far removed from its mythical namesake, the founder and first king of Rome. Nearby automobile factories had turned to manufacturing aircraft, and in August 1943 Romulus Army Airfield was home to the 3rd Ferrying Group of the Air Transport Command and also Hazel's new home. An established squadron of twenty-four WASPs, graduates of the first three classes, greeted her. The need to place all qualified male pilots overseas into combat positions had caused the WASP program to expand beyond all initial proposals, but it took time to train the women ferrying pilots, and so some men remained at Romulus until enough women became available to replace them.

Prior to Hazel's arrival, the male ferry pilots at Romulus had been delivering most of the P-39 Airacobra fighter planes, manufactured by Bell Aviation in Niagara Falls, across Lake Erie from Detroit, while the WASPs were assigned to trainer and liaison aircraft, what the military called "light planes." Bell was supplying P-39s to Russia and each week the output increased. The P-39 had its 1200-horsepower engine mounted behind the pilot, rather than in front as in other fighter aircraft, and its large fuel tanks sat below the cockpit, causing the weight to be farther to the rear than pilots were used to, and some of those pilots had not followed the tech orders precisely while taking off or landing, letting the nose of the P-39 rise too high. There had been crashes and deaths, causing the Airacobra to be called the "flying coffin," and male pilots came up with excuses not to fly them.

A woman ferrying pilot stationed at Romulus argued her way into the cockpit and for a day practiced takeoffs and landings while experimenting with various airspeeds, and found that the plane had to be landed at a higher speed than the men were using. After that, women began delivering the P-39s, and landing and takeoff accidents decreased significantly.

The WASPs did more than ferrying planes from one destination to another. One crucial job on every cadet training base across the country was that of test pilot. Hundreds of airplanes had to be maintained at a high standard of safety because they would be flown by future combat pilots. Air Corps pilots were far from eager to take on test pilot duties, which they saw as a crazy risk, and most would not fly the war-worn planes returned from Europe. If they were going to risk their lives, they wanted to do so in combat. One war veteran lieutenant couldn't get an old BT to recover from a spin. After coming within less than one thousand feet of the ground and crashing, he said he wasn't paid to test planes and stormed off. He told the chief maintenance officer that testing those "rotten planes" was too dangerous.

When male pilots refused to fly a dubious aircraft, WASPs said, *Sure.* They would fly anything. Three men had turned down a plane with gears not functioning, when a WASP stepped up and said she'd do it. On many bases, WASPs took over all test flying missions. Every plane they climbed into had something wrong with it, from a broken propeller to an exploded engine. Maintenance

units, overworked and short-staffed, depended on the sharp obser-
vations of test pilots to safeguard against oversight. Some of the
planes were so rickety the engine would fail on takeoff. WASPs
flew old planes to "bed" out in some Kansas field, where they were
literally put out to pasture.

General William Tunner, head of the Ferrying Division of
the Air Transport Command, who had been strongly opposed to
women pilots, and especially anything to do with Jackie Cochran, in
the beginning, changed his tune and began to prefer women pilots
to men. "Women, I found, would do what they were told to do. The
young men we had hired with little military training often found
excuses and generally, I might say, they were not as good. They were
not as well trained. They were not as knowledgeable as the women
pilots."[2] WASPs were often requested to fly on Saturday afternoons
over male pilots, who had a habit of not answering their pages fearing
they wouldn't get back in time for their dates.

WASPs performed the same ferrying tasks as their male counterparts, and also those the men refused to do, while receiving
two-thirds of the pay the men earned. Complaints regarding pay dis-
parities were ignored, and the women were told they were lucky to be
flying at all. "I was female, and he was male . . ." was an often-heard
refrain, followed by a shrug. Being paid less reminded the women
their work was considered less than equal to the same work being
performed by men. The argument for men supporting dependents
didn't sit well with the WASPs, many of whom were the financial
head of their households, supporting their parents or their children,
and sometimes both.

Hazel knew that repeating an action over and over again nor-
malized it, as she'd experienced in the treatment of Chinese Americans. Any behavior left unquestioned would never change. If male
pilots received larger salaries simply because they were male, it had
not been challenged because that was how it had always been. If
male pilots were the only pilots going into combat, then that's what

everyone would continue to believe was normal and as it should be. Long-accepted ideas that involved discrimination needed to be examined and challenged.

Three years of war had left the German Luftwaffe depleted. The Allies were suffering staggering losses, but so far had been able to recover thanks to American factories, staffed mostly by women, catching up to the demands. In 1943, eighty-four thousand airplanes rolled out of American factories, while German factories had been reduced to using slave labor that included French civilians who were forcibly taken from their homes and shipped to Germany. The country that had boasted the best air force in the world when the war began produced only ninety-four thousand planes during the entire war. Running out of men, Germany was forced to use boys to pilot their planes.

Working seven days a week in all weather, Hazel flew new planes right off the assembly line before they'd even been tested, often being the first to discover malfunctions or sloppy manufacturing. Some of her missions were flying Piper Cubs, which were good training aircraft with low horsepower. Made of balsa wood with a metal frame, they had no radio or heater, and their low horsepower made them difficult to land, and in addition, they were slow, at under one hundred miles per hour. Hazel took these planes from the factory in Lock Haven, Pennsylvania, to cadet training schools all over the country.

Bad weather could keep ferrying pilots grounded in small towns for days or weeks with nothing to do but wait. Some trips were as far away as Canada. When forced to stay overnight, they were required to send a telegram back to their station with the name of the hotel where they would be staying. They were forbidden from staying with family or friends. Flying all over the country, WASPs not only got geography lessons but a bit of American history. Held over in towns like Mandan, North Dakota, they went to rodeos, saw the art of native artists who recorded life of the local tribes, and learned about the Lewis and Clark expedition.

Traveling light was a necessity. Preparing for a mission, Hazel stuffed her orders, maps, and pilot log in a briefcase, stashed lipstick and a toothbrush in her shirt pocket, and was ready to go. Keeping her white shirt and khaki pants clean while ferrying a plane that had limited or no luggage space was a problem. Some planes had a small space in the cockpit for raising and lowering the pilot's seat. This worked fine if you were not too tall. The briefcase fit under the seat and the maps for the day's flight went into the pocket under the knee in her flight suit.

When she landed, she washed her underwear in the sink and hung it to dry, and then scrubbed her shirt collar and put the Gideon Bible on top of it so it would dry as if it had been ironed. Her slacks she placed between the mattress and the box spring.

The work, both dangerous and exciting and at times lonely, often included a succession of towns and a different hotel bed every night. Fatigue-induced inattention and carelessness could cost you your life, and it did for some. One of the youngest of Hazel's classmates, Mary Elizabeth Trebing, was delivering a P-19 when she lost power over Blanchard, Oklahoma. In a heavily forested area she spotted a farmhouse and beyond it a small field. She cleared the farmhouse, but her vertical stabilizer caught on electrical wires, causing her to crash nose-first into the ground. Mary ruptured an artery in her neck and died instantly.

As civilians, WASPs were forbidden to hitch rides on military planes, forcing them to spend many nights in bus and train stations trying to sleep on their parachute packs. After delivering an airplane, Hazel was to return to Romulus by the fastest method of transportation available. On some occasions, at certain fields, a

DC-3 would take the women back to base. The thirty-six-seater was the biggest airplane at the time, with metal bucket seats along one side. The WASPs were given the highest priority behind the President. Commercial airlines were ordered to displace any passenger if a WASP needed to be shuttled to an assignment. Once Vi Thurn bumped a passenger to get a seat on a commercial flight to Memphis. Disembarking, she was greeted by a crowd of teenagers looking bitterly disappointed. She had bumped Frank Sinatra.

Upon returning to Romulus, pilots were responsible for taking their parachute packs to the chute rigger, where the nylon was suspended on a hook overhead and each white panel unfolded and inspected, the lines checked, and the whole thing repacked. Then Hazel might receive her next delivery assignment that same day, or she might receive orders from the base where she'd delivered a plane. One woman's day trip turned into a four-week, seventeen-state, six-plane, eleven-thousand-mile trip.

Long flights required refueling, which meant that few flights were longer than a couple of hours. Hazel made a point to use the bathroom before leaving, and avoided drinking anything, especially tea and coffee. Upon landing, the ground crews knew that the WASPs needed to use the restroom facilities immediately and got out of their way. The relief tube, first encountered by the women in training, had been specifically designed for men during flight. Located near the pilot, it was a tube and funnel that deposited waste outside the aircraft. Women were out of luck. One WASP pointed out, "If we're sitting there piloting, how were we going to get our pants down? So it wouldn't work for us at all."[3] Jeanne Bennett out of desperation tried to use it by snaking the tube up her pant leg, but it was too short. She tried to get closer by scrunching down in her seat, but still had no success.

Women lived in barracks on all five ferrying bases across the country. They had PX (the post exchange that sold merchandise to military personnel) privileges, which meant they could buy necessities like lipstick and Kotex. Movies were shown on base, but not every evening. There was little free time during the day if you were not on a ferry trip. After checking early in the morning for your day's assignment, you might be sent for your skill upgrade in the Link trainer, which could save your life in a storm or fog.

Back in June when Jackie Cochran became the director of women pilots, she convinced General Arnold to grant her permission to create an experimental group of women to tow targets at Camp Davis, North Carolina. As with ferrying, the objective was to free more men to go overseas. Men wanting to fly overseas hated the towing assignment and were happy to give it over to the women.

The first group of twenty-five women handpicked by Jackie had no idea where they were going or what they were being assigned to do. They were told they had been chosen to be part of a special squadron of WASP pilots. Following orders, they reported to the Pentagon. When they arrived in Washington, D.C., Jackie told them they would be flying missions to train anti-aircraft artillery gunners.

At Wrightsville Beach, where the Wright brothers first flew, the women performed simulated dive bombings along the coastline while gunners fired at targets towed from their planes. Gunners fired live ammunition at the targets, which were mesh sleeves like an advertising banner reeled out a couple of hundred feet behind the plane. The WASP would fly up and down a prescribed course while a group of gunners tried to hit the target and not her plane. The women's assignment was dangerous not only because they would be fired at with live ammunition, but because the planes were in bad condition. Flying at night on the blacked out Atlantic coast meant a much more dangerous emergency landing, and they worried their planes were not in good enough condition for night flying. Worn-out tires often blew, and new tires were shipped overseas and therefore unavailable. Mechanics were overworked.

Replacement parts ran out constantly. Flap handles that would not lock into position weren't even considered worthy of a mechanic's attention. Sometimes engines died midair.

Their lives depended on the skill of gunners who were just learning how to shoot at a target. They experienced something of the feeling of being fired at during combat and began to suffer nervous symptoms like loss of appetite. Afraid that voicing their fears would bring down everyone's confidence, they never talked about it. Some quit, but not without fighting Jackie first.

On the evening of August 23, Mabel Rawlinson and her check pilot Lieutenant Harvey Robillard climbed into an A-24 for a flyover to become familiar with a swampy area on a moonless night. The first plane they tried to take off in didn't have a working radio, so they requested another and were given a plane that five days earlier had been marked for repair when another WASP discovered the engine wouldn't make horsepower. Mabel and Lieutenant Robillard experienced the same problem as they came in to land. Those watching on the ground saw the plane coming in too low and heard the motor starting and quitting as Mabel pushed the throttle in and out trying to get the motor to catch. They didn't make the runway and crashed into a swampy drainage ditch. Lieutenant Robillard, having been thrown from the plane, was alive. Mabel remained trapped inside the plane, struggling to release a faulty canopy hatch. By the time rescuers reached her, the plane and surrounding trees were engulfed in flames, and they could do nothing but watch. Her friends reported hearing her screams. Mabel's remains were charred beyond recognition.

The other women towing targets at Camp Davis in North Carolina, traumatized by Mabel's violent death, threatened to quit, and Jackie feared the worst if they carried out their threats. She refused to accept the resignation letters she received, although two of the women were allowed to resign and one of those joined the WAVES (Women Accepted for Volunteer Emergency Service) and served in Honolulu as a Link instructor and a crew member on a DC-5 transporting military officials.

Ferrying work was not all work and no play. The Mile High Club included a number of WASPs who had made love above five thousand feet. With someone else at the controls of the aircraft, WASPs found creative opportunities for intimate liaisons, including one reported in the panoramic Plexiglas nose of a B-17 over the Florida Keys. Military rules still existed, but the women were liberated of Dedie and Jackie and the restricted behavior expected at "Cochran's Convent."

Often the pilots flew in groups ferrying whole shipments of new aircraft from one location to another. Hazel enjoyed this aspect of the job, being in the air with friends, talking on their radios. If the trip was long enough, they shared a picnic in the sky. One pilot would radio the others that she was hungry and ready to eat, and they would eat together at the same time, discussing what they were eating and when they ate each item. "Okay, I'm having my apple." "I'm having my sandwich."[4] None of the WASPs interviewed ever failed to mention how close the women pilots became and that the friendships they made lasted throughout their lives.

In late September Hazel received news that a classmate, Betty Taylor Wood, had died in an accident. She was only twenty-two years old and a newlywed. On the same day in August that she and Hazel had graduated, Betty married her flight instructor, Harold Wood, who earned the tongue-in-cheek nickname "Shorty" because he was so tall. Despite the rule that students were not allowed to date their instructors, several trainees married their flight instructors after graduation. The couple had been married only forty-seven days when the accident occurred.

Betty had been assigned to Camp Davis, and on September 23, 1943, after flying for two hours towing targets, she experienced engine failure while attempting to land her A-24. When her left wing touched the runway on final approach, she radioed in her plan for another go-round, but when she gave full throttle, the engine surged and then stalled. The plane crashed into a four-foot embankment and rolled upside down, crushing Betty and the base chaplain riding as her passenger, killing them both instantly.

Jackie Cochran flew to Camp Davis the following day and inspected the plane herself, and discovered someone had put sugar in the gas tank. Even a mere teaspoon of sugar added to a gas tank could cause engine trouble. Enough sugar could cause complete engine failure in seconds. This was not the first time. Sometimes rags or grass were used. Jackie didn't say a word about her discovery and asked the mechanics involved to keep quiet, fearing that sabotage would scare the girls if they found out. She remembered the near insurrection that had occurred after Mabel Rawlinson's death and feared that if this news leaked and women quit, her program might be in jeopardy.

The official cause of Betty's crash was recorded as a "sticky throttle," without any further proof than another pilot's Form One reporting a throttle sticking when the plane was last flown. Acts of sabotage upon planes and the flying gear of women ferrying pilots, whether carried out by men who didn't want women flying, disgruntled airplane factory employees, or traitors to the United States, went unsolved and unpunished. Camp Davis had the most reports of sabotage, with eleven women forced to land due to engine failure.

19

CAVU

*I think I may not ever be able to see marriage except as a
cage until I am unfit to work or fly or be active—and of
course I wouldn't be desirable then.*[1]

—AMELIA EARHART

Mr. Harry Lee

Announces the marriage of his sister

Hazel Ying

To

Major Yin Cheung Louie

Saturday, the ninth of October
Marble Collegiate Church
New York City

O N A FOGGY MIDDAY, HAZEL HURRIED along 29th Street in New York City beneath maple trees that appeared to be on fire. Marble Collegiate Church's 215-foot steeple topped by a Dutch-style weathervane and rooster rose from the impressive neo-Romanesque gothic church built of locally mined marble. The funeral processions of both Presidents Lincoln and Grant had paraded past its doors. Inside, Hazel paused to take in the soaring interior and mahogany pews. She wore a cream-colored, belted, knee-length dress, pearls, and a corsage of lilies from Cliff, who waited at the altar in uniform, smiling.

Photos at her sister's house after the ceremony show the radiant couple cutting their three-tiered cake, holding hands, smiling and alight with happiness. Hazel likely wasn't given much time off. A weekend pass was customary although difficult to obtain even for weddings.

That same day, Hazel sent a telegram from New York to her friend Didi Johnson in Romulus. "KNOT TIED TODAY 1400 SNAFU CAVU FOR CLIFF AND ME. AH YING." CAVU was an acronym used by pilots meaning ceiling and visibility unlimited. As hopeful as her message sounded, Cliff and Hazel had no idea how they would be together or even if they'd be on the same continent until after the war ended, whenever that might be. SNAFU meant a confused or chaotic mess, and as a military term born during World War II stood for "Situation Normal, All Fucked Up." There must have been difficulties involved with the wedding or more likely traveling to New York. The following day, Sunday, October 10, Madge married Shay Minton.

Hazel and Cliff returned to Romulus, where she had a small apartment and roommates. Cliff stayed for another month, until he had to return to China. In November they parted not knowing when or if they would see each other again. Hazel kept Cliff's motorcycle helmet in the back window of her car.

◊ ◊ ◊

Hazel heard about a group of women who'd been chosen to train to fly the B-17s. Every pilot she knew wanted to fly a B-17. She took some comfort in the fact that they had chosen women who were over five-foot-four and she was five-foot-three, but had she been at Avenger Field she might have been chosen, and she would have insisted on being considered. General Tunner, with his new attitude about women flying for the military, believed that if women could fly the B-17, the 25,000-pound tail-dragging four-engined Flying Fortress, they could fly anything. He hoped women would be able to fly the bombers over to England. In the summer of 1943, the number of hours required for pilots training in the Army Air Corps was reduced due to the desperate need for crews in Europe. Pilots with less experience than recommended were nervous about the Atlantic crossing and with good reason. As well as having as little as half the required flight time, they hadn't flown in the winter conditions they would encounter on the "Snowball Route," a series of refueling stops that began in Goose Bay, Labrador, and took them to Greenland and Iceland before arriving at their stations in Great Britain. Between 1943 and 1945, four hundred bomber crews were lost enroute to their stations in Europe, most due to pilot inexperience.

Despite the costly loss of aircraft and trained airmen, women were not allowed to take the B-17s across the Atlantic. On September 2, 1943, Nancy Love and Betty Gillies, two of the first women to fly the B-17, got theirs all the way to Goose Bay before weather delayed them and General Arnold, who had never been in favor of women flying across the Atlantic, found out and canceled the flight. The women were heartbroken. They had more experience flying B-17s than the men. The expensive aircraft would be safer in their hands. They posed for a photo in front of their plane, with its name, *Queen Bee*, painted beneath Nancy's window, but they couldn't smile. Later, they watched the *Queen Bee* take off for Scotland piloted by men. Betty would later remember, "We had plenty of time to go to the bar and drink our sorrows that night." In 1955, Nancy wrote, "the disappointment is still with me." She would never be allowed to fly a B-17 to Europe. General Tunner, more than thirty years later, said the canceled flight had left him feeling "heartbroken."[2]

On October 16, 1943, seventeen graduates of classes 43-W-5 and 43-W-6 showed up on the flight line at Lockbourne Army Air Base in Ohio ready for instructions. All they knew was that they'd been chosen for a special assignment. Before them stood in regal alignment the largest planes they'd ever seen, seventy-five feet long and with wingspans more than one hundred feet. One of the women whistled. The rest stood in awed silence, hoping they would get a chance to ride in a B-17 or at least go inside and look around. "Let's go meet the 'Big Friend,'" instructor Lieutenant Mitchell said.[3]

The women climbed aboard and through the compartments, amazed by a ship so large that eleven of them would fit inside at the same time, and standing up in a cockpit was a first. After they saw the instrument panel, their awe became mixed with doubt. What kind of a mind would be required to fly something so complicated? Mitchell proceeded to tell them he was going to teach each of them to fly the B-17. One WASP, a Texan named Frances Green, said, "You're going to have to work your tails off."[4]

It nearly took two of them to push the throttles up as they pulled the big yoke back for takeoff. After the smaller planes they were used to, they said it felt like taxiing a hotel. The beast seemed too heavy to get off the ground, but Mitchell insisted the B-17 handled just like the smaller airplanes they already knew how to fly. Their arms strengthened, and they found the B-17s a joy to pilot. Soon a small group of women were flying the monstrous bombing machines alone across the country.

One of the most iconic photos taken of the WASPs is that of four women walking away from a B-17 named *Pistol Packin' Mama*. Frances Green, Margaret Kirchner, Ann Waldner, and Blanche

Osborn, in leather flying jackets and carrying their parachute packs, strut toward the camera shoulder to shoulder and smiling. Blanche Osborn wrote home about the B-17 that she was "simply nuts about the airplane. It's funny, I don't think of it as an airplane—but more like something alive."[5]

◊ ◊ ◊

Jackie Cochran wanted her girls in uniform. Americans didn't know the WASPs even existed, and her pilots needed visibility to gain public approval for militarization They looked less than military in tan gaberdine slacks and white shirts. A lieutenant colonel named Meyer offered her "hideous old WAC suits," castoffs from the Women's Army Corps, which she promptly refused. In that case, he told her, there was a lot of material in storage she could use and have made up any way she wanted. Jackie remembered, "When I saw the fabric, I was aghast. First of all, there was enough of it to make a tent to cover the entire United States of America. Secondly, it was terrible stuff. I told Meyer, 'You can give this to the starving Armenians. I'm not going to take it.'"[6]

Determined to have the WASPs stand out, and with her twenty-years in the fashion and beauty business, Jackie went to Bergdorf Goodman's department store in New York City and, using her own money, had designed a tailored custom uniform of Eisenhower jacket, shirt, slacks, and a beret she described as "cute." Jackie named the color of the fabric she chose Santiago Blue. At the Pentagon she searched out the most beautiful woman and dressed her in the Bergdorf Goodman uniform and dressed two other women whom she judged to be plainer in the WAC uniform and a uniform she'd had made from the "terrible stuff." Her presentation was persuasive, and General Marshall told her the army would pay for the new uniforms. The WASPs would be the first air force pilots in the United States to wear blue.

Although Army Air Corps second lieutenants received a $250

uniform allowance, the WASPs were not granted any money. The army would provide two basic jackets, skirt, slacks, and flying suits, but the women had to use their salaries to pay for the rest, including shoes. The women were issued ration cards, but the ration boards, believing women pilots would be issued clothing by the Army Air Corps, tore out the shoe ration stamps. Worn-out shoes became the norm. The official WASP uniform announced on November 16, 1943, included Army Air Corps lapel wings and a gold-lettered WASP insignia. Jackie was pleased with the uniforms and the timing.

In September a house resolution was submitted that would bring the WASPs into the Army Air Corps and grant them the same pay, rights, and benefits as male pilots. Once approved, the WASPs expected to be in the military as soon as Christmas.

But the bill died in committee. A new and more complex bill would be drafted, and the WASPs closely followed news about the progress of the "WASP Bill."

◊ ◊ ◊

On November 27, 1943, Hazel sent a postcard to Dorothea "Didi" Johnson.

> Didi:
>
> *How are you and the rest of the kids? I'm frightfully sorry not to have written you before this. After I reported back to the base as Mrs. Louie, I've been out on trips. Am staying over here for the night [South Bend, Indiana]. Cliff left last week for China and I am staying on with my flying. Will try to write you as soon as I get back to the base, as even tho I don't get a chance to write often we do think of you.*
>
> *Always, Ah Ying[7]*

Waiting for a letter or telegram or any news about Cliff filled Hazel's thoughts. She understood the danger and secrecy of his work in China. She kept busy to distract her mind, and keeping busy proved easy. There was plenty of work. She worked through Christmas and, on December 27, met up with Madge in Sacramento after they'd delivered their planes.

In January 1944, Sylvia Dahmes graduated from Avenger Field and was assigned to Romulus, where she became a part of Hazel's circle of friends, which included Pat Dickerson, Didi Johnson, Fran Snyder, and Hazel's bay mates from Avenger Treb (Joanne Trebtoske) and AJ (Alice Jean May.) When they found themselves in the same city overnight while ferrying planes across the country, Hazel took her friends to Chinese restaurants, which in a lot of small towns were upstairs over a pool hall. Hazel gambled and smoked cigars. She spoke loudly in her husky voice and laughed often and at everything. Life amused her. Her friends were both shocked and enthralled by her behavior. "Everyone she met was a friend," Sylvia said. "She didn't think of herself as a trendsetter."[8] But a trendsetter she was. Embracing her different-ness, accepting that she would never be like everyone else, freed her to be Hazel Ah Ying Lee.

AJ drew a cartoon sketch of Hazel ordering Chinese dishes at a restaurant in rapid-fire Cantonese while her friends listened in openmouthed amazement. They had never heard Cantonese spoken or eaten Chinese food. When the women said they were full, Hazel told them to "drink some more tea, and then you can eat some more."[9] Hazel could eat more than any of them.

Whenever their ferrying took them to New Jersey, Hazel would take her friends to her sister's home in New York where they were served a meal. Afterward, they rode transit back to where they were staying, and the train took so long that when they reached New Jersey she was ready to eat again. She had learned to cook at her family's restaurants in Portland and in the apartment she shared with other WASPs in Romulus; she cooked for her friends, and they remembered her macaroni with beef and spices and the copious amounts of macaroni and cheese they consumed thanks to rationing restrictions.

In January 1944, General Arnold asked the Deputy Chief of Air Staff, General William E. Hall, if the women pilots could be commissioned as had been done for male civilian service pilots. General Hall dropped a bomb on Jackie. Direct commissions into the army for the WASPs would not be possible; "the volunteer forms called for 'persons,' and the military defined 'persons' as 'men.'"[10] Jackie would not be so easily dissuaded.

20

UNNECESSARY
AND UNDESIRABLE

*When once you have tasted flight, you will forever walk
the earth with your eyes turned skyward, for there you
have been, and there you will always long to return.*

—Leonardo da Vinci

April 22, 1944
Dear Frances,

It's been a long time since I've heard from you. In fact,
Rose forwarded me your letter in which you mentioned seeing
Clifford. I'm glad you two had the chance to see each other. Since
then, I have also heard from Howard. What are the two boys
doing now? Cliff wrote me a month or so ago, saying that Howard and Daniel both wanted to enlist in the U.S. Army. I would
appreciate your writing me and tell me what is what with you all
from time to time.

I've been in the Ferry Command since last August. No
doubt, Clifford has told you most of the news concerning the
nature of my work. The flying keeps me pretty busy; in fact, we
hardly have any time off. We are on a seven-day week schedule.
Now, we may be placed directly in the Air Corp [sic]. At present,

we're known as WASPs (Women Auxiliary Army Service Pilots [sic]). The work is interesting and gives us many opportunities of going to all parts of the country including some parts of Canada. I have been able to visit Rose in New York during my trips and enroute back to my base.

Victor is somewhere on the East Coast—where he cannot say. However, I believe he is on his way overseas. We all try to write to him at least once a week. Someday I hope we can all be together again. The family is certainly scattered all over the world. Of course, you know I will return to China as soon as it is possible.

All of us are well here. Now that we know where to write to you, you can be sure you'll hear from us often. Keep well and let us know how you and the boys are. Do try to write when you can. If there is anything you want done, write. Best of everything to you + Herbert.

Love, Hazel.
Mrs. Yin-Cheung Louie WASP
3rd Ferrying Group
Romulus Army Air Base

H AZEL, WHO NEVER COMPLAINED and wore a smile while making jokes in the face of disaster, admitted to friends she was exhausted from flying seven days a week, exacerbated by the added stress of not knowing what was happening with Cliff. The future didn't look clear; in fact, she couldn't determine where she would be in a year's time or thereafter. The hours and the work were taking a toll. In her letter to Rose, the only need she expressed was hoping to see her family again and her desire to return to China. As important as her work had become and would continue to be, she missed the people she loved, especially her new husband. As the time stretched since they'd been together, she couldn't help wondering if she would ever see him again.

It was too disheartening to write her family about the latest WASP developments, although she knew the news had become biased and inaccurate. In March, members of Congress questioned the need for the women pilots, and the media followed suit. By May, the public's opinion had turned against the WASPs. The women pilots were no longer the "daring darlings" come to relieve men to fight overseas for world freedom. An article in the *Idaho Statesman* suggested the women had been allowed to fly for the war effort because of the "sentimental softness of American men in regard to their women. . . . In colleges the smooth, good looking gals can get A's without a lick of work; and in the armed services it may be that dimples have a devastating effect even on the generals."[1] The media described Jackie as "a shapely pilot" with "an attractive composition of wind-blown bob, smiling eyes and outdoor skin." General Arnold was accused of gazing into Jackie's eyes and taking "her cause celebre very much 'to heart.'"[2]

In the *Washington Times-Herald*, gossip columnist Austine Cassini also accused General Arnold of having a romantic interest in Jackie: "It's whispered he's battling like a knight of olde, or olde knight, for 'the faire Cochran.' So the announcement had to be expected any day that Jackie's commission has been approved, if the captivated general is victorious in his tournaments."[3] In truth, Arnold had been of little assistance to Jackie when she needed it most, through no fault of his own. On May 10, he suffered his third heart attack since February 1943.

On May 29, 1944, *Time* magazine, which had gushed over the ferrying trainees at Avenger Field a year earlier, ran an article titled "Unnecessary and Undesirable." And *The New York Times* speculated that male pilots might "soon be cleaning windshields and servicing planes for 'glamourous' women flyers who have only thirty-five hours of flying time."[4] The media called the WASP program an "expensive experiment."[5] And the message from the government to all women working for the war effort was that it would soon be time to step aside. The propaganda being released by the Office of War Information stressed that it was the role of women to heal men's emotional and physical wounds after the war, in order to ensure the best future for the next generation. Women should create a safe and happy home in which humanity would be restored.

Walter Brehm, Republican congressman from Ohio, said during a House debate about the future of the WASPs, "I think it is time to forget the glamour in this war and think more of the gore of war."[6] Glamour had been needed to sell the country on sending their young men off to war; now, to bring them home, apparently a different kind of mindset was necessary. It was time to forget the war and get back to work. Everyone had lost someone. Americans just wanted to go back to life as it had been before the war began.

Hazel leaned back into the sand and closed her eyes. An ancient colonel whose name she couldn't remember drawled on in a confusing Southern accent until she couldn't keep her eyes open any longer. Hoping not to appear rude, she pasted a smile on her face. With her sunglasses on he might not notice if she fell asleep, since he had required nothing from her in conversation. She and AJ were attending officer training at the Army Air Force School of Advanced Tactics in Orlando, Florida, for four weeks in June. Sundays were spent at one of the many lakes in the area. On Saturday evenings there was usually a general or two to dance with at the officers' club. Hazel got her first taste of what it would be like to be an officer.

Even though the future of the WASPs looked uncertain in Congress, General Giles, Chief of Air Staff in Washington, decided that since the women would at some future date be part of the military, they should have the same training as Army Air Corps officers. For eight hours a day, six days a week, throughout June, Hazel and AJ attended intensive classes where they studied military flow charts, military law, courts-martial, and the tactical and operational methods of military aviation. They were shown top-secret bombsights and radar equipment and trained in jungle survival, which included how to distinguish poisonous roots and ferns and cook rattlesnake meat, which Hazel declared delicious. In a chemical warfare course, they were given whiffs of mustard gas and cyanide. Without women's facilities, during breaks they had to yell into the men's room "Is anyone there?" and then line up outside to wait their turns.

On Sunday morning, June 6, 1944, Hazel and AJ woke to the news that the Allies had invaded France. Allied forces were moving inland but losses were significant. Later President Roosevelt's prayer on the radio reminded them that the nation was united in their hopes for the lives of the Allied men and the success of the massive invasion, far larger than anyone had anticipated, and an end to the war.

Although Hazel did not know of Victor's whereabouts overseas, she worried that he was involved in the invasion. And in fact his company landed on Utah Beach on the 23rd of June. After fighting their way across northern France, they took part in the Falaise Gap battles, and then moved through Lorraine in the late summer. Neither Hazel nor anyone in her family received word from him. His siblings and mother agonized over whether he was alive or dead, and every day a letter didn't arrive they grew more frantic.

While in Florida, Hazel and AJ heard that WASPs were traveling to air bases all over the country demonstrating to men that they had nothing to fear from the B-29 Super Fortress. After a terrible accident, the men had refused to fly them. When the bombers landed and four WASPs climbed out, the men were more than surprised and decided if a woman could fly the plane, so could they. But women showing up men had some unintended negative consequences.

On June 21, 1944, with seventy-three members abstaining, the House of Representatives rejected by just nineteen votes the request of the Army Air Corps to bring the WASPs into the military. It was the beginning of the end. Hazel and AJ wondered what General Arnold would do with the WASPs. Without funds from Congress, he didn't have much choice but to disband them. AJ and Hazel would complete officer training and report back to Romulus on the first of July more uncertain than ever about their future.

Jackie had been worried from the start that if her women appeared threatening to men and their jobs, it would lead to the end of the women flying for the war effort. From the beginning she spoke of women "relieving," not replacing, men. When the news of the WASP Bill became public, her worst fears were realized. A group of civilian flight instructors decided the bill would take away their jobs, with fewer combat pilots needing to be trained, and once that happened their draft deferments would end. Fearing they'd be drafted and sent into combat, they lobbied for the women's noncombat pilot jobs.

The media, which had glorified the WASPs' efforts in magazines, newsreels, and other outlets, turned against them as job stealers. What was happening to Rosie the Riveters was about to happen to the WASPs. They would be sent home to make their jobs available to men, the breadwinners. Suddenly the media began promoting false claims that men were better suited for piloting.

Although women were involved in fewer accidents than men, their accidents and especially deaths made headlines now. Twenty-three women pilots had been killed in service. That number would rise, and during 1944 a WASP would be killed almost every month, in large part because there were more planes than ever to deliver and more WASPs delivering them. Hazel's classmate Virginia Moffatt had been killed in a Basic Trainer near Ontario, California, in October 1943. Evelyn Sharp had died April 3, 1944. She was crushed when her P-38 Lockheed Lightning cartwheeled after an engine failed. Dorothy Nichols was killed June 11, 1944, in a P-39Q at Bismarck, North Dakota, due to engine failure at takeoff. Paula Loop died July 7, 1944, when the engine of her BT-13 Vultee Valiant quit and she crashed in the mountains near Medford, Oregon.

In the summer of 1944, it seemed the war was beginning to wind down. A House bill to provide WASPs with military status was defeated, stating that the program was "unnecessary," and "unjustifiably expensive." The recruiting and training of inexperienced women pilots would be discontinued. The war in Europe would continue for eleven more months, until victory was officially declared on May 8, 1945. Japan would surrender on September 2, 1945. It is believed that the militarization of the WASPs failed in large part due to the aggressive lobbying by male civilian pilots and instructors.

21

400 MILES PER HOUR

*I preferred single engine, and that's the difference
between a bomber pilot and a pursuit pilot. I like a Cub
and a sporty car.*[1]

—DOROTHY "DOT" SWAIN LEWIS,
WASP, CLASS 44-W-5

CAROLE FILLMORE WAS RUNNING out of daylight. She had
taken her P-51 the southerly route on her way to Newark,
New Jersey from Long Beach, California, to avoid winter weather.
When she called the tower at Athens, Georgia, for landing instructions, no one replied. Trying again to reach the tower and still receiving no response, she began to circle. When she called for a radio
check, an agitated voice shouted into her earphones, "Would the lady
who's trying to get in, please stay off the air! We are trying to bring in
a P-51." Carole looked around and, seeing no other P-51, called again
for clearance. She was given the same response. At last, realizing the
problem, she said, "For your information, the lady who is on the air
is *in* the P-51," and without waiting for an answer, she turned on final
approach and headed down the runway at 120 miles an hour.

◊ ◊ ◊

On September 4, 1944, Hazel returned to Texas to begin four weeks of intensive training at the new and expanded Pursuit Center in Brownsville, on the United States border with Mexico. Pursuit training continued despite the looming question of what would happen to the WASPs after their disbandment. As pursuit planes poured out of American factories, the women pilots had more work to do than ever and believed they would still be needed to fly in some capacity after the war ended. Any other outcome was inconceivable. Hazel had been selected for training that few would have the opportunity to receive, and had been given the choice between pursuit or bomber training. Some women preferred bombers, liking the security of a lot of metal around them and all the gauges, knobs, and dials. Hazel wanted speed, and fighter aircraft were the fastest planes on earth. WASP Jean Landis flew a P-51 from coast to coast in nine hours and thirty-five minutes total airtime, two hours faster than Jackie Cochran in her P-35 when she won the Bendix Race in 1938. For airline passengers such a flight still took two, and often three, days.

One of the uses of pursuit aircraft was to escort B-17 formations to their targets in Europe, fighting off enemy fire on the way. Early in the war, planes like the Spitfire and Hurricane gained heroic fame in the Battle of Britain intercepting German JU88 bombers before they could reach London. Built for speed, high performance, and maneuverability, they were able to peel off and dive through flak-riddled skies, engage in dogfights, and strafe bridges, railroads, and ships.

Flying at 300 miles per hour was something to get used to when the fastest they'd flown had been 140–150. One WASP came back to the airport after flying for a couple of hours, made a turn, and the airport was gone. She worried that she'd run out of gas before she could slow down enough to land. Pursuit instructors joked that "if a man could count to ten, he could not be a pursuit pilot. He thought too hard."[2] Those same instructors never dreamed they'd be teaching women. Hazel possessed the rare qualities needed to fly the fastest aircraft—determination to succeed and the ability to persevere under difficult conditions. Hazel believed in herself. She was confident, forthright, an intuitive thinker, and fearless.

The pursuit planes were so precious that WASPs were required to carry .45-caliber pistols. Many bound for overseas carried top-secret equipment. Should they be forced down under suspicious circumstances, WASPs were shown a spot on the fuselage to shoot that would blow up the airplane.

The men who flew pursuits in combat performed impossible-looking aerial acrobatics, all while shooting with precision and dodging other aircraft. They became revered like the World War I flying aces. Hazel had witnessed dogfights in China and had lost friends, both in practice and combat, flying pursuits. With only room in the cockpit for one, pursuit pilots flew, fought, and died alone.

Hazel's class would learn to fly a minimum of five types of pursuit planes: the P-40 Kittyhawk, the P-63 Kingcobra and its predecessor the P-39 Airacobra, the P-51 Mustang, and the P-47 Thunderbolt, the heaviest fighter airplane. Regardless of the prevalent doubt that women, who were smaller in size than men, could handle the larger, more powerful aircraft, General Tunner insisted that one WASP to every ten men be given the opportunity to learn to fly them. In some respects women were better suited than men as fighter pilots with their smaller size, ideally suited for the small cockpits, quick reactions, and lighter, more deliberate touch.

In December 1943, the first group of WASPs completed pursuit training and became the elite first women to fly fighter aircraft in the United States. The 117 WASPs who flew the high-performance airplanes across the country were among the first Americans to get an inkling of the new air age. After her first flight, Hazel earned the title of the first Asian American woman to fly a fighter aircraft.

Five of Hazel's bay mates from Avenger Field went on to fly pursuit planes: Joanne "Treb" Trebtoske, Madge Rutherford Minton,

Alice Jean "AJ" May, and Virgie Lee Jowell. There were thirty-four in Hazel's pursuit class of 44-18 Flight B, including seven other women from Romulus: Sylvia Dahmes, Jane Scott, Maurine Miller, Helen Barrick, Joanne "Treb" Trebtoske, and Fran Snyder.

The third day of pursuit training was washout day. Instructors unaccustomed to training women found it difficult to trust them with the powerful pursuit planes. Vi Thurn had been told she made a "lousy" landing. Unapologetic, she said, "Sir, that was not my landing. You've been on the controls the whole time." He admitted that he'd never trained a woman, and he could see her cracked up at the end of the runway and he would have been responsible. She didn't blame him, but said, "If I'm stupid enough to make a mistake it's not your fault, it's my fault." He let her fly the next day.[3]

The dream of every WASP, flying a P-51 Mustang, required experience and confidence due to its sensitive controls. The Mustang had been created to compete with the Luftwaffe's fighter aircraft inflicting terrible damage in Europe. At speeds of up to 441 miles per hour, it was one of the fastest planes in the world, and with only one seat it had to be flown solo. Vi Thurn called it "the love of my life, and I never felt any fear while flying it."[4]

In class one day, Hazel learned a lesson about the P-51 from another WASP's experience. Barbara Russell had picked up a brand-new Mustang at Long Beach, California, to transport to Newark, New Jersey, on a sunny, CAVU morning. The P-51 burned through sixty gallons of fuel per hour. After forty-five minutes, Barbara crossed into Arizona. When she switched the gas lever from the fuselage tank to the left wing tank, the engine began to cough, and then quit.

Looking down at the rugged, mountainous terrain below, Barbara decided bailing out would be her last resort. In pursuit school she'd learned the procedure for bailing out. Raising her eyes to the hatch, she knew she would have to release the hatch cover first. The canopy would likely be blown away by the force of the wind. Then she would need to move fast before the plane plummeted. With her parachute seat pack in one hand, she would need the other hand to hold on to the panel to keep from being blown out of the aircraft. Then all she had to do was climb from the cockpit and slide onto the wing and avoid the propeller as she slipped off. Definitely a last resort.

With three 85-gallon fuel tanks full and carrying five hundred pounds of gasoline, she would first burn off the fuselage tank, then switch every twenty minutes between the left and right tanks to keep the plane balanced. If the gas connection held, she could make it to Phoenix 150 miles away. She switched to the right tank and waited. The engine sputtered and caught. Her airspeed increased. Every minute, the plane burned off another pound of octane from the right wing. To compensate for the uneven weight, she pushed the left rudder pedal down with increasing force until her leg ached.

Finally reaching Phoenix, she called for an emergency landing. With the right wing tank almost empty, there wasn't enough fuel to circle. Upon approach, the plane listed, making holding the nose down the center line difficult. After a successful landing, Barbara waited for sensation to return to her left leg so she would not fall out of the cockpit. Jumping onto the tarmac, she told the ground crew, "Better iron the chinks out of this airplane before some lieutenant is being attacked by a bunch of Messerschmitts."[5]

Accidents and deaths were rare for the women flying pursuit aircraft, and that can be attributed to their flying skills and training, but also to the meticulous care and proficiency of the assembly line workers who received less appreciation than they deserved. Dorothy Scott had been killed in a midair collision flying a BC-1 when she was overtaken by a P-39 while shooting practice landings at pursuit school in Palm Springs, but such accidents were the exception and in this case the fault belonged to the P-39 pilot.

The women in pursuit training also learned to fly the P-47 Thunderbolt, nicknamed "the Jug" due to its globular shape. The largest and heaviest single-engine pursuit aircraft, twice the size of the British Spitfire, it flew at speeds of up to 433 miles per hour. Its thirteen-foot, four-bladed prop loomed in the pilot's line of vision. The Thunderbolt was highly combustible. Joanne Wallace Orr had been cleared for takeoff when a male pilot cut her off. Unable to miss him, she sheared his engine off and her plane burst into flames. From the cockpit she watched men come running and then stop, fearing the plane would blow up. She couldn't get the hatch to open. She continued to fight with the hatch as everything turned orange and the cockpit became an incinerator. The plane was engulfed in flames, and she knew as she struggled that she was going to burn to death, and it would be painful. Finally, the hatch released, and she climbed out onto the wing and jumped to the runway, only now aware that her teeth had been crushed when she was pushed forward into the gunsight.

Called "cumbersome," the P-47 landed like lead due to its heavy armor that saved lives. At pursuit school graduation a pilot came up to Vi Thurn and thanked her. He told her he kept calling in sick when he was scheduled to fly the P-47, and then one day he saw her land and all he could see was the top of her curly hair and he thought, "If she can do it, so can I."[6]

Hazel's first flight in the single-seat P-47 had to be done without an instructor. Every inch of space was taken in the snug three-by-three-foot cockpit, and the panel was a puzzle of dials, levers, and knobs. She methodically went through the pre-takeoff checklist. When she pressed the start button and pushed the throttle forward, flames shot from the exhaust pipes as the engine thundered to life. She called the tower and told them she was ready to taxi. Granted permission for takeoff, she took hold of the stick and settled her feet on the rudder pedals. Three cushions lifted her enough to see beyond the instrument panel, engine, and four-bladed prop. With a hand on the throttle and working the rudder pedals, she gradually moved the six-ton fighter down the taxiway. Looking down on the runway was like looking out of a second-story window. As she taxied toward the runway, the engine smoothed out. Every cell in her body was alive and alert. After a long, deep breath, she pushed the throttle all the way forward. The plane charged forward. Her body was forced back against the seat. At this point she knew some women had lost consciousness, but they came to once airborne.

As the plane leveled off, the sensation of floating belied the fact that she was speeding across the sky at three hundred miles per hour. With a gentle touch on the stick, the fighter banked to the right, and then moving the stick a little to the left, the plane recovered, and she was again speeding over the Gulf of Mexico's wide expanse of brilliant blue water lined with sandy beaches and rice fields, remembering LaRue's warning against landing in Mexico in an emergency. She flew at a speed she had never experienced, that few had experienced. The sensation must have been thrilling.

Back in Romulus, Hazel began delivering pursuit aircraft. Working seven days a week, she flew some of the country's most sophisticated planes, transporting them from factories to domestic airfields or to coastal debarkation points for shipment to foreign theaters. Many WASPs had never left their hometowns before the war. Now they were able to travel from coast to coast in a matter of hours. One pilot buzzed every state capitol in the nation and the Statue of Liberty.

A combat fighter pilot knew every inch of his airplane, a familiarity bred from flying the same plane on every mission. WASP fighter pilots flew a plane only one time and had to keep current on seventy different types of aircraft and their unique serial variations. Each new series brought quirks not mentioned in the tech manuals but talked about among ferry pilots. Hazel learned to listen when pilots talked about different aircraft and their unique quirks, knowing she might be flying the plane being discussed the next day.

Hazel flew over the Empire State Building before landing

in Newark. Parked on the ramp, she filled out her aircraft arrival report. She had picked up the P-51 fresh off the assembly line. Its engine had run for an hour, but it had never been flown. Untested aircraft and new engines posed numerous potential dangers, and the first entry on a pursuit's Form One was not always "A-OK." Hazel, like all WASPs, was proud to be the first to fly a new fighter to an embarkment center where it would be placed on a ship bound for combat. They didn't mind being guinea pigs. Vi Thurn said about taking off in an untested P-51, "Scooting down the runway at 100 mph, it occurred to me to wonder if everyone who worked on the plane did the right thing."[7]

Hazel jotted a note into the logbook, to the man who would fly the plane next and take her to Europe. Before jumping to the ground, she patted the fuselage. "Good luck," she told the Mustang. Then she headed inside to turn in her report to a clearance officer to sign and acknowledge that she had delivered the plane.

◊ ◊ ◊

On October 1, 1944, General Arnold announced the disbandment of the WASPs. The official date would be December 20 so that the women could be home for Christmas and New Year's. The women were still flying planes off the assembly line as fast as they came out, seven days a week without rest. They knew they were needed and couldn't understand how the planes would get delivered after they were gone. There wouldn't be enough ferrying pilots to keep up.

The invasion of Europe had been called successful, but the Germans were not going to give up easily, and the war continued as the Allies battled their way across France toward Germany, liberating towns along the way but losing lives too. With Paris liberated and the Allies making progress in Germany, pressure mounted to send the women back home to raise children and free up their jobs for the men returning from war. The men would be coming home, and women were no longer needed to fly. They were needed at home instead, they were told.

Stunned, they wondered if they would ever fly again. They mulled and discussed the implications. What about the government's investment? Their training and talent would be wasted. Many of the WASPs heard the news over the radio along with the rest of the country. On Tuesday, October 3, Hazel returned home from a flying mission to find an envelope from Army Air Corps Headquarters, Washington, D.C. Inside were two mimeographed letters. The first from Jackie Cochran began, "To All WASPs: General Arnold has directed that the WASP program be deactivated on 20 December 1944. Attached is a letter from him to each of you and it explains the circumstances leading up to this decision."[8]

Arnold's letter began, "I am very proud of you women. . . ."[9]

The WASP experiment was over. The women's dreams of flying for the military ended. They would not be commissioned. And worst of all, their flying careers were over too.

The final class at Avenger Field was supposed to have been shut down immediately, but Jackie won a small victory in convincing General Arnold to allow the girls to graduate. On December 7, 1944, class 44-W-10 became the final graduating class. Their ferrying careers would last only twelve days.

Like many of the WASP pilots, Hazel was exhausted from the long hours and grueling flights and frustrated by the shutdown of the program. Based on her logbook, she figured she'd flown around the world more than sixty times.

Hazel had been flying P-39s wearing the markings of the Chinese Air Force to the West, from where they would go on to fly in China. She was helping both the United States and China at last. As soon as she learned about the WASP disbandment, she began working to assist other women find flying jobs in China. Cliff, as a major in the Chinese Air Force, offered to help. Hazel had already accepted a job in China, but what the job entailed is unknown. She had long wanted to fly cargo planes with supplies over the Himalayas and Burma, to China, along the route known as the "Hump," a range of mountains in the eastern Himalayas, sixteen thousand feet high and notoriously dangerous to fly over. On January 8, 1945, Nancy Love would become the first woman to pilot an American C-54 over the "Hump."

◊ ◊ ◊

Hazel waited for a flight back to Romulus after a delivery. AJ joined her and asked if she'd heard the news about the disappearance. It was their classmate from Avenger, Gertrude Tompkins, whom everyone had called "Tommy." Hazel remembered a shy girl who stuttered, and she had enjoyed making her laugh. "She's missing. They can't find a trace of her."

They didn't always hear about accidents and deaths of fellow WASPs, unless it was someone they knew and they received a letter with the news, but with all the attention on the WASP Bill, this had made the national papers. Gertrude Tompkins had been learning to fly early in the war when her boyfriend, a pilot, was shot down and drowned. After his death, she was accepted into WASP training. Much to her embarrassment, she had always stuttered. During pursuit training, after her first flight in a P-51, she never stuttered again.

Two days after her wedding to Henry Silver, she returned to WASP duty. She would never see her new husband again. On October 26, 1944, she was flying a P-51 from what is today LAX to a stopover in Palm Springs on her way to New Jersey. She never arrived at Palm Springs. The flight controllers had not received her flight plan, and she was not reported missing until four days later. There was no black box, no radar to monitor her flight, no flight plan, and no evidence of her crash was ever discovered.

She was the only WASP to go missing, and the mystery remains unsolved. Archaeologist G. Patric Macha believed that her aircraft crashed in the shallow waters of Santa Monica Bay and was buried underneath layers of sand. Others believe she crashed in the mountains near Palm Springs. Most agree she likely became distracted or disoriented in the new P-51.

One evening in November, over a macaroni and cheese dinner at Hazel's apartment, AJ asked about Cliff; she knew it had been ages since Hazel had news of him. There could be any number of reasons. Mail ships were torpedoed and sunk. Mail became lost in less dramatic ways. Hazel had a premonition that she wouldn't see him again. She hoped he was a prisoner of war but feared he was dead. Hazel realized that she might not know what happened to Cliff until after the war ended. Maybe the feeling came from being surrounded by so many stories of missing boyfriends, brothers, and husbands. Hazel had met ferrying pilot Teresa James while waiting for transport back to their bases. Teresa had received the dreaded telegram telling her that her husband was missing in action. After months without news, she eventually learned that his plane had been shot down over Germany. Still no letter came, and she held on to hope that he had been taken prisoner. When the Allied prisoners were released at the end of 1945, he was not among them. His remains were never found.

22

SNAFU

To live without risk, for me, would have been tantamount to death.[1]

—JACKIE COCHRAN

A SEA OF OLIVE-DRAB P-63 KINGCOBRAS lined the Bell factory runway in Niagara, New York, like soldiers ready for battle. On each fuselage had been painted a red star outlined in white, marking it as bound for Russia and a product of the Russian Lend Lease Account conceived by President Roosevelt. The planes assembled that cold morning in November of 1944 were scheduled to be flown to Great Falls, Montana. Most, but not all, would make it there.

Hazel had arrived on the field early to monogram her friends' planes with their Chinese nicknames. Without enough red lipstick for six planes, she had used a large stick of chalk provided by the ground crew. The white letters in capitalized Disney font would be easy to spot in the air, and she'd be able to identify her friends while flying. The WASPs from Romulus going on the mission with Hazel were Fran Snyder, Claire Callaghan, Pat Dickerson, and AJ. They enjoyed seeing their names when they found their aircraft, even if they didn't always understand the meaning of Hazel's nicknames.

"FAE HOON" graced the nose of Pat Dickerson's plane. The Chinese nickname meant "Flying Rainbow."

Other ferrying pilots had flown in from their air bases in California and Texas to help deliver the large shipment of sixty to seventy planes. From Great Falls, Montana, male pilots would ferry the planes to Alaska, where they would be picked up by Russian fliers. They were equipped with a 37mm cannon that fired through the propeller, two .50-caliber nose-mounted machine guns and two .50-caliber machine guns under the wings. Russia used them as anti-tank weapons.

The Kingcobras were an updated version of the P-39 and flew at maximum speeds of 410 miles per hour. Dual wing tanks enabled enough fuel to be carried for the Russians to fly the distance from Fairbanks, Alaska, to refueling in Siberia. The new P-63s were built without belly tanks, which had proved to be dangerously unstable on takeoffs and landings.

Women were not allowed to fly to Alaska. The excuse given was that it would be dangerous for women to fly alone over the frozen tundra. Privately the fear of scandal weighed more heavily. Army commanders worried about the consequences of sending women into Fairbanks, where the men who were stationed there had not seen a white woman for as long as two years. Nancy Love tried and failed to get permission for women to be allowed to fly the P-63s all the way to Alaska. Because the disbandment was coming in December and they knew they might never fly again, the WASPs wanted to fly as much as possible. Joanne Wallace Orr said, "We were all crazy—just fly, fly, fly. Couldn't get enough."[2]

Although the P-63 was a more desirable plane to fly than its predecessor, the P-39, it had its own unique problems. According to General Tunner, with the power cut, the aircraft had the "glide angle of a brick."[3] A cartoon drawn by AJ showed a frustrated pilot in the cockpit of a P-63 pounding her fist, teeth clenched, expletives floating above her head while smoke poured from the landing gear and the front wheel support was tied in a knot. The caption read, "Good Old P-63."[4]

Before they took off, an instructor briefed the pilots on the finer points of the P-63 and sent them up for check rides. Some had never flown the Kingcobra but were familiar with the P-39. Conditions remained minimal. Weather in the northern states had been cold and stormy with snow, sleet, and ice. Pilots reported seeing Niagara Falls' frozen spray from the air.

When the weather cleared, as many pilots as could get clearance took off, leaving in small groups instead of all at once, before the clouds closed in again. Some were forced to wait it out for several days. Hazel made it out.

Like all pursuits, Bell products gulped high-octane fuel. The route from Niagara, New York, to Great Falls, Montana, required refueling stops in South Bend, Indiana, then Madison, Wisconsin, Fargo, North Dakota, and Bismarck, North Dakota. Hazel stayed over for two nights in South Bend due to weather and zero visibility. AJ had a mechanical problem and never made it any farther.

From South Bend, the pilots continued to be spread out as they took off in groups for Madison as the weather allowed. Again, the weather kept them in Madison for several nights. Hazel seemed to know Chinese restaurants in every town in America, and she took her friends to one in Madison.

Three days later, Hazel received clearance and left the city. As she prepared to taxi, a male pilot crashed shortly after takeoff due to ice on the runway. He survived with injuries, but his plane needed repair and would not go on to Montana. Some pilots only made it as far as Rochester, Minnesota, before they were weathered in again. Hazel flew through minimal visibility for two and a quarter hours before landing in Fargo, North Dakota.

Fargo was snowed in. The Roller Skate Hall near the Fargo airport had been converted into a hangar to protect the airplanes from the ice and snow. When Hazel arrived, the hangar was nearly full.

The planes had been packed in tightly, staggered with the first row nose-first and the next row tail-first.

Hazel waited six days in Fargo for the weather to clear. Waiting was difficult. Paperback books would not become available in the United States on a large scale until the 1950s. Hazel and AJ played cards, wearing their warm Montreal boots so they'd be ready to go if the opportunity arose. Montreal boots were men's, and fleece-lined, and a better fit than their standard flying boots. They read the telephone book. One night they went bowling and Hazel met Kay Gott. They talked late into the night. Kay wanted to know all the details of Hazel's fascinating life. It was a fortuitous meeting with consequences that would reach far into the future. Hazel's story made such an impression on Kay that she would later write a book about her life.

The trip to Montana should have taken only two days even with fueling stops. This was a long trip for everyone, one of the longest, and the delays meant they'd been working or waiting for thirteen days. Hazel was exhausted. Difficult flying conditions, waiting for weather to clear, and sleeping in unfamiliar beds had taken a toll physically and mentally.

Finally on November 23, Thanksgiving Day, the weather broke, and the day dawned calm and cloudy. Though the temperature remained bitterly cold, Hazel received a call she was cleared to go, and they needed to be off the ground at 8 a.m. She'd been invited to share the holiday meal with a family she'd met during dinner at the hotel the night before. There was no food service at the Fargo field, so it was even more disappointing to have to call and decline the offer of a home-cooked meal on Thanksgiving.

Hazel's airplane was one of the first towed out since she had been one of the last to arrive. Some of the planes that didn't arrive in Fargo in time to be inside the makeshift shelter were covered with ice and snow. Men were hard at work with brooms and snow shovels to clear the ramp and planes. The sound of engines warming up broke the muted morning silence.

With the oil checked, the fuel sump drained, and the preflight warm-up completed, Hazel received weather clearance, takeoff time, and her ETA to Bismarck, North Dakota. After takeoff, she followed the cleared railroad tracks west and saw the dark line of roads that had been cleared by snowplows. Everything below her was a blanket of white; the flat fields surrounding isolated farmhouses were all snowed in for Thanksgiving. Hazel's stomach growled. She thought resentfully of the meal she should be enjoying in Fargo and hoped there'd be something to eat in Bismarck. If they got delayed in Bismarck, there was one thing to look forward to. All ferry pilots knew the Prince Hotel in Bismarck would wash and iron a shirt overnight, but Hazel wasn't sure if they would be providing the service on Thanksgiving. She'd been wearing the same shirt for almost two weeks.

An hour after taking off from Fargo, Hazel landed before noon in Bismarck, where the temperature had dropped to thirty-five below zero. The mess hall was open and serving turkey with all the trimmings and pie, and because it was a holiday, in one of the metal tray compartments was a sample pack of four Lucky Strike cigarettes. Hazel smiled and put the pack in her pocket to enjoy after she made her delivery in Great Falls. If the weather held, she'd soon be on her way.

Kay came into the mess and told everyone to get going right away. Her plane had frozen outside the hangar, so she'd be delayed. The November darkness gathered early in Montana, and from Bismarck to Great Falls was two hours' flight time, so with luck they'd arrive mid-afternoon at the latest with some daylight to spare if the weather held.

As Hazel climbed into her plane, a Bell factory representative approached and asked if she'd had any problems with the plane.

"None," she replied and waved to him from the cockpit, flashing him a wide smile.

◊ ◊ ◊

The P-63 pilots in Fargo and at other bases, finally freed by a clearing in the weather, descended on Malmstrom Air Force Base in Great Falls, Montana, at the same time. Later described by pilots to have looked like a swarm of bees circling the airfield, the WASPs were reminded of their days at Avenger Field with so many planes in the air around them, but these were fighter aircraft, not the friendly little trainers of their early days. Many of the personnel at Great Falls Air Force Base were on leave due to it being Thanksgiving week, and with so many P-63s in the air, on the ground, and in all modes of landing, flying, and taxiing, the overwhelmed tower controllers had trouble identifying and communicating with the planes.

It was nearing two in the afternoon when Hazel approached Malmstrom East Base. For many of the WASPs, including Hazel, this trip to Montana had been the longest of any they'd flown for the Air Transport Command. Some pilots remained stranded and would be unable to deliver their planes until December 4, more than three weeks after they'd left the Bell factory.

Hazel received landing instructions despite the interference on her radio, which she assumed was caused by the chaos of bringing in so many planes at once. One by one, planes landed. Without clear communication from the tower, the pilots were relying on red and green lights. Despite clouds and a darkening afternoon, visibility was good.

Hazel lowered her landing gear on final approach and put the flaps down. Soon she would be able to relax, and this long ordeal would be over. Seeing no other planes on approach, a clear runway, and a green light, she positioned her plane for landing and headed in at an even attitude. Maybe the officers' club would be serving a turkey dinner with all the fixings. She was famished. Crossing over the fence, she was a hundred feet above the runway. *Adjust speed, eyes on the runway, bring her down gently, fifty feet more.*

Hazel felt a bump from something above her before a massive shock ripped through the compartment. An explosion followed and flames appeared. The force of hitting the ground jolted her body forward. She struggled to free herself but couldn't move. A sweet smell like putrid beef made her realize in horror that she was on fire. She must stay calm and still like a Chinese warrior despite the pain carving into her body. Trapped, her head fell back, and she blinked at the white sky streaked with pink and blue. Resignation. She knew she was about to die, and she hoped death came quickly.

Lieutenant Colonel Nimmo Thysson had been waiting with his driver in a jeep to cross the runway when the two planes came into land. One was directly above the other, and it appeared each pilot didn't know the other was there. At an altitude of fifty to sixty feet the propeller of the upper aircraft caught the lower aircraft's wing fuel tank and both exploded on contact. Flames enveloped them as the coupled mass flew another hundred yards before coming to rest at the end of the runway.

Thysson ran toward the burning wreckage. The pilot of the upper aircraft climbed out and jumped onto the tarmac. The other pilot remained trapped, badly burned but conscious. Carefully he lifted Hazel out of the flames and carried her to a waiting ambulance.

As many as forty pilots landing at the Great Falls air base either witnessed the crash or saw the tangled planes burning at the end of the runway. WASP Helen Turner was surprised to find herself the only one approaching the field with so many planes trying to land. She called for landing instructions and was prepared to move on final approach when she heard a message from the tower, "Planes on final approach pull up and go around." She turned and saw two planes approaching the runway, one above the other. "Then to my horror I saw them hit the ground, one on top of the other. And then the fire. I saw the ambulance and the fire engine headed toward the runway. Then after a time I was permitted to land."[5]

When Kay Gott reached the Great Falls air base after being one of the last to leave Bismarck, she saw smoke and a wreckage near the end of the runway. She received a message from the tower to circle the field until they could clear the landing strip. "Many planes arrived at East Base at the same time as Hazel, and some pilots felt as I did, that it was fate that they were spared death."[6]

The other plane had been piloted by Lieutenant Charles "Jeff" Russell, of the 5th Ferrying Group, Texas. His radio was not working, and since it was Thanksgiving Day there had been no one able to fix it at his previous refueling stop. Before taking off, he told a WASP that his radio wasn't working and asked her to alert the tower when they arrived at Great Falls, but due to the communication issues with the tower, her message about Russell's radio was not received.

The preliminary report typed up that same afternoon stated that "a number of P-63s were arriving at East Base, Great Falls, Montana at 1400 MT on 23 November 1944, simultaneously on individual flight plans. Approximately ten (10) P-63s had been, or were, in the traffic pattern at the time of the accident. Aircraft involved in the accident were on final approach two or three miles from boundary of field. Upper aircraft lowered gear on final; as they approached the field the vertical distance between the two planes gradually diminished until the two ships collided just short of the runway, 393, the upper ship (pilot Charles H. Russell, 1st Lt.), straddling 412, (pilot Hazel Lee) the right auxiliary wing tank on 393 exploded, enveloping both ships in flames. After colliding they struck about 500 feet from the north end of the runway '20' and slid to a stop 300 feet further down the runway."[7]

The subsequent official investigation revealed that Lieutenant

Russell had not established radio contact at any time with the tower. Hazel had called for and received landing instructions. Both pilots Russell and Lee were told verbally to "go around" while on final approach, and since no acknowledgment was received, a red light was given, accompanied by further warning that they should proceed around the field. Russell of course did not receive any verbal instructions because his radio didn't work. Hazel's was likely garbled by interference and inaudible. If she'd received it, she would have followed instructions, and she reported having a green light.

Three or four minutes prior to the accident, Russell had signaled to a WASP pilot that he was unable to contact the tower, after which she called in for landing instructions for him. "Tower was at no time able to establish the position of the aircraft without radio on final or determine whether or not they had radio communication."[8]

"As the planes approached the end of the field, the East Base Control Tower operator noticed that if they both kept coming and attempted to land, they would collide. He immediately flashed the red warning light from the Tower and instructed them to "pull up and go around. Apparently neither pilot was tuned to the tower or knew of impending danger."[9]

At the hospital, when Hazel's smoldering coat and down-filled flight suit were removed, smoke rose from her burning skin. Some of her friends believed the coat had exacerbated her injuries. Others understood that leaving her in the coat may have been done to keep her warm. Hazel remained conscious and in torturous pain from her burns and fractures for two days. The WASPs visited her in the hospital, and Virginia Luttrell Kahn said of her visit, "She was conscious the entire time. The doctor said they had never seen anyone so brave. She never complained."[10]

The other pilot, Lieutenant Jeff Russell, received first-degree burns, a slight concussion, and minor bruises, and was released from the hospital in a few days.

Lieutenant Colonel Thysson later received the Soldier's Medal for his courageous act of climbing into the burning wreckage to save Hazel Ying Lee. His wife, Harriet, had graduated from Avenger Field seven months before the accident. Assigned to Romulus, she undoubtedly knew Hazel. Both Lieutenant Thysson and his wife were killed in a car accident some time prior to September 1949.

Hazel died on Saturday morning, November 25, 1944, at 5:50 a.m. She was thirty-two years old. The cause of death was major burns, fractures, and injuries received from the midair collision on Thanksgiving Day, November 23, 1944. Did she lament the loss to the financers who had backed her and the government who had paid for her training, much of which she was just beginning to use flying fighter aircraft? She would have regretted the loss of the expensive P-63 she'd ferried across the country.

Pat Dickerson accompanied Hazel's body from Great Falls, Montana, home to Portland, Oregon. It must have been a lonely journey on the train accompanied by thoughts of death and the loss of her friend. Only a few of Hazel's effects were salvaged after the accident. Pat was given a small notebook burned around the edges, Hazel's qualification booklet, to deliver to Hazel's family. Her logbook, the one every pilot carried and filled in meticulously, must have been lost to the flames. Pat also delivered Hazel's car from Romulus to her sister in New York, with Cliff's helmet still in the back window.

Hazel's uniform was taken by the Romulus officer in charge of the belongings of people killed in service. He claimed he couldn't find any of Hazel's relatives. In 1974 his wife was wearing a WASP uniform while touring the Carlsbad Caverns and caught the attention of a WASP who asked about her service and learned the uniform had been Hazel's.

◊ ◊ ◊

There were conflicting reports about the accident in the two official reports produced by the government. One report said that Hazel, possibly having heard the direction to go around, had pulled up into Russell's plane. The other said Russell had dropped down. Kay Gott, in her book *Hazel Ying Lee: Women Airforce Service Pilot*, interviewed everyone who was at the scene of the accident. The women who witnessed the crash were never interviewed for any of the reports.

"She didn't ever pull up . . . she was landing." Martha Wagenseil said. "I just still see that scene in my mind." Martha had landed, delivered her aircraft, and gone back out to the flight line to wait for the others in their group. "It was just like a big circle of angry hornets buzzing around there. There were just P-63s all over the place. All coming in at once. I do not remember Hazel Lee pulling up. I was standing there watching her approach. She was flying a fairly shallow approach on final leg. She was just coming in at a nice slow, perfect approach and suddenly above her, at a much steeper angle of descent and directly above her, was another airplane. She was at about 40 degree attitude . . . he was at about a 60/65 attitude, and we stood there just transfixed with horror. Well, they both continued their path and he gently settled down on top of her and they both went down and crashed."[11]

Mary Darling witnessed the crash from the flight line. It appeared to her that Hazel had been cleared to come in, and she believed that the male pilot must have been coming in without permission. To her it looked like the male pilot landed his plane right on top of Hazel's. "Either Hazel never saw the red flashing light or she thought it was for a plane behind her and she continued landing." Whether or not she pulled up wouldn't have changed the outcome. Pulling up as the tower instructed would have resulted in her crashing into Russell.

According to Darling, "the whole thing was hushed up so fast it made your head spin, because it was a male pilot."[12]

In Kay Gott's interviews, some WASPs who thought they were at the scene of Hazel's accident were surprised to be proven wrong. Did such a dramatic event bring the women together on the field that day? Did the trauma cause them to believe they'd been with Hazel, together as they'd always been, even though they were physically separated?

The preliminary report done on November 23, the day of the accident, by Major Charles L. Smith, Air Corps Flying Safety Officer, Romulus, Michigan, read, "Preliminary report shows probable pull-up into another P-63 turning from short base and letting down at same time. PROBABLE tower error . . . Any action to be taken to be left to the discretion of Commanding Officers involved."[13] This did not go over well with the WASPs.

AJ looked at the photo of Hazel she held in her hands. It was the final photo taken of her friend. Pat had taken it in their Fargo hotel room while waiting for clearance on their way to Great Falls. Hazel, straight-backed and regal in a chair, looked as though she were conducting an interview. Wearing her regulation white shirt and tie, she flipped through a magazine, a cigarette in one hand and her black hair swept up and as usual without a strand out of place. The look in her eyes could be fatigue, but AJ wondered if it was sadness, and realized how infrequently she'd seen Hazel without a wide smile. "What's what?" she could hear Hazel ask, bursting into the room. AJ shook her head and placed the photo on her desk.

They had all been exhausted. Hazel was gone, and the shock was too much to comprehend.

Jackie Cochran received the news of Hazel's death as she sat down with a whiskey in a chair opposite her husband. She couldn't help but shudder at the agony Hazel must have experienced after the accident, for two long days. Jackie's greatest fear ever since she'd learned to fly was burning in a fiery crash and surviving.

None of the WASPs read the confidential, classified report of the accident until many years later when it was obtained with the help of Yvonne "Pat" Paterman, WASP class of 43-W-5, who later enlisted in the service and rose in rank to lieutenant colonel. The report, which had begun on the day of the accident, outlined the event in a two-paragraph narrative. The investigation revealed that Lieutenant Charles "Jeff" Russell had not established radio contact at any time with the tower, and the tower remained unaware that Russell had an inoperative radio.

The Aircraft Accident Investigation Board reached the decision that the accident was caused by the failure of Russell's radio, the failure of the WASP pilot to make a "check call" on "Base Leg" before landing, and the failure of either pilot to heed the red-light warning given by the tower.

What really happened is still up for debate. Those who witnessed the accident are gone. What is known is that the weather caused a deluge of planes to descend on Great Falls, and they were unable to assist that many pilots all trying to land at the same time. The pilots were tired. Russell's radio was not working. Neither Hazel nor Russell knew of the other's presence until the moment of impact. Could the tower have told Hazel there was a plane directly above her? With the radio interference, would she have received the message?

Mistakes with deadly consequences extinguished a life and haunted for the rest of their lives the memories of those who were present and those who knew Hazel.

At the time of Hazel's death, her brother Victor's company, having landed at Utah Beach on the 23rd of June, had fought their way across northern France. They had participated in the taking of Metz, France, and were approaching the German border with the Third Army, when on November 28, his unit joined with another at the western edge of a town southeast of Merten, France. They were met with more resistance than expected. Victor's tank was hit by anti-tank fire and he and several of his crew members were killed. The Lee family received word that Victor had died three days after his sister Hazel. He was thirty years old.

On the first day of December 1944, rain poured from an angry sky. The Lee family gathered on a hill south of Portland. Fussing children were lifted into their parents' arms and sheltered under umbrellas. Some of Hazel's childhood friends held each other's hands and cried. It was impossible to comprehend that a personality as big and a light so bright could be extinguishable.

Pat Dickerson had accompanied Hazel's body to Portland, where she was met by Hazel's sister Frances at a funeral home that refused to accept Hazel's body because they served only whites, forcing them to find another. The family wanted Hazel and Victor to be buried side-by-side, but because Hazel was not a military veteran, the siblings could not be buried together at Willamette National Cemetery. Instead they chose a hillside location at River View Cemetery. According to family lore, the cemetery at first refused their request to bury Hazel in the location they had chosen because it was an area for whites only, and it was only after a legal battle that they relented. The timeline, however, does not support this, since Hazel was buried less than a week after her death.

Chinese citizens had been buried at River View before Hazel—she was not the first—but there may have been a time when there were sections reserved for whites. Most likely, there had been some sort of struggle surrounding Hazel and Victor's burials that involved discrimination and offense, a story that has been passed down through the generations possibly becoming more dramatic with each telling. It seems clear, however, that even in death Hazel continued to break down accepted practices of inequality.

There were several accounts given in interviews by former WASPs that Hazel's body went unclaimed by her family for more than a year. This is untrue. Maybe confusion arose over the difficulty in locating her husband in China, which would be understandable since Hazel had not heard from him in a length of time that caused her to believe him either dead or imprisoned, or maybe because Hazel had used her sister's address in New York; many of the WASPs who were not close friends didn't know she was from Portland. But the truth is that Hazel returned to Portland, to the place she was born, grew up, fell in love, and learned to fly.

The Willamette River flowed thick and gray-green below the hill where the mourners stood. Their sister, auntie, and friend unimaginably occupied the simple coffin being lowered into the deep hole. As a civilian, Hazel did not qualify for a military funeral. Her family had paid for her body to be returned to Portland. There was no insurance money, and no service flag of the United States to drape over the coffin of the first Asian American female pilot to die in the service of her country.

On that day the Lee family made an unspoken agreement to never speak of Hazel again. Daniel broke the code from time to time over the years, telling his children stories about his sister's antics, her humor and courage, but mostly they left her in their memories, undisturbed, where she would remain laughing and full of life.

23

LEGACY

2022

Hazel was an excellent pilot. I never heard anything about her being not as responsible as she should have been or anything like that. She was one of the friendliest persons I think I ever knew. No matter where you met her, she knew your name, she knew you. Like an old friend, always. She was the first Chinese person I think I had ever met, and I thought she was so wonderful that I have never forgotten her. I just get goose bumps when I think of Hazel because I felt she was my real, true friend.[1]

—Sylvia Dahmes,
WASP, class 43-W-5

Dragging my luggage through Concourse E at Portland International Airport, I turn into a cocktail bar dedicated to women aviators called Juliett. Portraits painted by Sara Radonvanovitch of Bessie Coleman, Berta Moraleda, Micky Axton, and Hazel Lee line one wall. Hazel's familiar smile greets me and it's like seeing an old friend. There's a WASP cocktail on the menu made with tequila, lime juice, and cucumber agave. Wouldn't the Avenger girls love that? I order the "Hazy Hazel," a local beer made by Fracture

Brewing, and imagine its namesake sitting across the table and telling me in her deep voice, "I think I'll have one of those too." The large art deco light fixtures shaped like sago palm fronds create an ambience reminiscent of her era, and it's easy to imagine her here.

"I hope I've done your story justice," I tell her, and look around self-consciously. I wonder if all writers get this involved with their subjects. The bartender wiping the circular bar in the center of the room nods in my direction. I look out the floor-to-ceiling windows at the view of Mount Hood. Hazel and I, a couple of Portland girls, have come full circle.

I am no longer the same person I was when I began writing Hazel's story. To navigate a difficult chapter in my life I had no choice but to become fearless, and Hazel became my role model. After quietly accepting the roles assigned to me as a woman for my entire life, I stepped, tentatively at first, outside my lane, and with Hazel for inspiration, I stayed there. I learned to defy gravity. I learned to fly. Raising my glass, I thank Hazel for her story. She and the WASPs rescued me. And as so often happens, my thoughts return to them.

On December 16, 1944, the Battle of the Bulge began in Europe, and four days later the WASPs were officially disbanded. The women who flew for the United States Army Air Corps packed up and said their goodbyes not knowing if they would ever fly again. They turned in their WASP uniforms that would end up being worn by officers' wives who fished them from barrels of rejected army surplus clothing. It was cold in Romulus when Hazel's friends quietly gathered their belongings and cried. No one knew what they were going to do next, and they wondered if they would see one another again.

Their disbandment didn't involve common sense. On December 21, the day after the women went home, planes sat abandoned on runways needing to be delivered. There weren't enough male pilots to fly them. Three-fourths of all domestic deliveries of America's fastest airplanes had been accomplished by WASPs stationed at more than 120 bases all over America. Half of the Ferrying

Division's pursuit pilots were women. To replace them was going to cost the government $1,085,312.

The Battle of the Bulge would continue for more than a month, with tremendous loss of life. World War II raged on for eight more months. Shocking discoveries came to light when the concentration camps in Germany were finally liberated. The WASPs, like all Americans, had been unaware of the atrocities perpetuated against Jewish prisoners in the concentration camps until the liberation of Auschwitz a month after their dismissal. Finding out about the extermination of Jewish citizens only added salt to the wound. Reports of the number of people mercilessly put to death by the Nazis was unimaginable, and a collective grief settled over the newly disbanded WASPs. Ultimately the death number would be estimated at six million Jewish men, women, and children. Another five million prisoners of war—Romany, Jehovah's Witnesses, homosexuals, and others— were killed in the Holocaust, a word meaning "burnt offering." The WASPs had freed more than one thousand men to go overseas and help end the war and the staggering loss of life in the death camps, and in prison camps where Allied POWs were held.

The WASPs appealed to continue flying. Fighter aircraft were desperately needed and rolling out of factories, but Congress refused. Betty Gillies along with other ferry pilots wrote to the Pentagon offering their continued service for one dollar a year. Their offer was turned down. Men were taken off combat duty to replace the women pilots. The last pursuit school class that admitted women pilots graduated October 15, 1944. No women were admitted in the eight classes that followed.

The WASPs could not understand the politics behind their dismissal. Spending so much money on their training, evaluating their experience and their proven skills, and then dismissing them before the war ended was senseless and wasteful. Yet all WASPs serving at 126 bases across the United States were out of work and told to go home.

◊ ◊ ◊

The women wondered how they could go home and explain to their families they were no longer needed. Dismissed without ceremony, many were stranded so close to Christmas and with no military status to help them travel. While some of the air bases, sorry to see the WASPs go, assisted with travel arrangements, most of the women had to find their own way home.

Finding flying jobs proved impossible. Men were returning from the war, and the airline industry chose them over women, explaining that their customers were more comfortable with male pilots. Already cautious about getting in the air, if women were flying the airplanes, some passengers would refuse to fly. WASPs, desperate to find work, and sometimes the breadwinner in the family, took on the dangerous job of flying war-torn "junkers," planes too damaged to be fixed, to junkyards. A few became private pilot instructors. Vi Thurn couldn't find an airline that would hire a woman as a commercial pilot, so she took the only aviation job she could get, behind the ticket counter at Trans World Airlines. "It was painful," she said, "to be so close to planes yet so far from the cockpit." She soon left.[2]

With few options available to them, they returned home to anonymity. No parades or recognition ceremonies greeted the returning WASPs. Most married and had families, some returned to teaching, some attended college without the G.I. Bill benefits offered to military personnel including nurses and secretaries. Some traveled to Alaska, Mexico or Europe or any destination where they could get away and think for a while. Stripped of purpose, they missed their WASP sisters, and friends and family were often unable to understand. Men were able to continue their flying careers. They had choices no longer available to the WASPs.

Like many WWII veterans, the WASPs didn't talk about

their experiences. The records of their contribution and sacrifice were sealed for thirty-five years, and their stories were all but forgotten. "I was so disappointed that Congress would tell us to go home while we were still useful," said Kay Gott, ". . . and there was still a need for us to do the job we were doing. I was so disappointed that I never talked about what I did for years. It'll be 20 years I never talked about it at all."[3]

Due to the sentiment of the public surrounding their disbandment and their own grief over the loss of their jobs, livelihood, purpose, and joy, the WASPs may have failed to realize that the experiment put forth by Jackie Cochran had succeeded. They proved what the experiment set out to prove, that women could fly as fast and far as male pilots and with a better safety record. Their gender proved to be an asset and not a liability. They laid the groundwork for women being admitted into the military in the future.

The WASP missions, which totaled sixty million miles according to the Smithsonian National Air and Space Museum, were of critical importance and sometimes of life-threatening danger. They trained men to fly and fire at targets and encouraged them to tackle temperamental planes fearlessly. They were test pilots, ferrying pilots, target tow-ers, and instructors willing to risk their lives to help their country. Every WASP played a part in winning the war. They succeeded brilliantly in their mission. And their success would reach far beyond aviation. A precedent had been set that women could perform the same work men were doing and were worthy of equal pay. Nancy Love and Jackie Cochran believed the WASPs proved women could stand beside men in the military and in combat.

◊ ◊ ◊

I drive the familiar winding road up to River View Cemetery. Having lived in Portland all my life, I've been here many times, but today I'm visiting two graves for the first time. On this August day, thick smoke from nearby forest fires blankets the city and has turned the sun into a red orb. I find her on a hill where the view of the Willamette River with the passing years has now been obstructed by trees. Hazel's large marble marker is inscribed, "Hazel Y. Lee Louie, Aug 12, 1912, Nov 25, 1944," and adorned with the WASP medallion engraved with her name and class.

Four years after his death in France, on September 23, 1948, Victor Lee was buried with the full military honors denied his sister at River View Cemetery. His sister Frances purchased a plot and brought him home to Portland. He lies east and at the feet of his sister Hazel.

Clifford Louie survived World War II. After Hazel's death, he became reclusive. In 1945, after the Japanese surrendered, he served as a member of China's Military Commission to Japan, and later that year, he went to Karachi in British India as an instructor to Allied pilots. In 1946, he married Pearl Lowe, and they had three children. Cliff continued his work with the Chinese Air Force and after retiring from the military in 1974 became CEO and then chairman of the board at China Air Lines. He passed away in 1999 at the age of eighty-five.

Madge Rutherford and Shay Minton had three daughters and went on to work as a scientific team studying and collecting venomous reptiles. Together they coauthored two books. Some WASPs did not go on to marry or have children despite the messaging that the war was over and it was time for women to return to their roles and help the country recover. Having been told that motherhood was their duty, they politely passed.

In 1944 Arthur Chin, miraculously healed from the burns that should have ended his pilot career, began flying for the China National Aviation Corporation on dangerous cargo routes over "the Hump," something Hazel had expressed interest in doing after the WASPs disbanded. Art remarried and had a daughter, Susan. That marriage ended in divorce, and he married again and had a son named Matthew. On March 1, 1945, Art was discharged from the

Chinese Air Force. He went to work for the U.S. Postal Service in Beaverton, Oregon, a suburb of Portland, where a post office was renamed the Major Arthur Chin Post Office Building in his honor. In 1995 he was awarded the American Distinguished Flying Cross and Air Medal for wartime cargo and combat flying. He died on September 3, 1997, in Portland, after a distinguished career in which he is recognized as the first flying ace of World War II.

Jackie Cochran's accomplishments beyond her WASP program included being the first woman to break the sound barrier in the 1950s. Despite serious health issues throughout her adult life, she went on to break three world records, reclaiming her title as "the fastest woman in the world" and winning back the Harmon Trophy when she was nearly sixty years old.

On July 8, 1948, non-flying air force duty was authorized for women. Esther McGowin Blake became the first woman air force member, enlisting in "the first minute of the first hour of the first day."[4] In 1949 former WASPs were invited to join the new U.S. Air Force Reserve. They received letters from Jackie Cochran beginning "Dear Ex-WASP," offering them the commission of second lieutenant with a non-flying status if they met the standards and qualifications. Although they would not be allowed to fly, 165 WASPs took their commissions. Only 112 were able to serve for any length of time; the others were discharged for "dependency," meaning they had young children.

President Ford signed Public Law 94-106 in October 1975, allowing women to be admitted to all-male military colleges and academies. In the summer of 1976, 157 women entered the Air Force Academy, 119 entered the U.S. Military Academy at West Point, and 81 entered the U.S. Naval Academy.

Not until 1976, thirty-two years after the WASPs disbanded, were women again allowed to fly military aircraft in the United States Air Force. In 1993 Brigadier General Jeannie Leavitt became the air force's first female fighter pilot. With the passage of Public Law

95-202 in 1977, Congress finally granted the WASPs military status. President Jimmy Carter championed their cause for veteran's
status, which provided limited benefits. All WASPs were issued
honorable discharge certificates. In March 1979, an act of Congress
awarded veteran's status to all WASPs. Jackie Cochran lived to see her
dream realized. She died August 9, 1980.

The WASPs were awarded the WWII Victory Medal in 1984.
In 2009 they were inducted into the International Air & Space Hall
of Fame. In 2004 the Oregon Aviation Hall of Honor inducted
Hazel for her bravery and service. "I remember thinking here we
are—so close to the end of the program," Sylvia Dahmes said. "I can't
help but think she died doing what she really enjoyed doing."[5] And
AJ said in an interview, "I'm sure she'd be some kind of a leader now.
We enjoyed her so very much."[6]

"We were the first women military pilots," Dora Dougherty
said. "When the WASPs started, the military didn't know whether
we were emotionally stable enough to be military pilots. Women
were hysterical, they said. We opened the door."[7]

"The military can't deny women to fly anymore," said one proud
WASP in an interview, "because it's been done."[8]

This was the WASPs' legacy. The women who joined Jackie
Cochran's program enlisted because they wanted to help their country, not because they thought it "would be a cool thing for women to
do and that they were going to break down barriers," said WASP
documentary director Christine Bonn in the *Buffalo Times*. "It never
occurred to them that they had done something special or something worth remembering. They believed they'd been forgotten and
went on with their lives like everyone else did after the war."[9]

In 2010, President Barack Obama awarded the WASPs a Congressional Gold Medal, the highest award a civilian can receive from
Congress, in recognition of their contribution to World War II. One
of the recipients was Maggie Gee, who graduated from Avenger
Field November 9, 1944, in the second to the last class, and only

served six weeks before the WASPs were disbanded. She went on to become a scientist after the war, working on weapons systems, and lived to be eighty-nine. She died three years after being presented the gold medal.

Addressing a class at Helen C. Cannon High School in 2001, Hazel's friend Fran Snyder Tanassy told the audience that her generation proved "girls can do everything they want. It's just as easy for a woman to fly a plane as a man." She went on to say, "As a woman, you had one bad landing and you were out, where the men got three bad landings before they washed out. We had to fly under all kinds of conditions, including taking planes to Montana in winter in the snow. But women had safer flying records than the men."[10]

Hazel's courage continues to inspire today. In becoming the first Chinese American woman to fly for the military and the first female Asian American to receive a pilot license, she proved that anything is possible. Gender and racial barriers never stood in her way. She challenged labels and rose above them while embracing what others might call limitations and making them a part of who she became.

There is still a long way to go to close the opportunity gap for women and minorities. Hazel represents the best in all of us, and like her, we can break down barriers, overcome adversity, and risk it all in the pursuit of equality and justice for all people regardless of gender, race, or any other characteristics used to discriminate.

Hazel would tell us to spread our wings and fly—the conditions are CAVU.

ACKNOWLEDGMENTS

RESEARCHING AND WRITING Hazel Ying Lee's story has been an honor, and I'd like to express my deepest gratitude to two brilliant women for giving me the privilege. The first is Wendy McCurdy at Kensington Publishing, for knowing that Hazel's story needed to be told and then entrusting me with the project. And to my agent Jennifer Weis, who called me on a Friday afternoon with an idea that would change my life, a million prayer-hand emojis.

Many people generously shared their time and expertise to make this book possible. Thank you Nancy Ng Tam at the Museum of Chinese in America, New York City, for sharing Hazel's archives and photographs. For WASP and Avenger Field information, I relied on Shelia Bickel, Special Collections Research and Support, Texas Woman's University. My gratitude to pilot extraordinaire Meredith Datena, who always answered my aviation questions simply and thoroughly. I thank Steve Bollinger for his patient technical assistance and absolutely essential lighthearted banter, and Maureen O'Donnell for guiding me on a journey that allows me to write.

I understand how much Hazel's tribe meant to her, and I'm grateful for mine. Lornie McCormick, Mary Gathier, Judith Danaceau, and two-thirds of the three amigas—Paula Kurshner and Diane Gariety—you are my essentials. My sisters across the pond, Kate and Louise Van Laere, fueled me with gingerbread, tea, laughs, and love that meant more than they can ever know. Thank you John

Kupsick, my brother in history and possibly my biggest promoter, for convincing me to fly in a B-17 and so much more. My heartfelt appreciation goes to my cousin, Margaret Ward, who provided me a home surrounded by towering trees, wildlife, and a lush garden from which I finished the manuscript.

When I agreed to write a book in what seemed an impossibly short amount of time, the idea that I might be in over my head rarely occurred to me, and for that I have my parents Dean and Lillian Tate to thank. Although I've been without them for many years, the memory of their unwavering belief in me is the reason this book exists. Thanks, Mom. I wrote Hazel's story for you, about a woman with your strength and enormous personality, who also like you was a second-generation American. Thanks to your sacrifices that provided me with opportunities you never had, I'm living your dream.

ENDNOTES

PROLOGUE

1. Sally Van Wagenen Keil, *Those Wonderful Women in Their Flying Machines: The Unknown Heroines of World War II* (Toronto: McClelland & Stewart, Ltd, 1979; Saddle Brook, New Jersey: American Book-Stratford Press, 1979), pp. 152–153.
2. Keil, *Those Wonderful Women*, pp. 152–153.
3. Keil, *Those Wonderful Women*, pp. 152–153.

CHAPTER ONE: LITTLE HERO

1. https://www.brainyquote.com/quotes/amelia_earhart_752795, accessed August 19, 2023.
2. Gillian Flaccus, "Chinese American WASP Losing Her Anonymity," *Los Angeles Times*, May 11, 2003, https://www.latimes.com/archives/la-xpm-2003-may-11-adna-pilot11-story.html.

CHAPTER TWO: CHINESE NOT PERMITTED

1. David Kindy, "For Pilot Bessie, Every 'No' Got Her Closer to 'Yes,'" *Smithsonian*, January 21, 2022.
2. Alan Rosenberg and Montgomery Hom, producers, *Brief Flight: Hazel Ying Lee and the Women Who Flew Pursuit* (Los Angeles, CA: LAWAS Films, 2002), accessed on June 7, 2022, Evergreen State College library.

CHAPTER THREE: THE INVISIBLE GIRL

1. Mark and Christine Bonn, *Wings of Silver: The Vi Cowden Story* (Oshkosh, WI: 2010), documentary, accessed on amazon.com 6/3/22.

2. Leslie Long, "Rugged Individual," *Popular Aviation*, p. 43.

3. "Greenwood Attacked," *Oregonian*, May 2, 1932, p. 1.

4. Webster A. Jones, "Chinese Girl Flier Hopes to Aid Women of Orient," *Oregonian*, February 12, 1933, p. 13.

5. Rosenberg and Hom, *Brief Flight*.

6. Rosenberg and Hom, *Brief Flight*.

CHAPTER FOUR: ELEVATOR GIRL MASTERS FLYING

1. Margery Brown, "Flying Is Changing Women," *Pictorial Review Magazine*, June 1930.

2. "Leah Hing," Fort Vancouver National Historic Site, https://www.nps.gov/people/leahhing.htm.

3. Webster A. Jones, "Portland-Trained Chinese Flying to Oriental Fame," *Oregonian*, May 12, 1935, p. 2.

4. "Portland Elevator Girl Masters Flying and Gets License," *Oregon Journal*, November 1, 1932, p. 2.

CHAPTER FIVE: FEARLESS FATALISTS

1. Jones, "Portland-Trained Chinese."

2. Flaccus, "Chinese American WASP."

3. Trish Hackett Nicola, "I Think I'm Going to Fly: Chinese Pilots Trained in Portland During the 1930s," *Oregon Historical Quarterly* 122, No. 4 (Winter 2021).

4. Nicola, "I Think I'm Going to Fly."

5. Affidavit of Nancie D. Singleton, 4 November 1929,

Multnomah County, Oregon, National Archives, Seattle, Washington.

6. Chinese Exclusion Act Case Files of Virginia Wong.

7. Jones, "Chinese Girl Flier."

8. Untitled, *Oregon Journal*, May 3, 1933, p. 8.

9. Jones, "Chinese Girl Flier."

CHAPTER SIX: THE FLYING JOAN D'ARC IN CHINA

1. Hannah Chan, "The First Asian American Female Aviator," Federal Aviation Administration, https://www.faa.gov/sites/faa.gov/files/2022-08/Katherine%20Cheung_0.pdf.

2. Michael Little, *World War 2 Flying Ace Arthur Chin's Amazing True Story*, Disciples of Flight, 2016, https://disciplesofflight.com/world-war-2-flying-ace-arthur-chin/.

3. "Portland Girl Called Heroine: Chinese Aviatrix Trained Here Tells of Companion's Deed at Scene of Conflict," *Oregon Journal*, December 22, 1938, p. 17.

4. Rosenberg and Hom, *Brief Flight*.

5. Jones, "Portland-Trained Chinese."

6. Keil, *Those Wonderful Women*, p. 28.

CHAPTER SEVEN: REFUGEES

1. Keil, *Those Wonderful Women*, p. 32.

2. Taped interview with Faith Buchner "Bucky," 43-W-4, later first lieutenant USAF, in Kay Gott, *Hazel Ah Ying Lee: Women Airforce Service Pilot* (Eureka, CA: Veteran's Quality Printing, 1996).

3. "Portland Girl Called Heroine."

4. Rosenberg and Hom, *Brief Flight*.

5. RKO British PATHE newsreel, www.britishpathe.tv.

6. Chinese Exclusion Act, Hazel Ying Lee Case File, Seattle, Washington.

CHAPTER EIGHT: A HEROINE IN CHINATOWN

1. Jaqueline Cochran and Maryann Bucknum Brinley, *Jackie Cochran: The Autobiography of the Greatest Woman Pilot in Aviation History* (New York: Bantam Books, 1987).

2. "Portland Girl Called Heroine."

3. Little, *Arthur Chin's Amazing True Story.*

4. *Life*, December 22, 1941, nps.gov.

CHAPTER NINE: OPPORTUNITY

1. Vera S. Williams, *WASPs: Women Airforce Service Pilots of World War II* (Osceola, WI: Motorbooks International, 1994), p. 39.

2. Cochran and Brinley, *Jackie Cochran*, p. 200.

3. Katherine Sharp Landdeck, *The Women with Silver Wings: The Inspiring True Story of the Women Airforce Service Pilots of World War II* (New York: Crown Publishing, 2020), p. 74.

4. Cochran and Brinley, *Jackie Cochran*, p. 200.

5. Molly Merryman, *Clipped Wings: The Rise and Fall of the Women Airforce Service Pilots of World War II* (New York: New York University Press, 1998, 2020), p. 7.

6. Cochran and Brinley, *Jackie Cochran.*

7. Williams, *WASPs*, p. 41.

CHAPTER TEN: ENGINEERS, HOUSEWIVES, AND ROCKETTES

1. Keil, *Those Wonderful Women*, p. 144.

2. Keil, *Those Wonderful Women*, p. 144.

CHAPTER ELEVEN: PROSTITUTES OR LESBIANS

1. Williams, *WASPs*, p. 23.

2. Keil, *Those Wonderful Women*, p. 152.

3. Bonn, *Wings of Silver*.

4. Bonn, *Wings of Silver*.

5. Keil, *Those Wonderful Women*, p. 153.

6. Madge Rutherford's letters, Texas Women's University Archives.

7. Williams, *WASPs*.

CHAPTER TWELVE: RACING THE BOYS

1. http://www.quoteswise.com/amelia-earhart-quotes-2.html.

2. Madge's letters, TWU.

3. Rosenberg and Hom, *Brief Flight*.

4. Madge's letters, TWU.

5. Madge's letters, TWU.

6. Madge's letters, TWU.

7. Williams, *WASPs*.

8. Keil, *Those Wonderful Women*, p. 154.

9. Dr. Nels Monsrud, December 20, 1944, for the United States Air Force, provided by the National WASP Museum, Portal to Texas History.

10. Williams, *WASPs*.

CHAPTER THIRTEEN: KILLED IN THE SERVICE OF HER COUNTRY

1. Cornelia Fort, "At the Twilight's Last Gleaming," p. 19, *Woman's Home Companion*, July 1943.

2. Gott, *Hazel Ah Ying Lee*.

3. TWU Archives.

4. Virginia Luttrell Kahn, oral history, Texas Woman's University.

5. Taped interview with Faith Buchner "Bucky," 43-W-4, later first lieutenant USAF, in Gott, *Hazel Ah Ying Lee*.

6. Gott, *Hazel Ah Ying Lee*.

7. Katie Hafner, "Overlooked No More: When Hazel Ying Lee and Maggie Gee Soared the Skies," *New York Times*, May 21, 2020.

8. Keil, *Those Wonderful Women*, p. 153.

9. Keil, *Those Wonderful Women*, p. 153.

10. Williams, *WASPs*.

11. Madge's letters, TWU.

12. Madge's letters, TWU.

13. Madge's letters, TWU.

14. Rosenberg and Hom, *Brief Flight*.

CHAPTER FOURTEEN: COCHRAN'S CONVENT

1. Williams, *WASPs*, p. 52.

2. *Houston Chronicle*, May 1943; Gott, *Hazel Ah Ying Lee*.

CHAPTER FIFTEEN: SCANDAL

1. Madge's letters, TWU.

2. Landdeck, *The Women with Silver Wings*.

3. Madge's letters, TWU.

4. Caro Bayley's letters, TWU.

5. Madge's letters, TWU.

6. Madge's letters, TWU.

7. Madge's letters, TWU.

8. Madge's letters, TWU.

CHAPTER SIXTEEN: "ARE YOU CHINA GAL OR JAPANESE GAL?"

1. Adeline Blank's letters, TWU.

2. Madge's letters, TWU.

3. "Dad gum it! Why Don't I Watch the Weather?" *Avenger*, June 28, 1943.

4. "Dad gum it!"

5. "Dad gum it!"

6. Keil, *Those Wonderful Women*.

7. Merryman, *Clipped Wings*.

8. Madge's letters, TWU.

CHAPTER SEVENTEEN: CELEBRITIES

1. Bonn, *Wings of Silver*.

2. Madge's letters, TWU.

3. Inez "Woodie" Woods's letters, TWU.

4. Woodie's letters, TWU.

5. "Girl Pilots: Air Force Trains Them at Avenger Field Texas," *Life*, July 19, 1943.

6. Movietone Newsreel, 1943, Avenger Field, Sweetwater, Texas.

7. "WASPs," Army–Navy Screen Magazine, 1943, archived at TWU.

8. Gott, *Hazel Ah Ying Lee*.

9. Bonn, *Wings of Silver*.

CHAPTER EIGHTEEN: PICNICS IN THE SKY

1. Michael Hull, "Jaqueline Cochran: Blazing a Trail for Women in Aviation History," Warfare History Network.

2. Landdeck, *The Women with Silver Wings*.

3. Williams, *WASPs*, p. 41.

4. Bonn, *Wings of Silver*.

CHAPTER NINETEEN: CAVU

1. Written in a letter to a friend in 1930; Aurora Mackey, "50 Years Later, N. Hollywood Bears Traces of Vanished Aviator," *Los Angeles Times*, July 2, 1987.

2. Landdeck, *The Women with Silver Wings*.

3. Keil, *Those Wonderful Women*.

4. Keil, *Those Wonderful Women*.

5. Blanche Osborn's letters, TWU.

6. Cochran, *Jackie Cochran*.

7. Gott, *Hazel Ah Ying Lee*.

8. Flaccus, "Chinese American WASP."

9. Gott, *Hazel Ah Ying Lee*.

10. Landdeck, *The Women with Silver Wings*.

CHAPTER TWENTY: UNNECESSARY AND UNDESIRABLE

1. Landdeck, *The Women with Silver Wings*.

2. Landdeck, *The Women with Silver Wings*, p. 194.

3. Landdeck, *The Women with Silver Wings*, p. 195.

4. Landdeck, *The Women with Silver Wings*.

5. Landdeck, *The Women with Silver Wings*.

6. Walter Brehm, Republican congressman from Ohio, Debate on H.R. 4219, "Appointment of Female Pilots and Aviation Cadets in Army Air Forces," Congressional Record 6413.

CHAPTER TWENTY-ONE: 400 MILES PER HOUR

1. Williams, *WASPs*, p. 107.

2. Landdeck, *The Women with Silver Wings*.

3. Bonn, *Wings of Silver*.

4. Bonn, *Wings of Silver*.

5. Keil, *Those Wonderful Women*.

6. Bonn, *Wings of Silver*.

7. Bonn, *Wings of Silver*.

8. Keil, *Those Wonderful Women*, p. 290.

9. Keil, *Those Wonderful Women*.

CHAPTER TWENTY-TWO: SNAFU

1. Cochran, *Jackie Cochran*.

2. Jean Hascall Cole, Women Airforce Service Pilots Oral History Project, interview with Joanne Wallace Orr, 1989, Texas Woman's University archives.

3. Gott, *Hazel Ah Ying Lee*.

4. Gott, *Hazel Ah Ying Lee*, drawing on p. 76.

5. Gott, *Hazel Ah Ying Lee*, Helen Turner interview, pp. 43–45.

6. Gott, *Hazel Ah Ying Lee*.

7. Gott, *Hazel Ah Ying Lee*, p. 31.

8. Gott, *Hazel Ah Ying Lee*, pp. 62–63; Report of Major Accident, War Department AAF Form No. 14, November 25, 1944; "Report of Aircraft Accident," November 1944, in 1455th I & S files.

9. Gott, *Hazel Ah Ying Lee*.

10. Virginia Lutrell Kahn history archived at TWU.

11. Taped interview with Martha Wagenseil, in Gott, *Hazel Ah Ying Lee*, pp. 71–72.

12. Gott, *Hazel Ah Ying Lee*, p. 31.

13. History of Women Pilots in the Ferrying Division, ATC Collection, frame 1744, Walter J. Marx, Captain, Air Corps Historical Offices, February 1945, National Air and Space Museum, NASM.2021.0019.

CHAPTER TWENTY-THREE: LEGACY

1. Gott, *Hazel Ah Ying Lee*, p. 15.

2. Bonn, *Wings of Silver*.

3. Gott, *Hazel Ah Ying Lee*, p. 31.

4. Official United States Air Force website, https://www.af.mil/News/Article-Display/Article/109629/esther-blake-first-enlisted-woman-in-the-air-force/.

5. Gott, *Hazel Ah Ying Lee*.

6. Gott, *Hazel Ah Ying Lee*.

7. Landdeck, *The Women with Silver Wings*.

8. Thomas Baumann and Molly Merryman, *Women Who Flew*, video documentary (Lipstick Productions, 2002).

9. *Buffalo Times*, 2010, Christine Bonn interviewed by Mark Sommer.

10. "Women pilots share war stories, camaraderie," *Las Vegas Sun*, October 26, 2001.

INDEX